Legal Study on China's Sovereignty over the Nansha Islands

Cuibai Yang · Qianwen Zhang

Legal Study on China's Sovereignty over the Nansha Islands

南京大学出版社
NANJING UNIVERSITY PRESS

Springer

Cuibai Yang
Sichuan University
Sichuan, China

Qianwen Zhang
Southwest Jiaotong University
Chengdu, China

Translated by Cuibai Yang and Qianwen Zhang. Both authors contribute equally to this work.

The translation is supported by Chinese Fund for the Humanities and Social Sciences.

ISBN 978-981-15-8714-6 ISBN 978-981-15-8715-3 (eBook)
https://doi.org/10.1007/978-981-15-8715-3

Jointly published with Nanjing University Press
The print edition is not for sale in China (Mainland). Customers from China (Mainland) please order the print book from: Nanjing University Press.

This Springer imprint is published by the registered company Springer Nature Singapore Pte Ltd.
The registered company address is: 152 Beach Road, #21-01/04 Gateway East, Singapore 189721, Singapore

Preface

Legal Study on Chia's Sovereignty over the Nansha Islands is the revised edition of my Study on Jurisprudence of the Nansha Islands a decade ago which became a restricted publication due to multiple concerns of the publisher when it was to be published in July, 2003. Lots of readers have no access to this book for it was not sold publicly and one Singaporean Chinese even asked me to send her the book by mail.

South China Sea issues since then have never been resolved but exacerbated for the past decade. Even China's unilateral proposition of "shelving differences and seeking joint development" has been unable to achieve the goal.

Great powers outside the region such as the United States and Japan question China's sovereignty right over the Nansha Islands, and some other extraterritorial countries also are skeptical of China's claim in the South China Sea. There are many reasons for this situation. However, it is believed that one important reason is that China's claims in the South China Sea and the historical and legal bases are all recorded in Chinese which is beyond the reach of most foreigners, especially, the vast historical evidences written in classical Chinese, which is difficult to understand even for the majority of Chinese nowadays. Therefore, it is expected to reprint this book after enrichment, and to translate it into English for foreign readers through international copyright trade.

China has sufficient historical evidence and legal basis to prove its historic rights in the waters within the dashed line of the South China Sea, and has indisputable sovereignty and sovereign rights over the islands and adjacent waters. As early as in China's Han Dynasty two millennia ago, the Chinese people found islands and reefs in the South China Sea and conducted fishing activities there. Since then, the Nansha Islands have become an important place of production for Chinese fishermen, for those from Hainan Province in particular. And thus, an economic circle for Chinese people's production and life is formed. The governments of successive dynasties have established and improved the administrative institutions of the South China Sea. During the past two thousand years, the Nansha Islands were under the jurisdiction of China, in addition to the Second World War period when the Japanese imperialists invaded China and seized the Nansha Islands. In November

1964, according to the Cairo Declaration and the Potsdam Proclamation, Executive Yuan of the Republic of China ordered the Navy General Headquarters and the Ministry of the Interior to assist the Guangdong Provincial Government to take over the South China Sea Islands and send Taiping warship and Zhongye warship to receive the then named Tuansha Islands, and Yongxing warship and Zhongjian warship to take over the Xisha Islands. In December of the same year, the task was completed. To commemorate the event, it was ordered to rename Changdao as Taiping Island, and Lin Island as Yongxing Island. Government of the Republic of China also changed the name of Xiniao Islands into Spratly Islands for it is located in the distant South and is also known as Spartan Island. To adjust the names of these islands, the Ministry of the Interior then renamed Tuansha Islands, which was called Xinnan Islands by the Japanese and Spratly Islands by the Westerners, as Nansha Islands. And it changed the former Nansha Islands into Zhongsha Islands to make the name match its location in the South China Sea. The rest of the islands and reefs were named after Nanyang envoys in the past dynasties for commemoration. In 1947, the government of the Republic of China published "Map of the South China Sea Islands," drawn with 11 "dashed lines," as "the boundary between China and foreign countries", and published a lot of maps of China with Nansha Islands included. On January 16, 1947, the Ministry of Defense held the Implementation Conference for Construction in Xisha and Nansha Islands. It was decided in this meeting to set up the Hainan Special Administrative Region, and that Hainan Province had jurisdiction over Xisha and Nansha Islands. This decision was issued in Decree Yizi No. 1117 on January 27 by Executive Yuan. On June 6, 1949, according to the movements of France and the Philippines, the President of the Republic of China, Chiang Kai-shek, announced the "Hainan Special Administrative Region Organization Ordinance," and Article 1 of the Ordinance expressly provides that "Hainan SAR includes Dongsha, Xisha, Zhongsha, Nansha Islands and other big and small islands, beaches, sands and reefs." These are declarations of sovereignty in the sense of modern international law.

In 1949, the Chinese government changed, and the People's Republic of China was founded. In 1958, the Chinese Government issued the Declaration on the Territorial Sea, in which Article 1 states: "The territorial sea width of the People's Republic of China is 12 nautical miles, which applies to all the territory of the People's Republic of China, including mainland China and its coastal islands, as well as Taiwan and its surrounding islands, the Penghu Islands, the Dongsha Islands, the Xisha Islands, the Zhongsha Islands, the Nansha Islands, and other islands belonging to China." In 1959, the People's Republic of China established representative offices for Xisha Islands, Nansha Islands and Zhongsha Islands under Hainan Administrative Region, which governs islands and reefs as well as waters of Xisha Islands, Zhongsha Islands and Nansha Islands. In 1988, with the revocation of Hainan Administrative Region and the establishment of Hainan Province, representative offices for Xisha Islands, Nansha Islands, Zhongsha Islands also had been correspondingly set up under the jurisdiction of Hainan Province. Article 2 of the Law of the People's Republic of China on Territorial Sea and Contiguous Areas, adopted on February 25, 1992, by the Standing Committee of the Seventh

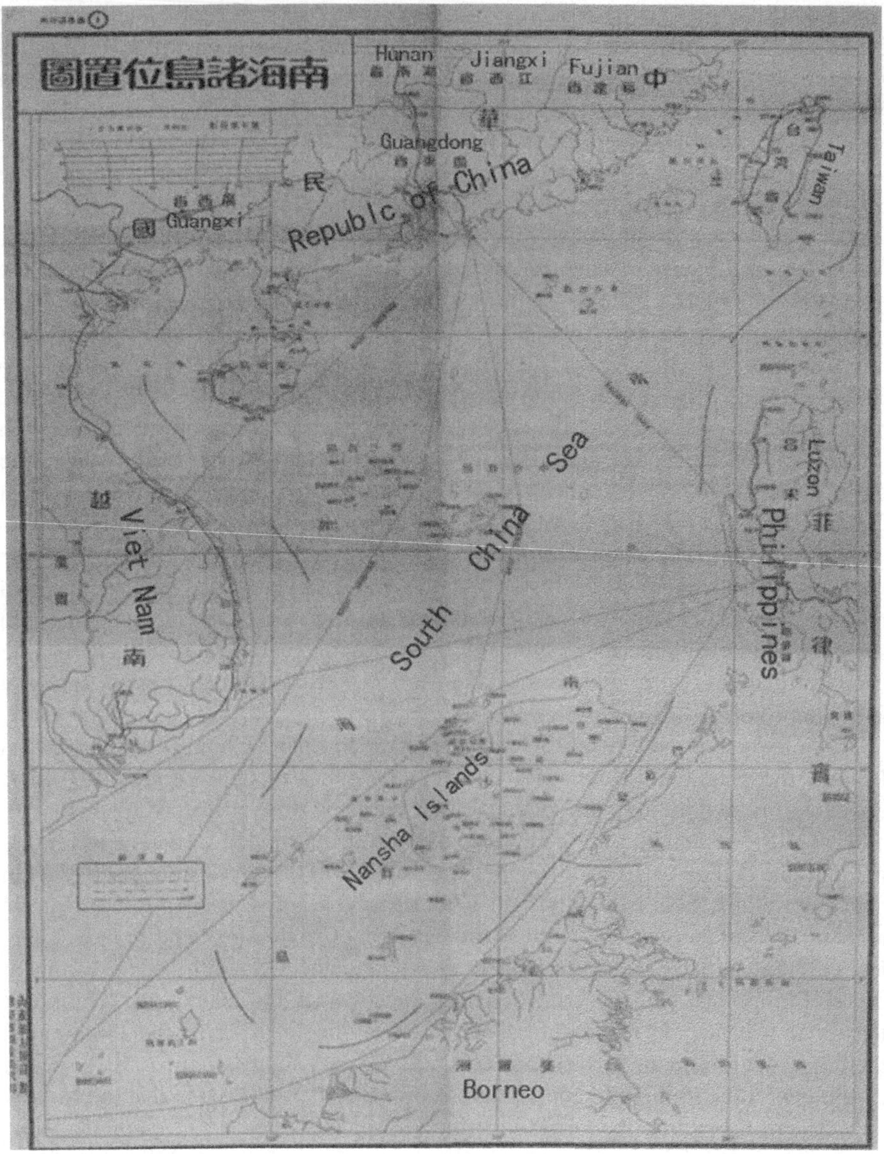

Fig. 1 Location Map of the South China Sea Islands drafted in 1946

National People's Congress of the People's Republic of China provides: "The territory of the People's Republic of China includes the mainland China and its coastal islands, as well as Taiwan and its affiliated islands including the Diaoyu Islands, the Penghu Islands, Dongsha Islands, Xisha Islands, Zhongsha Islands, Nansha Islands and all other islands belonging to the People's Republic of China."

On June 21, 2012, the Ministry of Civil Affairs of the People's Republic of China announced that the State Council has recently approved the revocation of representative offices for Xisha Islands, Nansha Islands and Zhongsha Islands under Hainan Province, and set up the prefecture-level city of Sansha to administer islands and reefs as well as waters of the Xisha Islands, Nansha Islands and Zhongsha Islands. The People's Government of Sansha is stationed in Yongxin Island. The establishment of Sansha City is conducive to further strengthen China's administration, development and construction on islands and reefs as well as waters of the Xisha Islands, Nansha Islands and Zhongsha Islands, as well as to protect the marine environment of South China Sea.

In addition, the United Nations Convention on the Law of the Sea (hereinafter referred to as "the Convention") entered into force in 1994, so it is inapplicable to China's sovereignty, sovereignty rights and jurisdiction over islands and reefs and related waters of the South China Sea, which have existed for more than two millennia. And the Convention does not apply to the adjustment of the ownership of the marine reefs, since the laws of the sea contain a rich legal system and not just the Convention. The United States is not a party to the Convention, so it is unreasonable for it to provoke China's sovereignty over the South China Sea while the Convention recognizes the historic rights of States over oceans and islands. And in this case, China has put forward the proposition of "shelving disputes and seeking joint development," showing China's principal and purpose of establishing friendly relations with neighboring countries as well as China's utmost sincerity and compromise.

In the two thousand years of sovereignty exercised by China over the Nansha Islands, the neighboring countries and regions either recognized China's sovereignty and rights in the South China Sea, or they had not yet formed a country. In other words, the neighboring countries have never questioned China's sovereignty not until the end of 1970s, that is, when a wealth of oil resources were discovered in the South China Sea. Not only that, when France wanted to occupy the Nansha reefs in 1933, it caused diplomatic disputes among China, Japan and France. Then, the Philippines belongs to the United States, and the US-controlled government of the Philippines claimed that "it does not consider the islands are Philippine territorial waters, and this issue is irrelevant to the interests of the Philippines, therefore, the Philippine governor-general did not care about it."[1] In 1956, a special committee of the Philippine government confirmed after discussion that the Nansha islands "are not within the territory of the Philippines."[2]

On June 15, 1956, when Yong Wenqian, Vice Foreign Minister of the Democratic Republic of Vietnam, and Li Lu, the Director of the Department of Asian Affairs of the Ministry of Foreign Affairs of the Democratic Republic of Vietnam met Li Zhimin, the ad hoc representative of the People's Republic of

[1]Japan, the 14th year of Showa 14, East Asia Information No.326, pp. 13–21, cited from Han Zhenhua, *Historical Data Compilation of the the Islands in Southern China Sea*, Oriental Publishing Center, 1988, pp. 260–261.

[2]*Guangming Daily*, June 1, 1956.

China in Hanoi, Yong Wenqian stated: "according to data of Vietnam, the Xisha Islands and the Nansha Islands have been China's territory as early as the Song Dynasty." And Li Lu added, "the Xisha Islands and the Nansha Islands have belonged to China as early as the Song Dynasty."[3] More than 2 weeks after China issued its territorial waters statement on September 4, 1958, Prime Minister Pham Van Dong of Vietnam wrote to the Premier Zhou Enlai of China, on behalf of the Government of the Democratic Republic of Vietnam, to acknowledge and endorse China's declaration on territorial waters. "The Government of the Democratic Republic of Vietnam respects this decision and will direct the responsible State authorities to strictly respect the territorial width of China's territorial sea of 12 nautical miles when there is a contact with the People's Republic of China in the sea."[4] Even textbooks of Vietnam's secondary schools recognize China's territorial sovereignty over the Nansha Islands: "The arc-shaped island ring formed from the islands of Nansha, Xisha to Hainan Island, Taiwan, Penghu and Zhoushan Islands constitutes a Great Wall to defend the Chinese mainland."[5] This indicates that the Vietnamese government and its people generally have no doubt on China's sovereignty over the territory of the Nansha Islands.

In 1943, the United States, Britain and China issued the Cairo Declaration, which explicitly recognized that: "(t)he purpose of the three nations is to return to the Republic of China the territory of China that was stolen by Japan, such as Manchuria, Taiwan and the Penghu Islands."[6] Since the First World War, Japan has stolen a large portion of Chinese territory, including the Nansha Islands. After the occupation of the Nansha Islands, Japan changed its name to "Shinnan Gunto" and placed it under the administrative jurisdiction of Kaohsiung, Taiwan. Therefore, the reference "return Manchuria, Taiwan, Penghu Islands and so on to the Republic of China" in the Cairo Declaration should include the Nansha Islands. In July 1954, China, the United States and Britain signed the Potsdam Proclamation and reaffirmed that: "(t)he conditions of the Cairo Declaration will be implemented, and the sovereignty of Japan will be restricted to Honshu, Hokkaido, Kyushu, Shikoku and other small islands determined by us."[7]

In 1971, a British High Commissioner in Singapore said that Spratly Islands, the fourth largest island in the south of the Nansha Islands, is part of China's territory and part of the Guangdong Province. When it was returned to China after the end

---

[3]Chen Jinghe, *Xisha Islands and the Nansha Islands—History Review*, Chuangda Asian Studies, 1989 No. 10, p. 53.

[4] *People's Daily,* September 22, 1958, Third Edition.

[5][Vietnam] *Geography Textbook for the Ninth Grade of Regular School*, "China" Section, Vietnam Education Press, 1974.

[6] *International Treaties Volume* (1954–1947), World Knowledge Publishing House, 1966, p. 407.

[7]*International Treaties Volume* (1954–1947), World Knowledge Publishing House, 1959, p. 77.

of the war, we cannot find any indication that it has been possessed by any country, and therefore can only conclude that it is still owned by Communist China.[8] The Soviet government believes that the part that the Japanese militarists split should be unconditionally returned to China. Foreign Minister Malik of Indonesia made a statement to reporters on February 4, 1974, claiming that China has sovereignty over the Nansha Islands and Xisha Islands. "If we look at the map nowadays, you can see that the Paracel Islands (Xisha Islands) and the Spratly Islands (Nansha Islands) are parts of China, which never has any protest." US Senator Mike Mansfield in April 1974 also made it clear that: "(t)his includes the current-contentious Senkaku Islands (Diaoyu Islands) among Taiwan, Japan and the People's Republic of China and other islands, and the People's Republic of China has put forward the claim of sovereignty to all of these islands, while according to the historical precedent, all China's requirements of these islands are very reasonable."[9]

It is thus clear that, after World War II, the world's major powers and the neighboring countries related to the South China Sea all advocate that islands and reefs in the South China Sea belong to China. Even today, countries in the international community who understand the history of the South China Sea still respect China's sovereignty over the South China Sea. On June 30, 2014, Singapore's Minister of Foreign Affairs and Minister of Justice, Shang Mugen, told a forum of nearly 200 foreign envoys and scholars at the International Institute for Strategic Studies: "I believe it is not the most correct view to say China failed to observe the international law when its position is antagonistic to the ASEAN's. Unfortunately, the international media tend to be anti-China, so we can't know the complete facts." He said, "I do not want to defend China or support others. Singapore is complete neutral. But the fact is that China claims to have sovereignty over many reefs and islands while the United Nations Convention on the Law of the Sea does not cover sovereignty over islands and reefs, which depends on a number of factors, including historical ownership, and the adequacy of the historical basis should be another pair of shoes."[10]

The neighboring countries in the South China Sea, represented by the Philippines and Vietnam, not only are unwilling to negotiate with China to solve the South China Sea issue, but are also constantly encroaching on China's territory in the South China Sea, and continuously taking the oil and gas resources there. The old warships of the Philippines, setting on beach, wantonly seize and detain Chinese fishermen who are conducting normal operations within the sea under China's jurisdiction while the Vietnamese ships constantly collide the "981" oil exploration ship within waters of the Xisha Islands. What is more, the Philippines violates the international law and basic norms of the international relations to

---

[8]*Hong Kong Far Eastern Economic Review*, December 31, 1973, p. 39.

[9]Cited from Han Zhenhua, *Historical Data Compilation of the the Islands in Southern China Sea*, Oriental Publishing Center, 1988, p. 557.

[10]Message posted to http://new.sina.com.cn/c/c2014-07-02/084330457695.shtml. Visited on July 3, 2014.

unilaterally take China to the United Nations International Tribunal. By the time the Convention was signed in 2006, China has issued a formal declaration that excludes arbitration on disputes over territorial sovereignty, including island reef disputes, military activities and so on, in accordance with the provisions of Article 298 of the Convention. However, as the biggest beneficiaries of the South China Sea, the Philippines and Vietnam constantly challenge the authority of international law and China's sovereignty over the Nansha Islands. The author believes that the Chinese government must continue to strengthen legislation, administrative jurisdiction and law enforcement activities in the South China Sea, and should speed up resource exploration and development as well as island construction there. At the same time, on the basis of respecting historical facts and international law, China should settle the disputes through peaceful consultation and negotiation with the direct parties.

Sichuan, China Cuibai Yang
Chengdu, China Qianwen Zhang

Contents

Chapter 1
Introduction

1.1 The Nansha Islands from Different Perspectives

1.1.1 The Natural Characteristics of the Nansha Islands

The Nansha Islands is located between 3°, 36 min north latitude to 11°, 57 min north latitude, and between 109°, 6 min east longitude to 117°, 50 min east longitude. Of the four archipelagos in South China Sea, the Nansha Islands is a group of Coral islands whose islands are most widely distributed with the largest number of reefs and neighboring countries. And it is also the farthest sea areas where ancient Chinese fishermen fished and worked.

The length of the Nansha Islands from east to west is about 905 km and the width of it from south to north is about 887 km. The area of the Nansha Islands is about 823,000 km^2. The easternmost part of the Nansha Islands is Haima Beach, and the westernmost part of it is Wan'an Beach. The southernmost part of the Nansha Islands is Zengmu Reef, and the northernmost part of it is Xiongnan Reef.

According to aviation and satellite pictures, there are 310 islands, sandbars and reefs in the Nansha Islands. So far altogether there are 189 islands, sandbars, reefs and beaches that are named, including 14 islands, 6 sandbars, 113 reefs, 35 shoals and 21 beaches.[1] There are more than ten large islands of the Nansha Islands, among which the highest one is Hongxiu Island with 6 meters above the sea level. The largest island is Taiping Island with an area of 0.432 km^2.

The distribution pattern of the Nansha Islands is related to submarine geology. The geologic structure of the Nansha Islands is very complex. Overall, the seabed looks like a huge rhombus basin, namely, the South China Sea Basin. A number of deep and huge fosses have been formed because of the crustal movement. The Nansha Islands is distributed in the continental slope steps in the southern part of the South China Sea. And these steps, the depth of which is around 2000–2500 meters, are in the middle of the continental slops. The Nansha Islands runs northeast to southwest,

[1] Wu (1999).

C. Yang and Q. Zhang, *Legal Study on China's Sovereignty over the Nansha Islands*,
https://doi.org/10.1007/978-981-15-8715-3_1

which is about 780 km long and about 320 km wide. The top of the Nansha Islands goes up and down in flat, and its fault structure gives rise to aulacogen nets that are up to hundreds kilometers in length and tens kilometers in width. These vast Nansha steps are the basis of the development of the Nansha Islands. Under the control of the basement structures, the distribution pattern of the Nansha Islands is from northeast to southwest, from northwest to southeast, from south to north and from east to west. Accordingly, Xie Yixuan classifies the Nansha Islands into four big groups, namely, middle north, east, west and south.[2] And Ju Jiwu classifies the Nansha Islands into five big groups, namely, north, northeast, southeast, south and southwest.[3] In his book *The Nansha Islands, the Dongsha Islands and the Penghu Islands*, Liu Baoyin classifies the Nansha Islands into five big groups, namely, the outside southern danger zone, inner and middle southern danger zone, inner southeastern danger zone, outside southwestern danger zone and northern and northwestern danger zone.[4] Each of the three classifications emphasizes different factors with its own merits and it is notable. Though the three classifications are different, they all reflect the basic characteristics of the Nansha Islands' distributions.

The latitude of the Nansha Islands is low, and thus this area is of tropical monsoon and equatorial climate. The northeast monsoon is strong from October to the coming April. The southwest monsoon is relatively weak from June to August. The transition period of monsoon is from May to September every year. It is partly cloudy from March to April, while cloudy from June to December every year. There is little fog all year round.

The temperature of the Nansha Islands is so high that its annual mean temperature reaches 27°–28°. The range of temperature rarely changes and the difference of annual temperature is only 2°–3°. The water surface temperature is high and stable, which reaches 26°–28°. The salinity of sea water is high, from 32° to 34°. The transparency of sea water is good, normally from 20 to 30 m, with maximum up to 47 m. There is rich rainfall and the difference between dry season and rainy season is significant. The average annual rainfall is 1800–2200 mm.

1.1.2 *The Geopolitics and Geo-Economics Meanings of the Nansha Islands*

Politics and economics, as two very basic social activities in human society, are closely related to geographical environment. Human activities have to take place in certain geographical space, which reversely has significant impact on human social activities. Therefore, when studying the legal status of the Nansha Islands, we must deal with it from the perspective of political and economic activities of the Chinese people.

---

[2] Xie (1991). Refer to Chen (1996), p. 140.

[3] Chen (1996), pp. 143–194.

[4] Liu (1996).

China is back on the Asian continent and faces the Asia Pacific. However, China is blocked and restricted by Russia, the Korean Peninsula, four big islands in Japan, the Ryukyu Islands, the Philippine Islands, the Malaysia Islands, and the Indonesia Islands when entering into the Asia Pacific area. Ever since the Second World War, the United States has been stationing large troops for long in the Korean Peninsula upper to northern China, big islands in Japan, the Ryukyu Islands, Philippine, etc. After the Cold War, the United States transferred its submarines in Europe to the Asia Pacific so that the intent of the United States is obviously reflected by the fact that 60% of its submarines are grouped in the Asia Pacific. In other words, China would be placed in a disadvantageous strategic position if the United States blocks all the above islands. Consequently, it is especially important for us to hold fast to the Nansha Islands.

China was once a big marine power in the Ming Dynasty, and thus was also a major power in the world at that time. Nevertheless, China began to decline because of the seclusion policy in the Qing Dynasty, and became of its semi-colonies status by some western marine powers. The world history has also proved that all big powers are related to the marine. In the future, in order to emerge as a big power in the world, China also has to emphasize marine and change some obsolete habits and thoughts. And we have to firmly control the Nansha Islands and nearby sea areas in order to be an international big power.

The Nansha islands are between the Indian Ocean and the Pacific, and a necessary place to cross the two oceans. Since ancient times, the Nansha islands waters along with three other islands waters are trade hubs to East Asia, Indochina, Nanyang islands, the Indian subcontinent, the Arabian Peninsula, eastern African and European countries. International economic exchanges will become increasingly frequent with the further development of economic globalization. The Nansha islands waters is the maritime traffic crossroads for American, Asia, Oceania, and Europe. A number of important international routes need to pass through the waters, including the routes from Singapore to Guangzhou and Hong Kong, Singapore to Manila, Jakarta to Guangzhou and Hong Kong, Singapore to Zhanjiang, Ho Chi Minh City to Manila, and from all the ports in Japan to Southeast Asia, South Asia, Middle East, Africa and Europe, etc. It has become the world's third gold waterway because the routes are crisscrossed like a spider web in the Nansha islands sea area. In this regard, the one who controls the Nansha islands and its waters owns controls over the strategic passage of the Pacific and Indian Ocean.

For China's national security, the Nansha Islands is important because the import of oil from the Gulf and Africa, Oceania, Europe and the trade with some Asian countries have to go through the Nansha islands waters. Therefore, China's economic development and social stability will face a huge threat if the Nansha islands and waters are occupied by hostile countries. Moreover, China's strategic point will be exposed and its strategic defense will be very difficult to hold without strategic defense zones in depth. The center of China's economic development is still in the southeast coast and the Yangtze River delta represented by Shanghai. China's economy will suffer a fatal blow in the event of a war. For a long time, the United States military surveillance planes have been conducting espionage activities in the northern South China Sea, which has indicated the importance of the location. The humiliating modern history and contemporary history of China also begins from the southeast coast. Both the opium and imperialism gunboats entered into China through the South China Sea. And the Colonists invaded our country and killed our people from the southeast coast. The lessons of history can not be forgotten!

It has been only 100 years since the British imperialism launched the opium war of aggression from the South China Sea. And although the 21st century just began, the hegemonists, the United States, cannot wait to launch a reconnaissance 104 km off the coast of South China Sea, planned an aircraft crush of Chinese planes, killed the Chinese and invaded China's sovereignty. What makes our people even more indignant is that the United States who conducted illegal invasion activities in China slandered that China's military aircraft has interfered their flights rather than sincerely apologize.

The Nansha islands not only are of special and profound geopolitical significance, but also have an important geopolitical economic sense.

The Nansha islands waters is rich in living and non-living resources. There are eight sedimentary basins in the Nansha islands and their waters, with a total area of 41 km^2, and about 26 km^2 in China's dropped boundary lines. According to incomplete statistics, there are totally 34.97 billion tons of oil resources in the eight basins. In addition, recoverable reserves of 11. 82 billion tons and 8 trillion cubic meters of natural gas have been discovered.[5] According to the analysis of Fan Kaiyi, an engineer from the offshore oil exploration and development research center in China National Offshore Oil Corporation (CNOOC), the Nansha Islands and the waters can realize the favorable petroleum exploration because of its excellent basic petroleum geological condition. "The stratum of the paleogene system presents a continuous layout with large area and even the paleogene system deposition can be found in the upheaval zones among basins, therefore there is a broad prospect for exploration; the geological advantages of large area of basins, deep hollow area, long development time and high geothermal gradient are conducive to the aggregation and accumulation of organic substances and formation of a large number of petroleum and natural gas; diverse reservoirs including sandy rock, carbonate rock, reef limestone and bedrock ensure the satisfactory physical property of oil storage and very large reservoir yield of petroleum and natural gas; polycyclic sedimentation forms multi-source reservoir-cap-rock combination; all kinds of entrapments are developed in the sedimentary basins with various genetic types to form the petroleum enrichment area with the petroleum super-system." According to Mr. Fan's estimation, there are 35.147 billion tons of oil in the Nansha sea area.[6] There is also rich oil in the Zengmu Basin in the southern South China Sea. According to relevant data, the basin began settling in about 37 million years ago, and bare about 8000 m of thick detritus sediment and carbonate deposits because it is located in the southern south China sea continental shelf, which provides a favorable geological condition for hydrocarbon generation. Detection results show that there is a large oil and gas basin with estimated

[5]Zhao (2000).

[6]Fan and Qian (2000).

reserves of 12 billion tons to 13 billion tons.[7] Various data show that in the Nansha islands waters, there are abundant oil and gas resources which are different from the oil and gas fields in China's inland areas. There is no worry about the exploitation of our inland oil and gas resources by other countries. However, it is different to develop the oil and gas resources in the Nansha islands waters because they are neighboring Vietnam, Malaysia, Brunei, Indonesia, the Philippines and other countries. Some of the above countries are in the same oil and gas layer which has been exploited by them for a long time since the 1950s and 1960s. By the late 1990s, there had been more than 680 drillings and 30 oil fields of various states in the continental shelf in the peripheral of the Nansha islands. Among those 30 oil fields, four of them were under exploitation, with an annual output of 26.07 million tons of oil and 17.74 billion cubic meters of natural gas.[8] Oil and gas are non-renewable resources. Moreover, oil and gas layers located in the border areas are beyond national boundaries. The more the oil and gas resources are exploited by surrounding countries, the more we are going to lose in our traditional boundary lines. The region's oil and gas resources may have been exhausted by the time our country has the ability to take them back. We spend a lot of foreign exchange in importing oils from the Gulf states every year. We should exploit the resources of the South China Sea waters in order to save the oil resources in inland China and to reduce oil imports from overseas.

In addition to oil and gas resources, there are other rich resources in the Nansha islands and their waters, such as the solar power, wind energy, tidal energy, ilmenite, chromite, phosphorite, bird droppings, fish resources, etc.

1.1.3 Regional Culture Characteristics of the Nansha Islands

The Nansha Islands are of humanistic features of Chinese culture and history, especially featured with the culture of China's southeast coastal area according to the fishery production activities of the Chinese fishermen in the Nansha Islands, the archaeological discoveries, the Chinese names of the Nansha Islands reefs, and the maps of territories drew by all previous dynasties. Thus, the culture of the Nansha Islands belongs to the Chinese culture. To be more specific, it belongs to southeast coastal Marine culture and its sub-culture of mainland China.

Since the Han dynasty, the Nansha Islands have been an important production site for Chinese fishermen, especially the Hainan fishermen, and thus have become an important economic circle for Chinese people's productivity and life. The fishermen in the Nansha Islands mainly fish nuts, red fish, shark, swordfish, tuna, Mackerel and catch sea turtles. The nuts and red sea cucumbers are shipped to Singapore for sales while dried sea cucumber, sea turtles and dried birds are brought back to Hainan.

The Hainan fishermen fishing in the Nansha Islands waters head for the South China Sea in winter, and return in the next summer. Some live on the island and do

[7] Xia et al. (1989). Cited form Ju and Pan (1996).

[8] Fan and Qian (2000).

not return to Hainan until April of the third year when southwest monsoon comes. People need to build houses, dig wells, and grow vegetables when living on these islands for a long time, so in the main islands, there are both, earth temples, wells and coconut trees left by the Hainan fishermen. These activities show the fishery resources, bird resources and fertile soil of Nansha Islands have become material foundations to the survival of Chinese fishermen. It is these fishermen's production activities that have left a rich Chinese cultural heritage in the Nansha Islands.

The cultural relics discovered in the archaeology of the Nansha Islands are characterized by the culture of the central plains.

The Nansha Islands archaeological relics can be divided into two parts: the surface of the building and underground excavation cultural relics. There are mainly earth temples in the earth's surface. There are earth temple ruins in the Taiping island, the Thitu Island, the West York Island, the Spratly Island, the Loaita Island, and the Namyit Island. Earth temples in the Taiping Island and the Thitu Island are made of pieces of wide slab frames which are three feet high and more than two feet wide. There are statues of the land god in the middle of the temples. After years of wind and rain erosion, the surface has been stripped off, but the clothes of the sculpture form are still faintly visible.[9] In the jungles of the Pacific island, there is also an earth temple which is more distinctive in that there are four Chinese characters "You Qiu Bi Ying" hanging on it.[10] The earth temples on the West York Island, the Spratly Island, the Loaita Island, and the Namyit Island are the same as those on the Taiping Island. And there is a censer in the earth temple on the West York Island. There are two porcelain cups and a wine pot in the earth temple on the Loaita Island. There are god statues, incense burners and sealing in the earth temple on the Namyit Island.

Worshipping earth temples in the reefs reflects Chinese traditional customs which has thousand-year-long history. Earth temples are the ones for worshipping the land god. The older generations of Chinese people as well as those from countryside are familiar with the land god. Chinese children who love watching *A Journey to the West* all know the land god. Every time when the Monkey King doesn't know where certain monsters come from, he will ask for help from the land god. The land god, which was called She God in ancient China, is the one who manages a small area of ground in Chinese folklore. It was recorded in *Gongyang Annals—Zhuanggong Twenty-Fifth Year* that Chinese people worshipped She God by beating drums and killing livestock. He Xiu made notes that She God was the master of the land. *Xiao Jing Wei* recorded that She God was the land god. The land was too vast to worship so that ancient Chinese people paid tribute to the She God to express their gratitude. *Gods and Ghosts in Folklores* also mentioned that She God has been called the land god from then on.[11] In our traditional customs, the purpose of building earth temples and worshipping lands is to pray for a good harvest. Evidently, building earth temples and worshipping the land god in the Nansha Islands is to pray for a good fish harvest, eliminate the evil and protect the fishermen. The habits and customs of building earth

[9]Zhang (1975), pp. 39–40.

[10]Zhang (1975), p. 16.

[11]*An Unabridged, Comprehensive Dictionary* (1989).

temples and worshipping the land god still remain in the vast rural inland of China. What's more, land is respected as god in Chinese Taoism. In this regard, though it is far away from the mainland, the Nansha Islands share common cultures with mainland China.

Professor Wang Hengjie, known as the first Nansha archaeologist, has discovered a lot of cultural relics which are as same as or similar to those in mainland China in the archaeological excavations of the Nansha islands. According to chronological order and era characteristics, these cultural relics can be divided into four types, namely the Qin and Han Dynasties, the Tang Dynasty, the Song and Yuan Dynasties, and the Ming and Qing Dynasties.

Hard potteries with plating are the oldest relics excavated in Loaita Bank and Reefs. These hard potteries have also been found in Qin and Han relics in Lingshui County, Hainan Province and some counties in Guangdong Province. Especially, they are "very close" in texture and pattern to one piece "in the Qin and Han Dynasties" excavated in Han relices in Guishan of Chenghai County, Guangdong Province. Professor Wang Hengjie believes that "the potteries are water bearers brought by fishermen from Hainan and southern China."[12] There are even more relics in the same period discovered on Taiping Island, two of which are typical hard potteries with plating. There is a Mi character on that potteries and they are the Qin and Han relics.[13]

Relics discovered in late periods are those in Tang Dynasty. Some pottery fragments of water bearers have been found underwater in Yongdeng Ansha. "In terms of type, temperature and color, it was made by people in the Tang Dynasty. They are similar to the Tang relics from the beach in Lingshui County of Hainan and Guangdong Provinces.[14]

Some celadon pieces of the Song Dynasty which were made in the folk kilns in Longquan and Fujian are also found on Taiping Island and in Nantong reef waters.

There are even more cultural relics from the Ming and Qing Dynasties, including porcelains, coins, navigation guide, iron anchor and so on. For example, porcelain bowls and jars made in the folk kilns in Guangdong in the Ming and Qing Dynasties have been discovered in Louisa Reef of Taiping Island and other waters. Ancient coins such as "Jiaqing reign," "Dynasty reign", "Xianfeng reign" and among others have been unearthed on Taiping Island. Anchors widely used by fishermen from Hainan, Guangdong and other places in late Qing Dynasty have been found in the Zhenghe reefs and Fulusi Jiao.

The discovered relics are similar to those in Hainan Province and Guangdong Province, which indicates that the waters of the Nansha Islands were areas for people in the southeast coast of China to conduct economic, productive and trade activities in as early as the Warring States period. As long as there are economic activities, there is culture. Now that the Nansha Islands are places for economic and productive activities for the fishermen along China's southeastern coast, so apparently the cultural traits

[12] Wang (1996), p. 443.

[13] Wang (1996), p. 444.

[14] See Footnote 12.

of the Nansha Islands are Chinese civilization, specifically part of the culture of Mainland China.

1.1.4 The Nansha Islands Discovered Early by China

The Naosha Islands were discovered by China as early as in the Han Dynasty. The Chinese were the first who navigated and produced in the South China Sea, and discovered the archipelago of the South China Sea. In the Eastern Han Dynasty, *Yi Wu Zhi* written by Yang Fu records that: "There are shallows and magnets in the islands (Qitou) of the South China Sea." In the Three Kingdoms, *Nan Zhou Yi Wu Zhi* written by Wan Zhen also records that "sailing northeast in the South China Sea, there are many shallows and magnets." "Qitou" was used by the ancient Chinese people to name the islands, reefs, banks and shoal of the Nansha Islands and the Xisha islands. KangTai, in the period of the Three Kingdom, mentioned the Nansha Islands in his *History of Funan.* It records that "sailing to the South China Sea and reaching the Coral Shoals, massive rocks with coralline on it are under the shoals". Chinese people's understanding of the Nansha Islands became even more comprehensive after the Tang and the Song dynasties. And they named the Nansha Islands and the Xisha Islands as "Shitang", "Changsha", "Qianli Shitang", "Qianli Changsha", "Wanli Shitang", "Wanli Changsha", etc. The Taiping Island in the Nahsha Islands was called Huangshan Ma Zhi and the Spratly Island is known as a bird Taipa Island in *Geng Lu Bu*, which is widely known and used among the fishermen of the Hainan Island. These names are still in use today.

It has been 2000 years since the Chinese people first discovered the islands of the South China Sea if judged by records in *Yi Wu Zhi* written by Yang Fu in the Eastern Han Dynasty. Moreover, it has already been more than 1000 years if judged by naming the Nansha Islands as "Shitang" in the Song Dynasty.

Vietnam "recognized the existence of the South China Sea islands through literature coming from China."[15] In the 17th century, the Vietnam atlas *Generalized Area Plan* documented the Nansha Islands for first time.

The Philippines entered into the Nansha Islands even later in the middle of 1950. In addition, it was only a retired US soldier in the Philippines rather than a Filipino who entered into the Islands.

Malaysia and Brunei had not claimed sovereignty over parts of the Nansha Islands until the 1970s.

[15] Urano Tatseo (1997).

1.1.5 The Nansha Islands from the Western's Perspectives

Today's South China Sea has always been what they called "Chinese Sea" or "China Sea" in the eyes of the West. Until the beginning of the 20th century, some colonists began to call it "South China Sea". As can be seen from the names, since they knew the East China, the West has naturally regarded that the South China Sea is China's territory because China has actual control over it. Since the West regards the entire South China Sea as "China Sea", it is natural that the Nansha Islands is taken as China's Nansha Islands as Chinese territory.

This fact can be clearly illustrated by historical maps about the South China Sea in the collection in Cambridge University. In January 2001, in the map rooms of Cambridge University, the British Museum and the University of Oxford, I read a lot of historical maps about the South China Sea which are published by the United Kingdom, France, Italy, the Netherlands and other European countries. It was clearly marked in the maps that the names used by different countries to address the South China Sea are Chinese Sea, China Sea,[16] Mar de la China,[17] Mar Cinese Merid,[18] Mer de Chine,[19] Chinese Sche Zee,[20] Mer de la Chine,[21] and Mar da China.[22] A map

[16]*Island in the Pacific Ocean* (1851). A. K. Johston National Atlas.

SOUTH HEMISPH (1816).

EASTERN ISLANDS OR MALAY ARCHIPELAGO. This map is a single one without publication date. In a atlas in the library of Cambridge University. Malay Archipelago or East India Islands, J. and F. Tallis, from the Illustrated Atlas of the World, 1851. Refer to R. T. FELL, *Early maps of South—East Asia* Oxford University Press 1991, Second Edition. R. T. FELL, *The East India Islands*, William Darton, c, 1812.

Nlle Galles Meridle (1995).

ASIA. W.& A. K. Johnston, Edinburgh. Refer to Keth Johnston: *Atlas of Political Geography*. W. &. k. Johnston: *SIAM, ANAM, CAMBODIA, COCHIN CHINA, TONG KING.* Limited, Edinbourgh & London. Refer to *The Victoria Region Atlas.* Second edition. London 1901. *Cyclopedian Atlas.* page 19, London 1865. *Cyclopedian Atlas* 1860, *Atlas of Generale Maps.* Edward Stanford, 6, Charing Cross.

ASIA (1902).

ASIA (1937).

EURASIA (1938–39).

[17]ASIA (1937).

[18]*EURASIA* (1938–39), *CARTA FISICA. Atlante Geografico Universale,* Baratta E Visintin, Sperling & Kupfer, Milano, 1938–39.

[19]*CARTE REDUITE DU GRAND OCEAN*, Compris entr. LASE et LAMERIQUE, Redigee dapres les observations les plus recentes et publiee pour le Service de Vaisseaux, Francais. Par Ordre du Ministre de la Marine au Depot General des Cartes et plans de la marine et des Colonies. LAn VI de la Republique. No publication date for another map, but there is a Call Number: Atlas 3.93.3 in the books of the library of Cambridge University. The map is on Page 95 and Page 96 with the name of INDOCINA, SIAM E ARCHIPELAGO MALESE. The bottom of the map is marked with scale: 1:10,000,000 (1 cm: 100 km).

[20]*AUSTRALIE.* C.COVENS, BIJ I.TIRION UITGEGEVEN. Te Amsterdam, Bij MORTIER, COVENS en Zoom.

[21]*OCEANIS* (1835).

[22]*OCEANIA* (1850).

of South China Sea found in the *Atlas of Chinese Culture* in the British Museum can serve as a particular evidence. The map draws a sealing line in the South China Sea, and listed Nansha, Xisha, Dongsha and Taiwan as Chinese territories. And "Nansha Is", "Xisha Is", "Dongsha Is" and "Taiwan" are marked in Chinese letters.[23] This map uses "South China Sea" among other names.

It is difficult to find the exact time for the West to change from using "Chinese Sea" to "South China Sea". However, it is clear that, initially, the West knew that it was China that held control over the South China Sea, and that the Chinese people were conducting productive activities and foreign trade or emigration in the South China Sea, so naturally they called the South China Sea as "China Sea". However, when they knew that Chinese people called it as the South China Sea and there were the East China Sea and the Yellow Sea in China, they, from the perspective of the Chinese, changed the name from "Chinese Sea" to "South China Sea" as the Chinese did. Mr. Chen Guohua, an English professor at Beijing Foreign Studies University, believes that both names themselves do not make any difference. The difference lies in the different angles. The former is from the standpoint of the West, while the latter is from the standpoint of China. In either way, the two names are marked with "China", which is an unchangeable fact. Moreover, the use of South China Sea, China Sea or Chinese Sea by the West has shown Western countries' recognition of the objective fact that it is China who possesses the sovereign rights in the South China Sea.

In addition, charts and books published and used in Western countries and Japan also acknowledge the names Chinese people use for the Nansha Islands and apply these Chinese names accordingly. In the 16th century, the Portuguese called Yongxing Island Paxo, which was transliterated of what fishermen of Hainan Island called "Bazhi". Japan's understanding of the Nansha Islands also came from the history books of China and the Chinese fishermen. In the 19th century, the British nautical chart called Hongxiu Island as Namyit, Jinghong Island as Sincowe, and Taiping Island as Ituaba. These names are transliterations of what fishermen called "Nanyi", "Chenggou" and "Huangshan Ma Zhi" in the past.

If it is the Vietnamese who discovered the Nansha Islands earlier than the Chinese did, then why don't Westerners and Japanese use the Vietnam names of the Nansha Islands?

[23]Cultural Atlas of China, Revised Edition. New maps and new photographs. Editor: Lauren Bourque, Map Editor: Tim Williams, Andromeda Oxford Limited for revised edition.

1.2 Current Situation of the Occupied Islands of the Nansha Islands

1.2.1 Current Situation of Partial Islands Seized by Vietnam

Hong Xiu Island was seized by Vietnam in July 1973, and was renamed as "Nam Yet" by Vietnam. In April 1975, North Vietnamese government took over the island from South Vietnam regime. 60 soldiers have garrisoned on the island where there is 1 helipad as well as cannons, communication equipment and chariots.

Hong Xiu Island is located at 10°11′00″N, 114°21′E, at the southern edge of Zhenghe Qunjiao and 11 nautical miles to the south of Taiping Island. The shape of the island resembles an ellipse. The length of the island reaches 0.46 km, width approximately 0.16 km, and altitude about 6.1 m. Among the islands in the Nansha Islands, Hongxiu Island is the highest, on which there are many trees and bushes. From the coast to the edge of the reef site, the width of the southwest part is about 1.9 km, and the width of other parts is about 650 m. There is a shoal patch, 4.5 m in depth, at the northeast direction 1 nautical mile away from the island. There is a riffle, 6.7 m in depth, at the southwest direction 2.3 nautical miles away from the island.

Nanzi Island or Nanzi Reef, S.W CAY (South West Cay) in English, and Song Tu Tay called by Vietnam, was invaded by Vietnam in February 1974 and then taken over by the North Vietnam in April 1975. There is a helipad on the island.

This island is located at 11°25′30″N, 114°19′20″E, 1.7 nautical miles away from Beizi Island at the southwest direction, and the altitude of it is 3.9 m. The shape of the island is like a long ellipse and it is the sixth largest island among the Nansha Islands. On this island, there are thick weeds and trees towering as high as 9.1 m. This island is a breeding place for seabirds and covered with guano, most of which has not been moved out yet.

There are patch reefs 5.4 m deep in the water channel −0.7 nautical mile away from the southwest of Beizi Island and are between Nanzi Island and Beizi Island; there are another patch reefs 9.1 m deep, 740 m away from the southwest of Beizi Island. The island is surrounded by coral reefs that are above the sea. The coral reefs extend from southwest of the island to the sea approximately 90 m and extend to the sea about 560 m at other directions. In the powerful southwest monsoon, people can land on this island from southwest side. There are two wells and a 12-m pillar in the middle of the southwest side of the island.

Dunqian Shazhou, Sand Cay in English and "Son Ca" called by Vietnam, was seized by Vietnam in February 1974. In April 1975, North Vietnamese government took over this island from South Vietnam regime. A reinforced platoon of Vietnamese army of 80 people has garrisoned on the island with 81 or 75 cannons (the number of cannons is uncertain and needs to be ascertained) supplied every 1, 2 or 3 months.

Dunqian Shazhou is located at 10°22′38″N, 114°28′10″E, 5.8 nautical miles from the east of Taiping Island, and is a round-shaped sand island. The altitude of the island is 2.5–4.6 m. It is surrounded by coral reefs and shoals with shrubbery and coconut palm in the flat depression which is in the middle of the sand bank. The 12–18 m deep shoal between Taiping Island and the sand bank is an ideal anchorage ground.

Jinghong Island, Sin Cowe Island in English and "Sinh Ton" called by Vietnam, is located at 9°53′N, 114°16′E. In February 1974, army of South Vietnam seized the island and North Vietnam took over it in April 1975. Vietnam has sent 60 soldiers garrisoning on the island where there is 1 helipad.

The island is located at the west of Jiuzhang Qunjiao, and 9 nautical miles away from the north of Chigua Jiao. It stretches from northeast to southwest with an altitude of 3.7 m. It is the largest one among Jiuzhang Qunjiao. There are weeds, low-quality fresh water but no trees on the island.

Nanwei Island, Spratly island in English and "Truong Sa" called by Vietnam, is at 8°39′00″N, 112°54′40″E, 13.8 nautical miles away from the east of Riji Jiao, 43 nautical miles away from the north of Nanwei Tan. The altitude of the island is about 2.4 m. In February 1974, it was seized by South Vietnam army, and taken over by North Vietnam regime in April 1975. On this island, there are 3 Vietnam barracks, 1 runway of sand and stone, 1 radio station, 1 helipad, 2 artillery positions, 1 fort and station troops of 20 soldiers.

In a flat shape, this island is the fourth largest island among Nansha Islands. It is also the most important one in the south of 10°N of Nansha Islands. There is coral sand and fragment along the coast and plenty of seabird inhabits on the island. In 1963, the island was covered with weeds.

The island is surrounded by reef frame and coral reefs above the surface of the sea. There is a reef flat which is 1 nautical mile long and 0.8 nautical mile wide at the south of the island. At the north side of the island, there is a 5.4-m-deep shoal which extends for 0.5 nautical mile. The east side of the island is steep and deep, and the depth of the water reaches 18.2 m within 190 m from the coast. At the southwest side and the west side, there is a shoal 5.4 m deep and 370 m away from the coast. It is the deep sea.

On the shoal at the northeast and southwest side of the island, ships could drop anchors. The shoal at the northeast side could be used as an anchorage ground even during in the period of northwest monsoon. However, the places 18.2 m deep or below are dangerous with irregular turbulence that sailors cannot drop the anchor. During the period of southwest monsoon, people can land on the island from the leeward side. However, there are many coral reefs near the coast which are dangerous when waves are roaring. According to the result of 24-h observations, there is only one high tide in summer. The height of this high tide in early July is 9 in. and the discrepancy is 1.6 m. At the northeast side of the shoal, the water flows to southwest when tide comes and flows from southeast to southwest when tide goes.

In April 1951, a British ship, Dampier, anchored at the place 18.2–21 m in depth and 0.6 nautical mile away from the island.

Anpo Shazhou, Amboyna Cay in English and "An Bang" called by Vietnam, is located at 7°52′00″N, 112°55′00″E, 19 nautical miles away from the southwest of Baijiao, 70 nautical miles away from the east of Nanwei Tan. In February 1974, the island was seized by South Vietnam, and taken over by North Vietnam in April 1975.

In this cay, there are 4 battery bunkers, 7 fire bunkers, four gun bunkers, 5 underground reinforced concrete bunkers, 2 rod antennas, 1 observatory and 1 helipad.

The cay is 1.8 meters above the sea, 300 m long and 140 m wide. The most part of the cay consists of sand and coral fragment. The west part of it is made of reef rock fragment and is covered with guano on the top. There are coral reefs in the waters extending from the coast to the sea. A reef which is 0.5 nautical mile long and 370 m wide is in the northwest of the cay. In northeast, there is reef which extends for 1 nautical mile and will appear above the surface when tide falls. The same coral reef stretching for about 650 m from the exposed beach is 7.3 m deep in water. The water of the reef fringes is 16.4 m deep and the depth of water drops steeply when the reef stretches out further. By observing 2 days before the neap tides of the cay, it is found that the flood current is at 23 o'clock and the ebb stream 6 o'clock; the water flows to the north when tide comes and to the west when tide goes, with a 1.5 flow velocity.

A British naval vessel, Rifleman, anchored at the place 9.1 m deep during southwest monsoon. A French surveying vessel, Astrolabe, anchored at the place 11.8 m deep and 650 m away from the cay, and overlooked the center of the cay above the water at an 106° angle. Overlooking the center of the exposed beach 1 nautical mile away at 224° angle, there is an ideal anchorage place 14.6 meters in depth. However, the water is deep and flows rapidly near the cay, so one should be careful when anchoring there.

Ranqing Shazhou, Grierson Reef in English and "Sinh Ton Dong" called by Vietnam, is located at 9°52′30″N, 114°34′00″E. It was seized by Vietnam in April 1978. It is a small cay above the bank reef which is 3 nautical miles away from the south of Changxian Jiao. At the south of the cay, there are black rocks above the water.

Zhong Jiao, Central Reef or Central London Reef in English and "Dao Truong Sa Dong" called by Vietnam, is located at 8°56′00″N, 112°22′00″E (or 8°56′N, 112°24′E and 8°55′N, 112°22′E). It was seized by Vietnam in April 1978. There is a 900-m-long atoll in the northwest part of Dongjiao, 5.2 nautical miles away from the northeast of Xi Jiao. A 7.3–14.6-m-deep lagoon has been thus formed by coral reefs. According to records, there is a shoal at the southwest of the reef, which will be submerged when tide rises. The difference between this reef and Dong Jiao and Xi Jiao is that it cannot be distinguished by waves.

Bisheng Jiao, Pearson Reef in English and "Phan Vhih" called by Vietnam, is located at 8°07′00″N, 114°07′00″E, 20.4 nautical miles away from the west side of Yuya Ansha and 13.6 nautical miles away from the northeast of Nanhai Jiao. When tide falls, reef rocks are above the surface and form shallow water lagoon, which is a small atoll. When tide rises, lots of reef rocks at the east side can be observed. There is no place for anchoring. Small ships can approach there when tide rises. This island was seized by Vietnam from March to April 1978.

Bai Jiao, including Danzhu shi, Wu Yuding shi, Bargue Canada Reef in English, is located at 8°10′00″N, 113°18′00″E (or from 8°04′ to 8°17′N, 113°15′ to 113°23′E), northeast of Anpo Shazhou, and 5.5 nautical miles away from the southwest of Danwan Jiao. It is a shuttle-like atoll which will be above the water when tide falls.

It extends to the northeast for about 33.2 km and there is a reef around 1.8 m high in the northeast of it. There is a lagoon in the reef center where ships can approach when tide rises. At the place 370 m away from the northern part of the reef, there is an anchorage area on the spit 36 ms in depth. However, the water here flows very rapidly. The maritime area of Bai Jiao is one of the major fisheries in the Nansha Islands. This reef was seized by Vietnam in February 1987.

Xi Jiao, West Reef in English and "Da Tay" called by Vietnam, is located at 8°52′00″N, 112°22′00″E (or from 8°52′N, 112°15′E to 8°49′N, 112°12′E), which is the westernmost reef of Yiqing Qunjiao, 16.4 nautical miles away from Dong Jiao in the east and 21 nautical miles away from northeast of Nanwei Island. The reef is an atoll which runs from northeast to southwest. There are several coral reefs on the top of it and a shoal 0.6 m high at the east side. The depth of the lagoon is around 10.9–18.2 m with several patch reefs. Many coral shoals are near the southwest side next to the center, and it is dangerous for sailing. The reef was seized by Vietnam in January 1988.

Riji Jiao, Ladd Reef in English and "Da Lat" called by Vietnam, is located at 8°39′00″N, 111°40′00″E (or from 8°38′N, 111°40′E to 8°39′N, 111°39′E), 13.8 nautical miles away from the west by north of Nanwei Island. It is a long small atoll with lagoon with white reef bottom and the length is 5.6 km and the width is 1.9 km. Part of the reef is above the water and there are shipwrecks in the northwest of it. When tide falls, ships cannot enter into the lagoon. The reef was seized by Vietnam in February 1988.

Wumie Jiao, Tennent Reef in English, is located at 8°52′00″N, 114°39′00″E (or 8°38′N–8°53′N, 114°38′E–114°41′E), north of Yuya Ansha, and its southwest is 25 nautical miles away from east of the northeast of Nanhua Jiao. It is a triangle-shaped reef with many rocks above the surface and it will emerge above the surface when tide falls. The atoll has no entrance and the water of the lagoon is deep and clear. Ships can approach it when tide rises. When northeastern wind blows, waves appear at the north side of the reef. The reef was seized by Vietnam in February 1988.

Dong Jiao, East Reef in English, and "Da Dong" called by Vietnam, is located at 8°49′N, 112°36′00″E (or 8°50′N, 112°34′E to 8°50′N, 112°35′E). It is 8.7 nautical miles away from Huayang Jiao in the east and 16.3 nautical miles away from the east of Xi Jiao. It is an underwater atoll with discontinuous edges and it runs from east to west. The Lagoon is from 7.3 to 14.6 m deep with shock waves above it which makes it easily to identify. In the west part, there are one or two rocks that cannot be submerged. According to reports, the inside and outside of the lagoon can be used for anchoring. The reef was seized by Vietnam in February 1988.

Daxian Jiao, East Reef in English, and "Da Lon" called by Vietnam, is located at 10°04′00″N, 113°52′00″E (or from 10°03′N, 113°52′E to 10°05′N, 113°52′E), 21 nautical miles away from the southwest of Zhenghe Qunjiao, 54 nautical miles away from the northeast of Yongshu Jiao by east. Most part of the reef will emerge above the water when tide rises. It is a long strip reef running from east to north. There are several reefs above the water and a lagoon in the center with deep water around it but no entrance. In 1867, a British naval vessel anchored at the place, 76 m deep and 0.5 nautical miles away from the north of the reef. According to the report of the fishermen from Hainan, there are rocks or shallows 10 nautical miles away from the northeast of the reef, where the depth is more than 73 m since the sounding plummet cannot reach the bottom. In February 1988, the reef was seized by Vietnam.

Nanhua Jiao, Cornwallis South Reef in English, and "Nui Le" called by Vietnam, is located at 8°45′00″N, 114°13′00″E (or from 8°44′N, 114°11′E to 40°N, 114°10′E). Northside of the reef is 6.5 nautical miles away from Liumen Jiao by east, which will emerge above the surface when tide falls. The reef is an atoll running from south to north with a lagoon which is 9 meters deep. In the south of the atoll, there is an entrance with less than 370 m in width, 9.1 m in depth and with several patch reefs. There are some dry reefs growing at the southeast side of the atoll. When northeasterly wind blows, the waves appear as the signal. The reef was seized by Vietnam in March 1988.

Guihan Jiao, Collins Reef in English, is located at 9°46′00″N, 114°15′30″E (or 9°45′N, 114°15′E). The reef is at the southwest of Jiuzhang Qunjiao, and its southeast is 1.8 nautical miles away from Chigua Jiao. The shape of the reef is like a quadrangle with many submerged rocks and dangerous shoals and only a few parts of it emerge above surface. There is a small coral sand dune in the southeast by its east. A deep-water channel is there to separate it from Chigua Jiao. In March 1988, the reef was seized by Vietnam.

Qiong Jiao, Lanstowne Reef in English, is located at 9°46′N, 114°22′E, 1.3 nautical miles away from the southwest of Quyuan Jiao and 5.5 nautical miles away from the northeast of Chigua Jiao. It is a reef flat that will emerge when tide falls among Jiuzhang Qunjiao. In March 1988, the reef was seized by Vietnam.

Liumen Jiao (Liumen, Liumen Sha), Alishon Reef in English, is located at 8°51′00″N, 114°00′00″E (or from 8°46′N to8°50′N, from 113°54′E to114°03′E). The northwest of the reef is 13.7 nautical miles away from Bisheng Jiao and its southside is 50 nautical miles away from the north of Nanhai Jiao. It is an oval-shaped atoll that extends to the east of the southeast and will emerge when tide falls. The shallow of the lagoon is dangerous. There is an entrance with a 9.1-m depth and a 650-m width, at the north side of the west of the reef. There are narrow water channels between each patch reef which emerges in the south. An anchorage is at the west and southeast of the reef with a depth of 60 m and another one at the west of it and outside of the north entrance of the lagoon has a depth of 9.1 m. In sunny days, spindrift can be seen 5 nautical miles away from the reef. The reef was seized by Vietnam in March 1988.

Bolan Jiao, Petley in English, and "Doi Thi" called by Vietnam, is located at 10°24′40″N, 114°34′00″E (or from 10°24′N, 114°34′E to 10°25′N, 114°35′E), at the northeast side of Zhenghe Qunjiao. It is 5.4 nautical miles away from the northeast of Dunqian Shazhou, and is near the external zone of deep and steep coral shelves extending for 5 nautical miles. In the coral shelf, there are shallows 5.4–8.5 m deep. This reef was seized by Vietnam in April 1988.

Nailuo Jiao, South Reef in English, is located at 11°23′00″N, 114°17′27″E (or 11°23′N, 114°19′E), at the southwest of Beizi Dao. It is 2.3 nautical miles away from Nanzi Dao, which will emerge above the surface when tide falls. During the southwest monsoon period, there are shock waves in its southwest side. The reef was seized by Vietnam in April 1988.

Guangya Tan, Princc of Wales Bank in English, is located at 8°08′00″N, 110°30′27″E (or from 8°04′N, 110°30′E to 8°08′N, 110°31′E), at the northeast of Xiwei Tan. It is 64 nautical miles away from the northwest of Nanwei Tan. It is an oval-shaped atoll which runs from northwest to southwest. The depth of the water varies and some reef patches are as deep as 15–19 m. From June to July 1988, the bank was seized by Vietnam.

Pengbo Bao, Bombay Castle in English, is located at 7°56′00″N, 111°42′30″E (or from 7°56′N, 111°43′E to 7°56′N, 111°44′E), at the northeast of Nanwei Tan, running from east to west, at a depth of 3 meters. It is an atoll at the shallowest place of Nanwei Tan. From June to July 1989, the island was seized by Vietnam and there are cannons and 12 Vietnamese soldiers garrisoning there.

Wanan Tan, Vanguard Band in English, is located at 7°30′00″N, 109°43′00″E (or from 7°30′N, 109°35′E to 7°28′N, 109°36′E), at the west of Nansha Islands and 35 nautical miles away from the southwest of Lizhun Tan. The island is crescent-shaped and 63 km long from east to west. It reaches an approximately 11 km in width on average. At the point of 112 nautical miles in the southeast-northeast of Wanan Tan, there is a reef patch with a depth of 64 m. There is a reef patch which is 82 m deep and 35 nautical miles away from the southeast of the Band. From June to July 1989, the island was seized by Vietnam.

Lizhun Tan, Grainger Bank in English, is located at 7°47′30″N, 110°29′00″E (or by Fu Kuncheng, 7°47′N, 110°29′E and by Valentia 7°52′N, 110°29′E), at the west of Renjun Tan and 12 nautical miles away from the south of Guangya Tan. It is a bank reef running from south to north, at a length of 9.6 km and a width of 3.7 km, with clear water. The shallowest place of the reef plat is around 11–15 m. The bank was seized by Vietnam in 1989.

Xiwei Tan, Prince Consort Bank in English, is located at 7°55′N, 110°58′E (or 7°52′N –7°53′N, 109°58′E–110°02′E), at the northeast of Wanan Tan and at the southwest of Guangya Tan. It is an underwater bank reef made by sand and coral, running from south to north, at a length of 29.5 km and a width of 16.6 km. The northwest edge is the shallowest part, with a depth of 18 m. The bank was seized by Vietnam in 1989.

Jinghong Dongdao, Sin Cowe East Island in English, is located at 9°55′N, 114°32′E. The possible time of being seized by Vietnam is 1988.

1.2.2 Nansha Islands and Its Waters Seized by the Philippines

Mahuan Dao, Nansha Island in English, and "Lawak" called by the Philippines, is located at 10°44′00″N, 115°48′E (from 10°43′N, 115°48′E to 10°44′N, 115°48′E), at the southeast of Xiyue Island and 10 nautical miles away from the northwest of Wufang Jiao by north. It is a long round-shaped island at an altitude of 2.4 m. On this island, there are coconuts trees, growing weeds, wells with good quality water and it is available for planting vegetables. There are many shallows where ships can anchor at the western edge of the reef flat in the south. The island was seized by the Philippines in September 1970, and there are about 80 soldiers garrisoning there.

Feixin Island, Flat Island in English, and "Patag" called by the Philippines, is located at 10°49′00″N, 115°49′30″E (from 10°49′N, 115°51′E to 10°49′N, 115°50′E), 5 nautical miles away from Mahuan Dao. It is a sand island with flat terrain without trees and importable water. It is 2 nautical miles extending from the edge of the island to the southeast and the northeast and 1 nautical mile extending to the south of Mahua Island. The water is 45 m deep and there are huge reef flats without precise measurement but available for anchoring.

Zhongye Dao, Thi Tu Island in English, and "Pagasa" by the Philippines, is located at 11°03′40″N, 114°16′20″E, 13 nautical miles away from the northeast of Zhubi Jiao, the west of Tiezhi Shuidao, and 3.4 meters above the sea. It is the second largest island among Nansha Island. It is like a triangle, where there are growing weeds, arborets. It has 18 meters tall coconut trees at the southwest. Along the coast, there are wells with drinkable water in the coconuts trees. Reef patches in the northeast above the surface around the island extend for 0.5 nautical mile. During northeast monsoon period, with an entrance, the central part of the west side of the island is the best landing ground. From May to July 1971, the island was seized by the Philippines. In 1978, a meteorological observatory with 80 marines was established there by the Philippines. In February 1978, the Philippines built a simple airport.

Nanyao Island, Loaita Island in English, and "Kota" called by the Philippines, or called as South Island of Horsbung, is located at 10°40′20″N, 114°25′20″E (from 10°41′N, 114°25′E to 10°40′N, 114°25′E), with an altitude of 1.4 m, which is the lowest island of Nansha Island. The island is covered with katus and coconut trees and bushes grow there. The island is 16 nautical miles away from the north of Zhenghe Qunjiao, at the southern edge of Daoming Qunjiao. Extending 0.5 nautical mile away from the island, the island has reefs above the water. There is a shallow 5.4 m deep, which is 2 nautical miles away from the island at the west. There are two reef flats 5 nautical miles away from the northwest of the island and 1 nautical mile apart at the northeast side. One reef flat is 0.8 nautical miles away to the east of Xinan Jiao with a 5.4 m deep shallow and the other one which is called Dongbei Jiao has a sandbank exposed in the center. In 1868, at the northeast of the above-mentioned two reefs, there is the northwest edge of Nanyao Island, and the surrounding water is measured to be more than 7.3 ms deep. 2 nautical miles away from the eastnortheast of Nanyao Island, there are some reef patches emerging above the surface. In 1933, no one inhabited on the island. According to the documents of scholars from China mainland, the island was seized by the Philippines in May-July 1971. However, according to Fu Kuncheng, the Philippine army had garrisoned on the island with 80 soldiers in total in 1968.

Beizi Dao, North East Cay in English, and "Parola" called by the Philippines, is located at 11°27′40″N, 114°22′43″E (or from 11°27′N, 114°21′E to11°27′N, 114°22′E), at the northwest side of Shuangzi Jiao, and 1.5 nautical mile away from the west-southwest of Gongtu Jiao. The island is the fifth largest island of Nansha Islands, which is a long oval sand island with an altitude of 3 m. It is covered with weeds and surrounded by shrubs, among which some are of 6.1–9.1 m tall. There is fresh water as well. Reef rocks in the northeast extend for 0.6 nautical mile. Between the northeastern edge of the reef rocks and Gongtu Jiao, the separation distance of the 5.4-m deep contour is about 560 m, and several 3-m deep shallows are in the middle but the channel is not available for navigation. Mr. Fu Kuncheng believes that the Philippines may seize the island in 1968, and 80 soldiers garrisoned in the island in 1971. However, other domestic documents show that the Philippine seized the island in May-July 1971, and a navy commander of the Philippines announced that a beacon was established on the island in March 1974.

Xiyue Island, West York Island in English, and "Likas" called by the Philippines, is located at 11°05′00″N, 115°00′E (from11°05′N, 115°01E to 11°05′N, 115°02′E). The southwest of it is 56.9 nautical miles away from Taiping Dao, and it is 13.3 nautical miles away from the southeast of Mengzi Jiao. It is an isolated island of the reef, and the third larges island of Nansha Island. Trees and shrubs cover it and several coconut trees of 25 m tall are there in the south. The submerged rocks 1.8 m below the water extend for 2 nautical miles from north to the ocean. There is a small bay in the southeast which can be a shelter from northwest wind. The water in the vicinity of the island is ideal for fisheries. In May-July 1971, the island was seized by the Philippines, and about 80 soldiers garrisoned on the island.

Siling Jiao, Commodore Reef in English, "Da Cong Do" called by Vietnam, "Rizal" by the Philippines, and "Terumbu Laksamana" in Malaysian, is located at 8°22′00″N, 115°13′00″E (8°22′N, 115°13′E–115°11′E). It lies in the northeast of Yuya Ansha and its northwest is 39.5 nautical miles away from Wumie Jiao and the westernmost is 25.8 nautical miles away from the easternmost of Yuya Ansha. The reef is an atoll that will emerge entirely above the surface when tide falls. On the reef george between the two lagoons, there is a sand bank 0.3 m above the water and 0.3-m tall rocks are there at the east of the reef. Boats can approach the lagoon in the west when tide rises and they can also approach somewhere of the lagoon when tide falls. The best place for anchoring is in the north and south 2 nautical miles away from the west of the reef. Most part of the lagoon in the west is 5.4–14.6 m deep but reefs are everywhere closing to the surface. The lagoon in the east with some dangerous shallows has not been measured precisely. The cliff of its outer part is steep and the water there is more than 2000 m deep so it is difficult for ships to anchor. The Philippines seized the reef in 1980.

Shuanghuang Shazhou, Loaita Nan in English, and "Panata" called by the Philippines, is located at 10°43′05″N, 114°31′35″E (10°43′N, 114°31′E–114°3′E), at the southwest edge of Daoming Qunjiao. It is 6.5 nautical miles away from east-northeast of Nanyao Dao, and is at the center of the reef rocks extending for 0.5 nautical mile to the ocean. There are two rocks above the surface at the northeast which is 3 nautical miles and 4 nautical miles away from the shoal respectively. From the rocks 4 nautical miles from the northeast of the sand bank, the water within 10.9 m deep extends for 1 nautical mile to the north; The shoal patch of 10.9 deep is located at the north of the reef flat which is in the northeast of the sand bank. Shuanghuang Shazhou is seized by the Philippines and there are two fresh water factories and two squads of marines of about 10 soldiers.

Ren'ai Jiao, Second Thomas Shoal in English, and always called as "Duanjie" by Chinese fishermen, is an atoll of Nansha Island of South China Sea. It is located at 9°39′N–9°48′N, 115°51′E–115°54′E, 14 nautical miles away from southeast of Meiji Jiao. The length from south to north is 15 km and the width from east to west is 5.6 km. Most part of the reef will emerge above the surface when tide falls. The north half part is relatively complete and the southern half part is divided into several sections which form several reef gates. Ren'ai Jiao is under the administrative jurisdiction of SanSha City of Hainan Province. Chinese garrison strictly monitor the reefs and regularly patrol there. Chinese ships berth at the lake within the reef.

1.2.3 Illegal Activities by Malaysia on the Nansha Islands and Its Waters

In 1968, Malaysia illegally delimited Nankang Ansha, Haining Jiao Beikang Ansha, and Zengmu Ansha into its territory, and rent them to an American company, Sarawak Shell, for oil drilling.

Malaysia conducted illegal exploration in Nankang Ansha and Beikang Ansha in 1970, Haining Jiao and Tanmen Jiao in 1971, Kangxi Ansha in 1972 and in Mengyi Ansha in 1973 as well.

In the maps published by Malaysia in December 1979, it could be seen that Siling Jiao, Polang Jiao, Nanhai Jiao, Anbo Shazhou, Nanyue Ansha, Xiaowei Ansha, and the waters in the south of the island and reefs were delimited into the territory of Malaysia.

The Islands seized by Malaysia include:

Danwan Jiao, Swallow Reef in English, and "Terumbu Layang Layang" called by Malaysia, is located at 7°23′N–7°25′N, 113°50′E, 27.5 nautical miles apart from the northeast of Huanglu Jiao and 13.9 nautical miles away from the southwest of Andu Tan. It is a shallow lagoon surrounded by a long and narrow coral reef zone with several 1.5–3 m tall rocks at its northeast. There are rocks above the surface in the southeast. The reef has developed into an island, which is an ideal navigational mark. During daytime, the spoondrift can be seen 8 nautical miles away. There is a shipwreck in the west. In August 1983, the island was seized by Malaysia with a commando of 45 people. In May 1991, Malaysia declared that the island would be developed into a tourist attraction. In September 1992, Malaysia established simply-constructed airport on the island.

Guangxingzi Jiao, Ardasier Bank in English, and "Terumbu Ubi" called by Malaysia, is located at 7°37′30″N, 113°56′00″E (7°36′N–7°37′N, 113°56′E). It is a triangle-shaped atoll in the southwest of Andu Tan and 14 nautical miles away from north-northeast of Danwan Jiao. Reef rock that surround the shallow lagoon can be seen when tide falls and ships can approach the lagoon when tide rises. Except for the east side of the reef joint with Andu Tan, other edges of the reef are extremely abrupt. In 1986, the reef was seized by Malaysia.

Nanhai Jiao, Marivels Reef in English, and "TerumbuMantanani" called by Malaysia, is located at 7°56′N–8°00′N, 113°56′E–113°58′E, 35.2 nautical miles away from west by south of Yuya Ansha, and the south of the reef is 18 nautical miles away from Andu Tan. When tide falls, the reef rocks will emerge above the surface, which will form a shallow lagoon. It is a small atoll where some reef rocks can be seen when tide rises. There is no place for anchoring and can be approached when tide rises. The reef was seized by Malaysia in October 1986.

Boqi Jiao, Erica Reef in English, "Terumbu Siput" called by Malaysia, is located at 7°30′N–7°57′N, 113°56′E–114°02′E. The island was seized by Malaysia.

Until today, there is no complete and authoritative data which record the total number of islands, reefs and shoals in Nansha Islands. According to *Nansha Islands, Dongsha Islands and Penghu Islands* written by Liu Baoyin, it is 142. And, there are 185 listed in the appendix of *Research on Legal Status of South China Sea* written by Fu Kuncheng. And, there are 93 islands, reefs and shoals listed in *Sharing the Resources of the South China Sea* written by Valencia who is from the East and West Center. However, the mentioned three data are not complete. Nevertheless, the islands, reefs and shoals listed by Mr. Fu Kuncheng are relatively comprehensive.

Vietnam, the Philippines and Malaysia are continuously seizing the islands, reefs and shoals listed above. The total number is about 40, which accounts for one third of the number counted by Liu Baoliang, almost close to one third of the number counted by Fu Kungcheng, and over half of the number collected by Valencia. No matter which number is taken as reference, it suggests the grim situation that those countries have seized plenty of islands, reefs and shoals within the traditional territory of China. After their invasion, they have intensified their rule on the territory through the means of migration, establishment of harbor, airport, and satellite state, attempting for de facto "legitimization". China should be vigilant, and figure out the solution.

After their invasion of the islands, reefs and shoals, Vietnam, the Philippines and Malaysia have speeded up to explore petrolatum and pillage the resources that belong to China. Through pillaging the resources, Vietnam has developed from a country lack of petroleum into an oil exporting country. Malaysia and the Philippines have also benefited a lot from oil exploration. The worst situation for China is that the involved countries gang up on us. It is an indisputable fact that Malaysia and Vietnam jointly develop and explore the petroleum within the traditional territory of China.

China pursues peaceful means to deal with international disputes. China also proposed an assumption that on the premise that the sovereignty of the invaded territory belongs to China, shelving differences and seeking joint development can be achieved. It reveals that China has made a concession. However, the involving states didn't accept the concession and denied the assumption proposed by China. They have continuously conducted illegal activities, explored and developed oil resources within traditional territory of China. They even strike down Chinese fishery ships which conduct legal and regular operation. The situation is not in favor of China.

Scholars and experts from Chinese mainland and Taiwan have already proposed some assumptions. Related departments should speed up to draw up plans and implement them. China should be prepared for both eventualities in order to respond to the activities of involving states. China should seek peaceful settlement, as well as strengthen its power. Meanwhile, China should explore effective ways as well as take practical measures, such as immigrating into these islands.

References

An Unabridged, Comprehensive Dictionary. (compact edition), Shanghai Lexicographical Publishing House, 1989, p. 583.

ASIA, The XXth Century, Citizen's Atlas of the World. Gorge Newnes, Limited 1902.

ASIA, Refer to Justus Perthes: Altals Portail Decima Septima Ediction, Gotha: Justus Perthes 1937.

EURASIA, CARTA FISICA, Atlante Geografico Universale, Baratta E Visintin, Sperling & Kupfer, Milano, 1938–39.

Chen Keqin, *The Islands in the South China Sea*, Hainan International News Press Center: 1996, p. 140.

Fan Kaiyi, Qian Guanghua, "The Partition of Kainozoic era sedimentary basin and the prospect of petroleum resources in the Nansha Islands waters" printed in *The Nansha Island in 21st Century: Proceedings of Problems and Prospects Seminar*, 2000, pp. 150–160.

Ju Jiwu, Pan Jiangang, "Abundance Products and Precious Treasures", printed in Chen Keqin, ed., *The Islands in the South China Sea*, Hainan International News Press Center: 1996, p. 259.

Liu Baoyin, *The Nansha Islands, the Dongsha Islands and the Penghu Islands*, the China Ocean Press: 1996, pp. 1–28.

Nlle Galles Meridle. Ou Cote Orientale de la Nouvelle Hollande. RIGOBERT BONNE (1788). This map is used by *TERRA AUSTRALIS DISCOVERED* (1600–1800),refer to Robert Clancy: *The Mapping of Terra Australis*. Universal press, 1995.

OCEANIA (1850). DETALHES DA COLONIA DA NOVA GALLES MERIDIONAL.

OCEANIS (1835). Dressee, Par. A. R. FREMIN, Paris.

SOUTH HEMISPH (1816). Projected and Engraved for Thomson's New General Atlas, 20th, Sep.1816. Projected on the Plane of the Horizon of London, By Geo. Buchanan, J. G. Menzies, Sculp. Edin.

Urano Tatseo, *Sea power: the History of Disputes in the South China Sea and the Current Situation of the South China Sea*, 刀水书房(とうすいしょぼう) 1997, p. 37.

Wang Hengjie, "Archaeological survey of Nansha", in Chen Keqin,ed., *The Islands in the South China Sea*, Hainan International News Press Center: 1996, p. 443.

Wu Shicun, *The Origin and Development of the Dispute of the Nansha Islands*, China Ocean Press, 1999, p. 56.

Xia Kanyuan, et al. "Comprehensive geophysical analysis and oil and petroleum characteristics of Zengmu Basin", printed in *Report of Comprehensive Research on the Nansha Islands and the nearby Waters*(一)Vol. 1, Science Press, 1989 .

Xie Yixuan, "The Elementary Characteristics of the Topography of the Nansha Islands", *The Symposium of Study on the Geological physics and reefs of the Nansha Islands and Sea Areas Nearby*, China Ocean Press, 1991.

Zhang Zhenguo, "A Trip to the Nansha Islands", refer to No. 8 *of the Documentation of the Islands in South China Sea*, Taiwan Students Book Store, 1975.

Zhao Huanting, "Characteristics of regional environment and resources in the South China Sea", printed in *The Nansha Island in 21st Century: Proceedings of Problems and Prospects Seminar*, 2000, pp. 150–160.

Chapter 2
Application of International Law Theories to the Dispute on the Nansha Islands

2.1 Territory Acquisition and Change in International Law

2.1.1 Territory Acquisition in International Law

There are two types of territory acquisition and change, namely, traditional and modern ways in international law. Traditionally, there are five ways in terms of territory acquisition and change: occupation, accretion, prescription, cession and conquest. Among the five ways, occupation, accretion, conquest and prescription are ways of original acquisition, while cession is a way of derivative acquisition. With the development of modern international law, two new ways have been created: self-determination and referendum.

Occupation is derived from the preoccupation system of private property in Roman law. Some famous international law scholars take the preoccupation system as the "only natural and original way of territory acquisition."[1] The object of preoccupation is *terra nullius*. And *terra nullius* could become part of a state's territory through this country's effective occupation. On May 4th, 1493, Pope Alexander VI issued a decree to assign the newly-discovered territories to Spain and Portugal, rendering "Discovery" as one element of territory acquisition. However, because the competitions among European countries for the colonies were so fierce in the 18th century, "Discovery" alone did not lead to territory acquisition. In other words, "Effective Occupation" became a prerequisite for territory acquisition. The elements of "Effective Occupation" contain subjective and objective factors. The subjective factor means that the occupant must have the intent to occupy, while the objective factor refers to the occupation actions. It is acknowledged that Effective Occupation is the prerequisite for non-state territorial acquisition in both the arbitral award on the Kripke island (France v. Mexico) held by the Italian King on January 28, 1931 and

[1] H. Grotius, De jure belli ac pacis, Eng. Trans. ,Bk. 11, Chap. 111., Fenwick (1965).

C. Yang and Q. Zhang, *Legal Study on China's Sovereignty over the Nansha Islands*,
https://doi.org/10.1007/978-981-15-8715-3_2

the judgment concerning the legal status of Eastern Greenland (Norway v. Denmark) held by the Permanent Court of International Justice.[2]

Effective Occupation is that a state intentionally exercises jurisdiction over non-state territory. The intent could be reflected by state's declaration, announcement, domestic legislations, administrative measures and other means. The intent could be to permanently control the *terra nullius* which is occupied, to incorporate the area in a state's own territory or to take concrete measures to exercise occupation so as to exercise a state's power peacefully in this area. In other words, a state is exercising effective occupation or control in the area through legislative, judicial or administrative measures, such as setting up a settlement, hanging national flag, establishing administrative institutes, etc. It is obvious that effective occupation requires that a state should lay military and police who are able to sufficiently exercise a state's power in its occupied areas in order to specifically realize occupation. And the occupant should peacefully exercise a state's power. Huber confirmed the two points above in the Island of Palmas arbitration case.

---

[2]The Norway government announced that Norway had sovereignty over Erik the Red's Land (71° 31 min north latitude to 75° 40 min north latitude) in Eastern Greenland on July 10th, 1931. The legal basis of the announcement was that this area was *terra nullius* instead of territories of Denmark. Afterwards, Demark resisted in response to this announcement, and filed a litigation before the Permanent Court of International Justice based on the court's optional mandatory clause. The Denmark government held that the land occupied by Norway actually belonged to the Denmark royal family, and thus the land could not be occupied by other countries. In this regard, the Denmark government insisted that the court judge the Norway government's occupation announcement and related steps taken consist the destroy of current legal situations and therefore illegal and invalid., and acknowledge Denmark had sovereignty over Eastern Greenland and deny Norway's claim on its sovereignty over Eastern Greenland in the announcement.

The court held that Norway's occupations announced on July 10th, 21,931 and related steps taken were both illegal and invalid. The reasons are two: from the historical perspective, no country had raised any objection against Denmark's sovereignty over Eastern Greenland before July 10th, 1931. Denmark had been exercising its sovereignty continuously and peacefully. From 1380 when Denmark and Norway united as a real union, the Denmark king's right in Greenland was equal to sovereignty. At the beginning of 17th century, Denmark had sent expeditions to the islands and excluded foreigners' engagement in business there. In 1721, Denmark set up colonies in the islands, which further indicated and exercised Denmark's sovereignty over the islands. According to the Treaty of Kiel signed in 1814, the Denmark-Norway Union ceded Norway to Sweden, while Eastern Greenland still belonged to Denmark and Denmark continued exercising its power. For instance, Denmark released a series of licensed document on conferring exclusive rights of trading, hunting and mining in the eastcoast in Greenland to the English people Taylor. Between 1915 and 1921, the Denmark government mailed foreign countries to request them acknowledge Denmark's sovereignty over Greenland. On May 10th, 1921, the Denmark government issued a decree to strengthen its rule in Greenland. All the above facts indicate that Denmark has been exercising effective governing over the all Greenland, certainly including Eastern Greenland. Consequently, the court should confirm that Denmark has sovereignty over Eastern Greenland. Another reason is that Norway's activities indicate its acknowledgement of Denmark's sovereignty over Eastern Greenland. For example, Norway became the state party of international agreements on the dispute of Greenland, which guaranteed Denmark's rights. These international agreements reflect that Greenland is the colony of Denmark, or permit Denmark exclude Greenland from the scope of validity of the agreements. In addition, the Norway foreign secretary Helen announced orally when he met the Denmark minister in Christian on July 2nd, 1919 that the Norway government would not thwart Denmark's sovereignty

It is notable that with the development of international community, there is no longer *terra nullius* in strict sense in the world when the 20th century began. Non-state territory does not equal to *terra nullius*.

With respect to the ways of accretion, in accordance with international law, the original territory which is expanded because of natural reasons and human factors still belongs to the original state. Accretion could be divided into natural accretion and artificial accretion. Natural accretion is territory increase owing to natural reasons, such as delta area expansion because of sediment accumulation in the mouth of river, new island appearance in territorial waters, etc. Territory expansion by reclamation of land from lakes and seas, dam construction, artificial facilities construction in the reef is the so-called artificial accretion.

Cession refers to a state's transfer of its partial territories to another state through agreements. Cession could be divided into mandatory cession and non-mandatory cession. Mandatory cession means that a state forces another state to transfer its territories through agreements by military force. And this transfer is achieved through military threat or war, and therefore is obviously unequal. There are several mandatory cession incidents in history, such as the Treaty of Frankfurt in 1871, through which France ceded Alsace and Lorraine to Germany. And in the Treaty of Brussels in 1919, Germany ceded two cities back to France. Non-mandatory cession refers to that a state transfers its territories to another state peacefully on an equal basis. For instance, Russia sold Alaska to the United States in 1867. Another example is that China and Burma exchanged partial territories along their boundaries in 1960.

Traditional international law allows resorting to wars to settle international disputes, so mandatory cession is legal. The two Hague Peace Conferences in the late 19th century and the early 20th century respectively, the General Treaty for Renunciation of War as an Instrument of National Policy in 1928 and the Charter of the United Nations require that all states should abandon war, and take peaceful measures instead to settle international disputes. Consequently, mandatory cession has already been denied by modern international law, while non-mandatory cession is still legal because it is on an equal and free will basis.

Conquest is that a state occupies all or part of other states' territories through military force, and annexes the territories after the war ends so as to acquire territories. Because this way to acquire territories violates the Charter of the United Nations and other basic principles of international law, conquest is not acknowledged as a valid way to acquire territories by modern international law.

Prescription means that a state acquires sovereignty over other states' territories through exercising its administrative power long-term and peacefully after it has occupied part of their territories. "Exercising administrative power peacefully" means that other states don't raise protest or objections, or stop protest or objections against a state's occupying the territories so that the state's occupation is not disturbed. The principle of prescription could not be applied alone, and instead must be considered

over Greenland and would not occupy any Greenland land. The court held that this announcement was binding to Norway. And Norway at least bore the obligations not to raise any objection against Denmark's sovereignty over the whole Greenland.

together with other territory acquisition measures. However, modern international law goes against invading other states' territorial sovereignty, and against occupying other states' territories illegally. Moreover, in the modern international community, no state is willing to have their own territory occupied by others. In this regard, it is not realizable to acquire territories through prescription.

2.1.2 Ways of Territorial Change in International Law

Self-determination, referendum and reversion of territorial sovereignty are new ways of territorial change developed in modern international law.

Self-determination is a territorial change when a nation is separated from its colonizing state or metropolitan state to be an independent sovereignty state or join another state. In accordance with this principle, a number of independent nations have been founded in Asia and Africa after the Second World War.

Referendum or general polling is that citizens in a land decide the territorial entitlement fully independently by polling. According to this principle, Saarland was incorporated into Germany in 1935; West Ukrainian People's Republic and the Republic of Belarus which were Poland's territories were incorporated into Ukraine and the Republic of Belarus in 1939; West Irian was incorporated into Indonesia in 1969.

Reversion of territorial sovereignty or revendication refers to a state's reversion of its territories which were illegally occupied by other states and reversion of its historical title on the territories. Modern international law does allow neither invading other states' territorial sovereignty by military force or military threat nor acquiring other states' territories by military force or military threat. In other words, modern international law acknowledges states' reversion of its occupied territories. There are peaceful and otherwise measures to reverse occupied territories. China, by resorting to peaceful measures, took back its sovereignty over Hong Kong and Macau. By war, China regained its sovereignty over Taiwan and the Penghu islands from Japan's illegal occupation; India regained its sovereignty over its boundary river, Dammam and Diu from Portugal; Kuwait took back its sovereignty over Iraq. To conclude, modern international law allows reversion of occupied territories by war measures.

2.2 Ways of Territory Acquisition and Change Applied to the Nansha Islands Dispute

All above indicate that conquest, cession and prescription are all applied to the land which were under other states' sovereignty jurisdiction. Hence these ways of territorial acquisition are cannot be applied to the Nansha Islands. Referendum and self-determination, another two ways of territorial change, are applied to the condition where there are a number of citizens or indigenous people on the land, and thus cannot be applied to the Nansha Islands either. Therefore, only preoccupation, accretion and reversion of territorial sovereignty could be applied to the Nansha Islands dispute.

Nansha Islands are far from Chinese mainland, and there are several big reefs, such as Taiping Island, Xiyue Island, Zhongye Island, Nanyue Island and Hongjing Island. Moreover, life on these islands is just manageable but not pleasant. And the rest of the more than 90% of reefs, sands and submerged reefs are not suitable for living. Consequently, the way of territorial acquisition with respect to the Nansha Islands sovereignty could only be original acquisition rather than ways of land territorial acquisition.

The objective of preoccupation is "*terra nullius*", "Territories inhabited by tribes or peoples having social and political organization were not regarded as '*terra nullius*'".[3] Early in the Han Dynasty, the Chinese people named the Nansha Islands and recorded the incident in history to certify that Chinese discovered the Nansha Islands at that time and brought it under China's administrative jurisdiction. Chinese fishermen were living on the islands and built temples and other living facilities. Nansha Islands were obviously *terra nullius* to the Han Dynasty or even later in the Song Dynasty. Vietnam, the Philippines, Malaysia and other countries surrounding the South China Sea did not claim their sovereignty over the Nansha Islands until the fiftieth of the 20th century, or even late in the eightieth of the 20th century, when the Nansha Islands were not *terra nullius* any more.

Accretion also applies to the Nansha Islands since the reefs in the Nansha Islands originate from corals. It is recorded in China's *Book of the Later Han* that "rising sea in all the seven countries of the Giao Chi quận reaches seven to eight hundred miles. At the bottom of water there are monoliths, on which corals grew."[4] This means ancient Chinese had realized that the Nansha Islands were formed by corals. Corals constantly secrete calcium and make coral calyx, which can grow thicker and bigger due to the pile up of calcium. According to the experts' measurement, the growth rate of top coral reefs which are in the southernmost point of the Nansha Islands is named Zengmu Reef. The water is 17.5 m deep with an increase of 5.5 cm per year. "The average growth rate of coral reefs in Xisha Islands is about 1 mm per year."[5] As Nansha Islands are formed by piles of corals, the islands of natural accretion belong to China.

There are also artificial accretions in the Nansha Islands. Under the delegations of UNESCO, oceanographic stations have been built in the Yongshu Reef of the Nansha Islands in order to provide scientific statistics for global marine observations. The Yongshu Reef runs northeast-southwest direction, and is an elliptic atoll made by several reefs exposed by ebb-tide, including the coral shoal patches washed up by

[3] *Encyclopedia of Public International Law*, Vol. 2, Decisions of International Courts and Tribunals and International Arbitrations, North Holland Publishing Co., p. 291.

[4] *Imperial Readings of the Taiping Era*, Vol. 69.

[5] He and Zhong (1979).

seawater. The reef edge is steep and deep with inter-reef between 14.6 and 40 m. In high-tide, only exposed patch reefs in southwest and the reefs with 0.6 m in southeast are above water, while the rest reefs are all underwater. In 1988, Chinese constructers built a lot of land facilities such as observation stations, wharfs, roads, buildings, oil depots, reservoirs and playgrounds on the reef sites of the Yongshu Reef. In addition, China also built pile dwellings on some reefs. It is evident that these facilities manually made by China also belong to China.

With respect to the principle of revendication, it has already been applied to the return of Hong Kong and Macau to China. Considering that more than forty reefs of the Nansha Islands are occupied by such countries as Vietnam, the Philippines and Malaysia, China's oil and minerals round the Nansha Islands are illegally exploited and pillaged. One day, China will take whatever means to take back its occupied islands, reefs and sands so as to regain its legal rights over the Nansha Islands.

2.3 The Complexity of the Dispute on the Nansha Islands

2.3.1 The Categories of International Disputes

In 1927, the Permanent Court of International Justice held in *Lotus* case (France v. Turkey) that "international disputes only arise when a particular application of the laws in question shows them to be at variance with international law". In brief, international dispute is different legal or factual claims, or the conflict owing to political interests or particular rights among subjects of international law. Accordingly, international dispute is divided into two categories, namely legal dispute and political dispute in traditional international law.

Legal dispute or dispute of rights refers to the dispute between states involved with respect to concrete rights and obligations. The characteristic of legal dispute is based on international law. According to Article 36(2) of the Statute of International Court of Justice, legal dispute could be divided into four categories: (1) the interpretation of a treaty; (2) any question of international law; (3) the existence of any fact which, if established, would constitute a breach of an international obligation; (4) the nature or extent of the reparation to be made for the breach of an international obligation. Arbitration or judicial proceedings could be resorted to in order to settle legal dispute. Consequently, legal dispute is also called "judiciable dispute".

Political dispute or conflict of interests refers to political interest conflict between states involved and the dispute could not be effectively solved in accordance with legal criteria. Political dispute involves essential political issues such as state sovereignty and independence, national security, national reputation and national sentiment. It is virtually impossible to deal with political dispute through legal means. Therefore, political dispute is also called "non-judiciable dispute".

It is proved by practice of international relations and development of modern international law that it is very difficult to simply categorize international disputes into legal dispute and political dispute. Many international disputes contain both legal and political factors and thus mixed international dispute arises. Additionally, among mixed international disputes, some contain more legal than political factors while some include more political than legal content. All in all, it is difficult to completely separate political and legal content. Thus it is necessary to study and further discuss every dispute case by case. In order to settle the mixed international disputes, we could simply take legal ways or political ways, or take both of them simultaneously.

Apart from the three international disputes above, another factual dispute arising from states' different opinions towards a fact, a situation, or the truth of a matter may also exist. It is advisable to deal with the disputes whose facts are unclear or controversial through political ways such as investigations, reconciliations etc.

2.3.2 The Dispute of Nansha Islands Is a Mixed Legal and Political Dispute

International dispute is very complicated according to the categories of international disputes above. The dispute of the Nansha Islands is also complex at the moment. It is complex "at the moment" because the dispute of the Nansha Islands initially did not virtually exist. Though some foreign experts insist the dispute of the Nansha Islands has existed for long, and use such vocabularies as "international dispute of the South Sea", "the South Sea is international common sea area".[6] Obviously, they intend to involve the states besides the neighborhood countries in the dispute of the Nansha Islands. We firmly disagree with this attitude and must pay great attention to it.

The dispute of Nansha Islands involves six countries including China, Vietnam, the Philippines, Malaysia, Brunei and Indonesia.

The sovereignty dispute of the Nansha Islands is in fact not complicated. The dispute becomes so difficult to settle largely due to the fact that China has not been building solid foundations as always after the Second World War, or enter and garrison on the habitable islands of the Nansha Islands.

References

Charles G. Fenwick, *International Law*, 4th Edition, Meredith Publishing Co., 1965, p. 404.
He Jisheng, Zhong Junliang, *A Study on the Growth Rate of Coral Reefs in the Xisha Islands from the Perspective of Archaeological Discovery*, 1979.

[6]Professor Urano Tatseo from Law School of Nihon University clearly refers to these vocabularies in a unpublished paper and in *The History of Disputes in the South China Sea* published by 刀水水房 in 1997.

Chapter 3
The Legal Meaning of Maps and Its Applications to the Sovereignty Dispute on the Nansha Islands

Maps have played important roles in dealing with the sovereignty dispute of the channel islands between the United Kingdom and France, the sovereignty dispute of Preah Vihear Temple between Thailand and Cambodia, and some modern international borderline disputes such as the dispute between Jordan and Israel. The role of maps could be concluded as follows: Territorial maps reflect the scope of jurisdiction of a state's sovereignty. Military maps even demonstrate a state's sovereignty. Various maps could be used as evidence in dealing with borderline disputes. When a state publishes its territorial maps and when other states follow these maps, or no states raise any objections against the maps, these conducts should be regarded as acknowledgement and acquiescence in international law. The legal force of maps is equal to treaties and quasi-treaties when borderline maps are acknowledged as the appendices of treaties. It is indicated in majorities of maps, both in China and abroad, that Nansha Islands belong to China, including maps from the dispute-involved states. All the above functions of maps could be applied to disputes on the Nansha Islands and thereby prove that China has indisputable sovereignty over the Nansha Islands.

3.1 The Legal Meaning of Maps

3.1.1 General Functions of Maps

In accordance with the explanations in *the Geographical Chapter of Encyclopedia of Chinese Dictionary*, map is, according to specific mathematic rules, to minimize natural and human phenomenon on the ground to a two-dimensional graph by specific signals through cartographic generalization.

Maps can be used to effectively deal with the conflict between sphere and two-dimension, complicated content, and clear and readable pictures. Map signals, such as points, lines, plans and colors, could represent content as abundant as possible with least space. Moreover, map signals could also significantly minimize area of

C. Yang and Q. Zhang, *Legal Study on China's Sovereignty over the Nansha Islands*,
https://doi.org/10.1007/978-981-15-8715-3_3

diagram and amplify important phenomenon which could not be shown by plotting scales. Map is characterized by perceptual intuition, geographical orientation, abstract conceptualization and geometrical accuracy, and has basic functions such as information delivery, graphic modeling and graphic understanding. The tendency of geo-analysis may appear in many departments and fields owing to the special functions of maps, the development of scientific technology, especially the popular application of geographic information systems on account of the combinations of mathematics, computer technology and maps. It is certain that cartographic method is going to be more widely applied and further developed, following the mathematic method.

3.1.2 Legal Functions of Maps

3.1.2.1 The Function of Maps in the Sovereignty Dispute on the *Minquiers and Ecrehos* Case (France/United Kingdom)

In the case concerning sovereignty dispute of Jersey of the English Channel and both the Minquiers and Ecrehos along the French coast, all the judges reached consensus that the United Kingdom has sovereignty over the islets and rocks in the Minquiers and Ecrehos groups. One of the critical bases of the judgment is a letter and two charts that French Maritime Affairs Minister gave to the French Ministry of Foreign Affairs. In the two charts, the Minquiers and Ecrehos were not incorporated in French territory.[1]

The Minquiers and Ecrehos are very far from the United Kingdom, while the Ecrehos is only 6.6 nautical miles far from the French coast and the Minquiers is 16.2 nautical miles far from the mainland of France, and only 8 nautical miles far from the Suoxi Islands of France. Only a few of these islands are habitable, while they are normally used to make it convenient for fishermen and summer tourists as temporary shelters to escape the wind.

After the Second World War, both France and the United Kingdom intended to exercise sovereignty over the Minquiers and Ecrehos, and thus were against each other to take the two islands as *terra nullius* or condominium. France and the United Kingdom signed a special agreement in which both the states consented to submit the dispute to the International Court of Justice in December 29th, 1950.

In order to acquire the sovereignty over the Minquiers and Ecrehos, the United Kingdom and France submitted a large amount of historical evidence. The United Kingdom claimed that the whole English Channel, including the Minquiers and Ecrehos, has belonged to the United Kingdom ever since the Duke of Normandy conquered the United Kingdom in 1066. Nevertheless, France claimed that besides the main channel islands, namely Jersey, Guernsey and Alderney belong to England,

[1] Report of the International Court of Justice (1953), Vol. 47, p. 71, cited from *American Journal of International Law*. 1963, vol. 57, p. 785.

while the rest French King fiefs owned by King John of England had already been deprived according to a French court judgment on April 28th, 1202. The King of France Philip Augustus conquered Normandy in 1204 and excluded Anglo Normans from it. Hence the Minquiers and Ecrehos and other islands along the French coast have belonged to the King of France ever since the disintegration of Normandy.

The United Kingdom and France submitted a lot of bilateral treaties between the United Kingdom and France as well as other documents so as to support their claim of rights. By reviewing the treaties, the court held that none of those treaties, namely, Treaty of Paris of 1259, Treaty of Calais of 1360 and Treaty of Troyes of 1420, have specified the ownership of the two islands. A convention on fishery between the United Kingdom and France, concluded in 1839, only agreed to establish a shared fishing zone outside the fishing zones of the United Kingdom and France instead of addressing on the sovereignty of the inland basin of the shared fishing zone, where the Minquiers and Ecrehos are located.

Nevertheless, the judges noted a letter and two charts that French Maritime Affairs Minister gave to the French Ministry of Foreign Affairs among the documents that the two states submitted. This letter and charts were delivered to the Foreign and Commonwealth Office of the United Kingdom from the French ambassador. The letter as well as one of the charts indicated that the Minquiers and part of the Ecrehos belonged to the United Kingdom, though the line of territorial water of the Ecrehos had not yet been drawn. And the rest of the Ecrehos was taken as *terra nullius*. The memorandum of the Foreign and Commonwealth Office of the United Kingdom indicated that the letter and charts showed France took the Ecrehos as "a state belonging to none" rather than belonging to France, and regarded the Minquiers as belonging to the United Kingdom.[2] The French representative held that the letter and charts were made when distinguishing the fishing activities of the fishermen of the United Kingdom and France, and thus were irrelevant to the borderline demarcation. The legal consultant and chief representative of the United Kingdom Harrison rebutted that the letter and charts delivered by the French Maritime Affairs Minister is a state action and therefore represented the standpoint of the French government. Accordingly, the letter and charts should be taken as important base for the judgment of the International Court of Justice.

Both states submitted a lot of maps to support their own submissions in the litigation procedures. Harrison, the chief representative of the United Kingdom, specifically prepared two editions of maps of Germany in order to avoid just referring to maps of the United Kingdom. Two maps of Germany incorporated the Minquiers and Ecrehos into the United Kingdom. Accordingly, the English representative insisted that the court should refer to the two maps of Germany because the maps were evident and essential. The French representative acknowledged the importance of maps in territorial disputes. Nonetheless, he argued that the court should attach more attention to other states' maps which were neutral and more accurate. Subsequently, France showed maps of Italy, Switzerland, Hungary, Germany and the United Kingdom.

---

[2]*American Journal of International Law*, Vol. 57, 1963, pp. 785–786.

However, the English representative argued that the maps shown by France indicated the islands belonged neither to France nor to the United Kingdom.

The judge of this case Levi Carneiro noted the maps and held that the maps were evidence that indicated the exercise of sovereignty and territorial entitlement, though not decisive in setting the dispute on territorial legal status.

3.1.2.2 The Important Function of Maps in the Sovereignty Dispute on the *Preah Vihear Temple* Case (Thailand v. Cambodia)

The importance of maps is fully demonstrated in the dispute on Preah Vihear Temple along the borderline between Cambodia and Thailand.

Preah Vihear Temple is located in the eastern extension of the Dangrek Mountains juncture of Cambodia and Thailand. Siam (current Thailand) and France, the protectorate state of Cambodia then, signed a demarcation agreement to confirm that the demarcation point of the eastern Dangrek Mountains was the watershed on February 13th, 1904. Siam and France agreed to establish a demarcation committee which was responsible for field exploring and demarcation of the borderline. In the end of 1906, the demarcation committee, taken charge by French, investigated the eastern Dangrek Mountains, including the Preah Vihear Temple. France and Siam agreed on a new agreement in terms of further demarcation on March 23rd, 1907.

After signing borderline agreement and field exploring, France and Siam moved to the last procedure of setting borderline dispute, that is, to make more detailed protocols and maps. Siam itself did not take part in making maps, but instead delegated the French to do it. And the French completed making borderline maps in 1907. In 1908, the French gave completed maps to the Siam government. And the maps were appendices I of memorials to the borderline agreements between Siam and Cambodia. However, as one of the appendices, one map delimited the Preah Vihear Temple (located in the Siam side of the mountain watershed), which was supposed to be incorporated into Siam, to Cambodia. The Siam government then, nevertheless, did not raise any objections against this mistake, but instead thanked the French for their work. Forty years later, Thailand discovered the mistake on the map in 1948 and sent military forces into the temple. The French government and the independent Cambodia successively protested and insisted that Thailand had evacuated its military forces, which were rejected by Thailand.

On 1959 September 30th, Cambodia brought a litigation to the International Court of Justice according to the demarcation map between France and Siam in 1907. After reviewing the evidence submitted by Cambodia and Thailand, the International Court of Justice held that the fact that the maps drawn in demarcation that marked the Preah Vihear Temple in the Cambodia side was not consistent with the demarcation principle that demarcation point of the eastern Dangrek Mountains was the watershed. As one of the appendices, the map was not ratified by the bilateral committees and thus was not legally binding preliminarily. Nevertheless, reasons as follows could demonstrate that map, instead of articles in the agreement, should be referred to by

Cambodia and Thailand. For one thing, the map was handed to the Siam government as a demarcation result. The Siam government acquiesced by having not raised any objections at that moment and many years afterwards. For another, the map was delivered to the representatives of Siam government and none of them opposed. In this regard, the Siam government accepted the map as Appendix I without any investigations, and therefore they could not deny the truth that they agreed with the map by turning to any mistakes.[3] The Thailand accepted the map as well as the demarcation in the map, which therefore constituted the acknowledgement of Cambodia's sovereignty over the Preah Vihear Temple.[4]

3.1.2.3 The Function of Maps in the Sovereignty Dispute on the *Frontier Lands* Case (Belgium/Netherlands)

In the frontier lands disputes between Belgium and the Netherlands, maps played critical roles again. On November 29th, 1836, the Belgium Mayor Baerle-Duc and the Dutch Mayor Baarle–Nassau reached a Memorandum of Agreement when classifying tax areas. On April 19th, 1839, Belgium and the Netherlands signed a separate London Protocol, according to which a mixed boundary commission was established. On November 5th, 1842, Belgium and the Netherlands signed a boundary agreement. Both countries agreed to take "detail described and detail surveyed maps and topographic maps as the appendices to the agreement. And the Appendices are equally binding as the agreement." Belgium, however, could not agree with the Netherlands with respect to the explanation of protocol memorandum as well as boundary agreement. From the standpoint of Belgium, two villages belonged to Belgium according to the protocol memorandum, whereas the Netherlands insisted that those two villages belonged to the Netherlands.

By reviewing the records of the boundary commission, the court held that maps played significant roles for both commissions because they needed careful preparation and verification. Moreover, the maps that demonstrated the disputed land belonged to Belgium and were equally binding as the agreement itself and therefore were part of the basis to settle the dispute.[5] The court also referred to the military map which demonstrated that the villages mentioned above belonged to Belgium

[3]Liang (1999).

[4]Chen (1998).

[5]*Report of the International Court of Justice*, Vol. 209, p. 220, p. 216, cited from *American Journal of International Law*. 1963, Vol. 57, p. 788.

and was published by Belgium. The Belgium representative defended that "military map is the demonstration of sovereignty".[6]

Judge Moreno Quintana held that the dispute between Belgium and the Netherlands was a dispute on the explanation of agreement. Both states could not reach an agreement due to some mistakes and thus a judgment should be made in accordance with maps.[7]

It is evident that maps were given certain importance in the territorial dispute between Belgium and the Netherlands, and was especially essential for Belgium to rebut the Netherlands.

In the Palmas dispute brought to the Permanent Court of International Justice in 1928, Judge Huber held that maps played indirect function in territorial dispute. "Evidence could be found out in maps…among indirect evidences". And maps were especially important in the following two situations in which "draftsmen draft the map by collecting abundant materials instead of merely basing on maps available", or "official and semi-official maps".

To conclude, a map is legally essential in settling modern international boundary disputes.[8] Generally speaking, a territorial map, especially a military map, demonstrates the fact of a state's sovereignty. Varieties of maps serve as evidence in settling boundary disputes. It is regarded as acquiescence or acknowledgement in international law if a state publishes its territorial map and other states follow it or do not raise any objections against it. Moreover, a map is equally binding as agreement especially when boundary maps are accepted as appendices to an agreement.

3.2 Maps at Home and Abroad that Demonstrate the Nansha Islands Belonging to China

The Chinese was the first to discover and occupy the Nansha Islands and the Chinese government was the first to exercise its sovereignty over the Nansha Islands. The fact that the Nansha Islands belong to China is demonstrated in a lot of maps at home and abroad which show that the Nansha Islands are within the Chinese territory.[9]

---

[6] *Indictment of the International Court of Justice*, Sovereignty over Certain Frontier Land Case (Belgium v Netherlands), cited from *American Journal of International Law*. 1963, Vol. 57, p. 789.

[7] *Report of the International Court of Justice* (1959), Vol. 209, p. 254.

[8] Refer to Zou (1997).

[9] Zhang (2000).

3.2.1 The Chinese Government Reconfirmed the Evident Fact the that Nansha Islands Belonged to China by Publishing Maps

3.2.1.1 The Territorial Map in the Qing Dynasty Demonstrated that the Nansha Islands Belonged to China Through Municipal Administrative District

Yu Changhui drafted "Wanli Changsha" and "(Wan Li Chang) Sha" in the Coastal Map in Zhi Province, which was in the first page of the preface of his book *An Abstract of Coast Defense* in 1842, the twenty-second year of the Daoguang Emperor in the Qing Dynasty. Wanli Changsha referred to the Dongsha Islands and the Xisha Islands while the (Wanli Chang) Sha referred to the Zhongsha Islands and the Nansha Islands. It was clearly demonstrated that the Nansha Islands belonged to China in the map.

Wu Changfa drafted "Wanli Changsha" and "Wanli Shitang." when revising Geographic Maps of All Administrative Unites of China in 1904, the thirtieth year of the Guangxu Emperor in the Qing Dynasty. Wanli Shitang referred to the Zhongsha Islands and the Nansha Islands. The drafter indicated that "Wanli Shitang" was a provincial administrative unite in China. Evidently, the map demonstrated the fact that the Qing Dynasty exercised jurisdiction over the Nansha Islands.

In 1905 (the thirty-first year of the Guangxu Emperor in the Qing Dynasty), Wang Xingshun revised Geographic Maps of All Administrative Unites of China in the Qing Dynasty. He also incorporated the Zhongsha islands and the Nansha Islands into China, referred to as "Wanli Shitang", which was marked as a provincial administrative unit by a rectangle legend in the map.[10]

3.2.1.2 The Map in the Republic of China Demonstrated that the Nansha Islands Belonged to China

The maps in the Republic of China published both by individuals and the government demonstrated the Nansha Islands belonged to China. Those maps could be divided into two categories. In the first category, there were eight editions of maps demonstrating the fact that the nine small islands of the Nansha Islands belonged to China after the French colonists declared the occupation of the nine small islands in 1933. In the second category, the Nansha Islands, the Zhongsha Islands, the Xisha Islands and the Dongsha Islands were incorporated as a whole into China's territory. And there are sixty editions of maps in the second category.[11] The first category includes A Survey on Current China (one copy) and A Survey on Current World (one copy), written by Tong Shiheng and proofread by Chen Haoji. Both of the illustrated books incorporated part of the Nansha Islands into China's territory. Additionally, another

[10]Refer to Han (1988), p. 309, pp. 311–312.

[11]Han (1988), p. 319.

six maps published in 1934 and 1935 also incorporated part of the Nansha Islands into China's territory.

In the second category of maps, for example, the second map of the New Construction Maps of China (applied to middle schools), published by Beiping Construction Library in 1936, incorporated the four islands of South Sea into China's territory and marked all around by range lines. The southernmost was at 4° north latitude and Zengmu Reef was within the range line. Moreover, the author noted in this map that the Nansha Islands were where the Chinese fishermen lived and grew and thus its sovereignty undoubtedly belongs to China. The way of lineation remained the same when the book was republished in 1937. In July 1947, the Shanghai Yudi Student Association compiled the New Geographical Textbook of China. The book marked the Nansha Islands and other three islands by range lines and such letters as "territory of the Republic of China" in the Administrative Map of China in page four to indicate they belong to China. The southernmost was also at 4 degrees north latitude. The ninth map of the Geographical Textbook of the World, published in July 1947 in Shanghai, also marked the four islands in the South Sea by range lines and incorporated the Nansha Islands into China's territory with the southernmost 4° north latitude. The same lineation that incorporated the Nansha Islands into China's territory with the southernmost 4° north latitude could also be viewed in the New Provincial Maps of China published in July 1947 in Shanghai, on page four of the Administrative Map of China and page twenty of the Map of Guangdong in the New Geographical Textbook of China published by Commercial Press, page twelve of the Map of Fujian, Taiwan, Guangdong and Guangxi in the Geographical Textbook Maps in China and Abroad published by Yanguang Yudi Press in 1947, the Introductive Maps of Current China published by Wuchang Press in August 1947, the Map of the South China Sea Islands in the Maps of Modern China published by Yanguang Yudi Press in September 1947, the Territory Transition Maps in Recent China in the New Maps of China published by Shanghai Commercial Press in December 1947, the Location Maps of the South China Sea Islands made by the territory department of the Ministry of the Interior and printed by the measurement bureau of the Ministry of National Defense, the Location Maps of the South China Sea in the Administrative Area Chart of the Republic of China made by the territory department of the Ministry of the Interior and printed by Commercial Press in February 1948, the Maps of Modern China published by Yanguang Yudi Press in March 1948, the Political Area Maps of China in the New Maps of China published by Oriental Yudi Press in April 1948, the Map of Guangdong in the New Provincial Maps of China published by Shanghai Press in July 1948, the Maps of Islands in South China Sea in the New Maps of the Republic of China published by Yanguang Yudi Press in January 1949, the Islands of the South China Sea in the Latest Big Maps of China published by Xinya Yudi Press in April 1949, and the Maps of Islands of the South China Sea in the New Maps of China published by China History and Geographic Press in September 1949 etc.

There are up to 60 maps that incorporate the Nansha Islands wholly into China's territory, which demonstrate that it is widely acknowledged that the Nansha Islands are China's territory just viewed from the quantity of the maps. It is notable that the

Map of Islands in the South China Sea, which was edited and published by the Land and Water Map Review Board of the Republic of China in 1935, incorporated the Nansha Islands today into China's territory as Tuansha Islands. The Land and Water Map Review Board was constituted with staffs from the General Staff, Ministry of Interior, Ministry of Foreign Affairs, Admiralty, Ministry of Education and Mongolian and Tibetan Affairs Commission. The Board was responsible for reviewing land and water maps published all over the country. On March 22nd, 1935, the Board demanded all territorial maps in political divisions to mark out the Tuansha Islands (namely the Nansha Islands) and other three islands by No. 29th conference resolution. Ministry of Interior decided to rename Tuansha Islands as Nansha Islands and afterwards formally authorized and issued it in 1947 and from then on the names of these Islands have been used. The governmental actions of the Republic of China have laid the foundation of maintaining China's territorial integrity.

With respect to the demarcation of range line of the Nansha Islands, the map which was formally and publicly published by territorial department of Ministry of Interior in February, 1948 marked the southernmost line as approximately 4° north latitude, including Zengmu Reef. And this demarcation is still in use.

3.2.2 Maps of State Parties Concerning the Disputes on the Nansha Islands that Demonstrate the Nansha Islands Belong to China

In the current territorial dispute on the Nansha Islands, Vietnam seized more than twenty of China's islands. Nevertheless, the previous maps published by Vietnam clearly indicate that Vietnam acknowledged China's sovereignty over the Nansha Islands. The World Map published by the map department of the Headquarters of the General Staff of Vietnam People's Armed Forces in 1960 clearly demonstrates in Vietnamese that "Nansha Islands" belong to China. This map inevitably reminds us of the military map shown by the Belgium representative in the territorial dispute between Belgium and the Netherlands who declared that "military map stands for state sovereignty". Similarly, the military map of Vietnam also stands for Vietnam's state sovereignty, which also means Vietnam could not exercise its state sovereignty over the Nansha Islands. Nansha Islands belong to China. The fifth map of Vietnam Atlas, published by the Bureau of Survey and Cartography of Vietnam in 1964, spelt the Nansha Islands in Chinese phonetic alphabet. The World Atlas and the World Political Maps, published by the Bureau of Survey and Cartography of Vietnam respectively in 1972 and in 1974, also marked "Nansha Islands" based on its Chinese name in Vietnamese.

The Vietnam maps had not yet incorporated the Nansha Islands into Vietnam's territory while the Chinese maps have already incorporated the Nansha Islands into China's territory. This fact indicates the Vietnam government acknowledged Chinese maps' lineation and hereby acknowledged China's sovereignty over the

Nansha Islands. None of the following maps incorporates the Nansha Islands into Vietnam's territory, and reversely, marked the Nansha Islands in Chinese phonetic alphabet: the Vietnam Atlas published by the Bureau of Survey and Cartography of Vietnam in 1964, the Vietnam Terrain Roads Maps published by the Vietnam National Geographic Department in 1966, the Vietnam Administrative Regions Maps published by the Vietnam Education Publishing House in 1968, the World Atlas published by the Bureau of Survey and Cartography of Vietnam in 1972, the Vietnam Traffic Maps and the Vietnam Territories published by Saigon. These maps should be regarded as acquiescence of China's sovereignty over the Nansha Islands.

As another state in the sovereignty dispute on the Nansha Islands, many Philippine maps also acknowledge that China has sovereignty over the Nansha Islands. None of the Philippine Survey and Statistics Maps (many volumes) published by Philippine Statistics Authority in 1940, the Philippine Maps published in 1950 and the Atlas published by the Coast and Land Hydrographic Department of Manila Investigation Committee in 1969 incorporate the Nansha Islands into Philippines's territory.

As two major states involved in the Nansha Islands dispute, the Philippines and Vietnam neither raise any objections after the Chinese government approved and publicly published a large number of maps that certified the Nansha Islands belong to China, nor incorporate the Nansha Islands into their territories in their domestic maps, which evidently demonstrate that the Philippines and Vietnam acknowledge China's sovereignty over the Nansha Islands.

Among the states not involved in the Nansha Islands dispute, Japan and France belong to a special category. Both Japan and France once evilly invaded China's Nansha Islands, but acknowledged China's sovereignty over the Nansha Islands after their invasion.[12] The Japanese and French official maps also incorporate the Nansha Islands into China's territory, which is strong evidence to rebut the sovereignty claim on the Nansha Islands from the Philippines, Vietnam, Malaysia and Brunei.

The fifteenth of the Standard World Atlas published by Japan National Education Publishing House in 1952, namely the Asia-pacific map, shares the same lineation with the map of China. The Asia-pacific map marked the that Nansha Islands belong to China by national boundary line and also marked the Nansha Islands in Chinese phonetic alphabet.[13] It is notable that there is autography from the Japanese Foreign Minister Katsuo Okazaki in the title page of the map. New edition of the map published by Japan with the autography from the Japanese Foreign Minister evidently makes sense in international law, hereby acknowledging that China's effective governing area includes the Nansha Islands.

The nineteenth of the World New Atlas, edited by Tanaka Kakuei in 1964, named "the Philippines", drew a maritime boundary line near west Palawan, including the Nansha Islands in China's territory and marked the islands in Chinese phonetic alphabet. There is a recommendation letter from the Japanese Foreign Minister Ohira Masayoshi in the title page of the map, which indicates that Japan invaded China and

---

[12]The author of *The History of Disputes in the South China Sea,* Professor Urano Tatseo from Law School of Nihon University.

[13]Han (1988), p. 615.

Asia-pacific regions, but returned the Nansha Islands to China and acknowledged China's sovereignty over thc Nansha Islands.

The 11th page of the World Map (new edition), published by Japanese Heibonsha in 1968 marked the Nansha Islands with "CN" letters in brackets indicates that the Nansha Islands belong to China.[14]

The relation between France and Vietnam is even special. From the middle 19th century, Vietnam, Cambodia and Laos of Indo-China were colonized by France by colonial wars. Therefore, France has decisive influence on the political, economical and diplomatic affairs of indo-china. It was France who marked "the Nansha Islands (Spratly Islands) (China)" in the No. 13B map, namely an Asia-pacific map, of the Larousse World Political and Economical Atlas, published by the Larousse Bookstore in 1956. The mark indicated that France acknowledged the that Nansha Islands belong to China. The 98th to 99th pages of the Larousse Atlas, published by the Larousse Bookstore in 1969 drew a maritime boundary line outside the Nansha Islands. And the line was basically consistent with that of China. Page 100 to page 101 of the Pocket World Atlas published by the French General Bookstore in 1970, recorded the Nansha Islands as "Spratly Islands (China)". Here "Spratly Islands" refers to the Nansha Islands, which again indicated that France acknowledged China's sovereignty over the Nansha Islands.[15] Moreover, there are seven French maps that have not incorporated the Nansha Islands into either Vietnam's or Philippines's territories, such as the 28th map of the World's Natural Geographical and Political Geography Atlas published in Paris in 1889, the Indo-China Map attached to French Indo-China Maps published in 1907, Volume 2 attached map of Indo-China Political Regions Maps attached to the French Indo-China Colonial Empires published by France in 1927, Volume 2 of the Economic Maps attached to the French Indo-China Colonial Empires published in 1929, Volume 2 attached map of the Indo-China Maps attached to the French Indo-China Colonial Empires published in 1929 and the Indo-China Maps attached to French Indo-China Colonial Empires whose publish dates are unknown. None of the above maps have incorporated the Nansha Islands into the French colonial territories, which indicates the French government acknowledged the fact that the Nansha Islands belonged to China.

The United States was once the sovereign state of the Philippines, and thus attitude from the United States towards the Nansha Islands should also be considered. The Philippine Map published by the United States in 1905 marked Philippines's territories by black lines. The map also verifies "the line of Treaty of Paris", and indicates affirmatively that the Nansha Islands are not in the territorial line of Philippines. The Philippine Map published by the United States in 1938 marked the Philippine territorial line by imaginary lines and noted the line is "a line of international treaties", indicating affirmatively that the Nansha Islands were not in the sea boundary line of Philippines. The sea border in Indo-China and East India, in page 160 of the Gute School Applicable Maps, published by the United States in 1939 and 1943, is the line confirmed in the Treaty of Paris of 1898 between Spain and the United States.

[14]Han (1988), p. 637.

[15]Han (1988), p. 658, p. 632, p. 636, p. 658.

The map excluded the Nansha Islands from Philippines's territories. The Philippine Islands Maps, edited and published by Military Atlas of the United States in 1944, also excluded the Nansha Islands from Philippines's territories. In view of the special relations between the United States and the Philippines and the lessons learned from the Island of Palmas arbitration case, the United States would definitely be very serious about dealing with the ownership of the Nansha Islands. The United States, nevertheless, did not include the Nansha Islands within Philippines's territorial line, which indicates that the United States does not regard Nansha Islands as part of Philippine territory.

3.2.3 *Maps Published by Other Countries*[16] *that Acknowledge China's Sovereignty Over the Nansha Islands*

Maps published by many other influential countries such as the United Kingdom, Canada, the former Soviet Union, Switzerland, Spain, Portugal, Italy, Australia, former East Germany, former West Germany, Romania, Czech, Hungary, Poland and Bulgaria have incorporated part of the Nansha Islands into China's territories.[17] According to incomplete statistics, there are more than 200 such maps.[18] And there could be even more if the number of maps that do not incorporate the Nansha Islands into the territories of Vietnam, Philippines, Malaysia and Brunei is counted.

The 141st and 142nd Asian Map of the World Atlas published by Soviet Narodnyy Komissariat Vnutrennikh De (NKVD) in 1954 both incorporated the Nansha Islands and other three islands in the Southern Sea into China's territories. The Atlas published by Soviet NKVD in the same year also regarded Nansha Islands as Chinese territory. The Map of China edited by Surveying and Mapping Bureau of Soviet NKVD in 1956 marked "China" behind the words "Nansha Islands" so as to indicate that the islands belong to China. Page 186 to page 187 of the World Atlas edited and published by Military Topography Department of the Soviet Union General Staff in 1958 also noted "Nansha Islands (China)", "Spratly Islands (China)" as well as "Amboyna Cay (China)", indicating the islands belong to China. Page 107 to page 108 of the World Atlas edited and published by Surveying and Mapping Bureau of Soviet NKVD in 1959 marked the that Nansha Islands belonged to China. Many other maps also incorporate the Nansha Islands, along with the Zhongsha

[16] With respect to the fact that maps published by many other states which incorporate the Nansha Islands in China's territories and thereby acknowledging China's sovereignty over the Nansha Islands, majorly refer to Han Zhenhua, (eds.) *Historical Data Compilation of the Islands in Southern China Sea.* A few maps were collected from the library map room of Cambridge University and the British Museum in January 2001 by the author of this book.

[17] For example, the introductions at page 116 of *Times World Map* (6th edition) published by the United Kingdom in 1980 acknowledged that China brought the Nansha Islands under the administrative jurisdiction of Guangdong Province and marked the Nansha Islands and its affiliated major islands by Chinese phonetic alphabet.

[18] Li (1990).

Islands, the Dongsha Islands and the Xisha Islands into China's territories. They are such maps as the Asia-pacific map, attached map of the Concise Geographic Encyclopedia (volume 2, page 296) published by the Soviet Union in 1961, page 49 of the World Atlas published by Moscow in 1962, page 101 "map of Asia-pacific", page 86 "map of Asia" and page 89 "map of China" of the World Atlas published by Moscow in 1963, page 102 to page 103 "map of Asia", page 105 to page 106 "Asian political map", page 117 to page 118 "map of middle and southern China", page 128 to page 129 "map of Indonesia" of the World Atlas (English version) published by the CCCP-affiliated Surveying and Mapping Bureau in 1967, page 85 to page 86 "map of Asia" and page 89 to page 90 "map of China" of the Pocket World Atlas edited and published by the CCCP affiliated Surveying and Mapping bureau in 1975.

Some other maps also incorporate Nansha Islands and Xisha Islands into China's territories, such as page 168 to page 169 "map of China" attached to the Bolshaya Sovetskaya Entsiklopediya published in 1953, page 46, page 62 to page 63 of the Atlas published in Moscow in 1954, page 85 to page 86 of the Pocket World Atlas published by CCCP-affiliated Surveying and Mapping Bureau in 1955, page 140 to page 141 of the Foreign Administrative Area published by Moscow Geographical Publishing House in 1957, the World Administrative Zones Wall Maps published by Surveying and Mapping Bureau of Soviet NKVD in 1957, the Pacific Wall Maps and Atlas for Middle Schools published in 1958, attached map of the Concise Geographic Encyclopedia published in 1960, attached map of the Soviet Union Small Encyclopedia published in 1961, page 34 to page 35 of the World Atlas published by the Soviet Union in 1962, the Bolshaya Sovetskaya Entsiklopediya published in 1963, Map of the Northern Hemisphere published in 1965, Map of Asia published in 1966, the World Atlas published in 1967, Map for the Soviet Union Middle Schools published in 1968, Chinese illustrations in Bolshaya Sovetskaya Entsiklopediya published in 1973, page 280 to page 281 "Map of Pacific Regions" of the Atlas Maps of Oceans published in 1974, and page 101 to page 102 of the Pocket World Atlas published in 1975. The above maps were published by the Soviet Union government or published after being reviewed by the official department of the government. Therefore, they are authoritative and could be a strong support for China's territorial sovereignty over the Nansha Islands.

In addition, Map of Indonesia published in Moscow in 1966 and in 1974 incorporated the Nansha Islands into China's territories.

Page 27 of the World Atlas published by Romanian State Publication Bureau in 1957 also regards the Nansha Islands as belonging to China. Asian Natural Geographical Maps published in 1964 notes in Chinese phonetic alphabet that the Nansha Islands belong to China. And No. 116th map of the Atlas published in 1974 also marks that the Nansha Islands belong to China.

And many maps of Czech mark the that Nansha Islands belong to China, such as page 103 of the Pocket World Atlas, published by Czech Surveying and Mapping Bureau in 1957, page 103 (map No. 26a) of the Pocket World Atlas edited by Czech Surveying and Mapping Bureau in 1958, map No. 27a of the Pocket World Atlas published in 1960, page 22 of the Pocket World Atlas published in 1960, and page 23 of the Pocket World Atlas published in 1963 and 1964.

Moreover, some Hungarian maps also mark the Nansha Islands as belonging to China, such as No. 60 and No. 61 of the World Atlas published in Hungary in 1959, page 60 of the Asian Wall Maps and Atlas published in 1959, page 116 to page 117 of the World Political and Economical Atlas published in Hungary in 1961, page 74 of the Pocket World Atlas published in 1965, and page 116 to page 117 of the World Political and Economical Atlas (with illustrations) published by the Hungarian Map Publishing House in 1974.

Former East Germany also had published a lot of maps which acknowledged China's territorial sovereignty over the Nansha Islands, such as the World Atlas in 1956, the Harker World Atlas published in Leipzig in 1968 (No. 28 in volume 4, No. A4 and A6 in volume 5, No. A6 and No. 12 in volume 6, No. 12 in volume 7), No. 128 and No. 129 of the Latest World Atlas published in 1970, and page 193 of the Atlas for Harker's Family published in 1973. Besides, the boundary line outside the Nansha Islands marked in the Atlas for Harker's Family is the same as that of China.

Additionally, the Map of Middle, East and Southern Asia published in Bulgaria in 1959 to 1960 notes the that Nansha Islands belong to China.

Map of Asian Administrative Zones published in Poland in 1957, Asia-pacific Wall Maps published in Poland in 1960 and Pergamon World Atlas published in 1968 all mark Nansha Islands as Chinese territory.

Because of the Cold War after the Second World War, some capitalist countries such as the United Kingdom, France and the United States were hostile to China, a communist country. Even under such a situation, their published maps still acknowledge China's territorial sovereignty over the Nansha Islands. In fact, their acknowledgement represents Western countries' attitude towards China's sovereignty over the Nansha Islands.

Page 40 of the Penguin State of the World Atlas which was published in the United Kingdom in 1956 marks the Nansha Islands as Chinese territory.

The 9th map of the World Atlas published in West Germany marks the Nansha Islands as Chinese territory.

Page 226 to page 227 of the Aguilar World Atlas published in Spain in 1970 notes the that Nansha Islands belong to China, and also marks some important reefs of the Nansha Islands in their Chinese names. The 63rd, 67th and 73rd maps of the Atlas of Integrated World Economy and Geographies published in Spain in 1973 and Layered Atlas of the World published in Spain in 1971 both mark the Nansha Islands as Chinese territory.

The Wilder Mike Countries Encyclopedia, published in the United States in 1963, says that the islands of People's Republic of China "include the islands and cays extended to 4° northern latitude of the South China Sea. The islands and cays include the Dongsha (Pratas), Xisha (Paracel), Zhongsha and Nansha Islands."[19] In addition,

[19]"China has indisputable sovereignty over the Xisha islands and the Nansha Islands—document of the Ministry of Foreign Affairs of People's Republic of China" (January 30th, 1980) in *The Xisha Islands and the Nansha Islands have been China's Territories since Ancient Time*, People's Publishing House, 1982, p. 8.

some maps published in the United States mark the islands in their Chinese names, thereby acknowledging China's sovereignty over the Nansha Islands.

What's more, western countries did not incorporate the Nansha Islands into either Philippines's or Vietnam's territories, such as the attached Map of Far India of Tokyo or France in the Far East published in the United Kingdom in 1884. The attached map of Indo-China of the Surrounded Tokyo and Siam published by the United Kingdom in 1894 does not incorporate the Nansha Islands into French territories. Map of Indo-China attached in During Annam's Tenure and after His Quilt published in the United Kingdom in 1910 does not incorporate the Nansha Islands into Indo-China's territories. The attached map in the preface of Indo-China published in Paris and London in 1930 does not incorporate the Nansha Islands into French territories, neither.

3.3 China Has Indisputable Sovereignty Over the Nansha Islands from the Legal Functions of Maps

Different roles of maps could be viewed from the sovereignty dispute on the Minquiers and Ecrehos case (France/United Kingdom), the Preah Vihear Temple case (Thailand v. Cambodia) and the Frontier Lands case (Belgium/Netherlands). In addition, many published maps of influential countries, including China, Vietnam, the Philippines, France, and Japan, indicate China has sovereignty over the Nansha Islands. In this regard, the above cases concerning boundary and territorial disputes as well as a number of historical maps of China and foreign countries should play essential roles in carving out maritime boundary lines between China and other countries surrounding the Nansha Islands such as Vietnam, the Philippines, Malaysia and Brunei. The South China Sea national boundary dropped line defined by China in 1947 is acknowledged both by China and countries surrounding the South China Sea and it is natural that it is the most important basis and standard.

There are two reasons for the origination of the South China Sea national boundary dropped line. One is France's invasion of southern Hainan, which invoked strong resistance from the Chinese government and people. The other one is the Policy of the United States with respect to the Natural Resources of the Subsoil and Sea Bed of the Continental Shelf, issued by President Truman of the United States. The proclamation stated "the natural resources of the subsoil and sea bed of the continental shelf which are beneath the high seas but adjacent to the coasts of the United States subject to the jurisdiction and control of the United States".[20] Under the particular circumstance, it has legal significance that the Chinese government maintained China's sovereignty over the Nansha Islands by national boundary dropped lines.

In the 1930s, the Map Review Committee established by the Government of Republic China consisted of such state powerful departments as the General Staff, the Ministry of the Interior, the Ministry of Foreign Affairs, the Admiralty, the Ministry of

[20] Wang (1995).

Education, and the Mongolian and Tibetan Affairs Commission. On April 14th, 1947, the Ministry of the Interior re-invited the government and some other departments to discuss about the area of the South China Sea. After the discussion, all attendants agreed that "it should be maintained that the southernmost of the South China Sea reaches to the Zengmu Reef, which had been confirmed by the government and schools as well as press publications of the Republic of China before the Anti-Japanese War, and recorded by the Ministry of the Interior as well." "After the Ministry of the Interior's review and reference from the national government, it was to declare sovereignty over the Xisha Islands and the Nansha Islands, attached with maps. The navy general headquarters was to enter and garrison all the affiliated islands before the declaration."[21] The intermittent national border line of the South China Sea was formed "through the process growing out of nothing, the continuous to the intermittent and from the folk to the official". "In terms of its development, the national boundary dropped line of South China Sea is the declaration of Chinese government's sovereignty over the Nansha Islands"[22] "we should persist and maintain our sovereignty within the national boundary dropped line of the South China Sea."[23]

Judge Huber held that "official and semi-official maps" could play certain roles in dealing with territorial disputes.[24] Consequently, it is reasonable that Chinese government follow all previous Chinese governments' consistent stands. Charles. C. Hyde, an American jurist, clearly pointed out that "a map, published by sponsorship or statement of a state…, could be taken as a state's claim of its territorial boundaries" in his article "Map Evidence in International Boundary Dispute". "Conclusions could be reasonably drawn, from a series of similar maps published in decades which reflect the same facts and carved the same boundary, that these maps could confirm the boundary as long as no related states raise any new convincing ways of (territorial) acquisition." Hyde continued "maps, published in accordance with specific litigants' support or request, should have binding force to litigants in boundary arbitrations."[25] Here Hyde clearly acknowledged official maps' significant roles in dealing with boundary disputes. Moreover, Merdey pointed out in his article Boundary and Maps that "official maps are strongest evidences for a state to claim its sovereignty within territorial boundaries provided that they are publicly published and distributed by a state."[26] Another British, an international law scholar, also held that "originally, courts and arbitral tribunals consistently acknowledge the importance of maps to serve as evidence for both parties in dispute with respect to boundary disputes."[27]

Article 38 of the Statute of International Court of Justice states that "judicial decisions and the teachings of the most highly qualified publicists of the various

[21]"A Measurement of the Boundary Stone of Sha Tau Kok in the Xi'sha and the Nansha Islands", Guangdong Province Governmental Achieves. Cited from Li (1999), p. 112.

[22]Wu (1999).

[23]Li (1999).

[24]Cited from *International Journal of Marine and Coastal Law*, vol 1, 1999, p. 49.

[25]Hyde (1933).

[26]Merdey (1964).

[27]McEwen (1971).

nations are subsidiary means to the determination of rules of law". To conclude, China should use a number of maps that reflect China's sovereignty over the Nansha Islands as maritime boundaries of the Nansha Islands sea areas. Chinese government has indisputable sovereignty over the Nansha Islands according to a number of maps published by the Chinese government and other countries as well as the fact that China's exercise of sovereignty over the Nansha Islands in history. The South China Sea national boundary dropped line is the Chinese government's explicit declaration of China's territories, and thus could be the most crucial ground on which China deals with surrounding countries in terms of boundary issues in the Nansha Islands.

References

Charles. C. Hyde, *Map Evidence in International Boundary Dispute*, American Journal of International Law, 1933. Vol. 27, p. 315.

Chen Zhizhong, ed. *Cases of International Law*, Law Press. China, 1998, p. 156.

Han Zhenhua, eds. *Historical Data Compilation of the Islands in Southern China Sea*, Oriental Publishing Center, 1988. P. 309, pp. 311–312.

Li Jinrong, ed. *International Law*, Sichuan People's Publishing House, 1990, p. 116.

Li Jinming, *A Study on South China Sea Boundaries*, Fujian People's Publishing House, 1999, p. 113.

Liang Shuying, ed. *Study Cases of International Law*, China University of Political Science and Law, 1999. p. 68.

A. C. McEwen, *International Boundaries of East Africa*, Oxford, The Clarendon Press, 1971, p. 54.

T. S. Merdey, *Boundary And Map*. India Journal of International Law, 1964. Vol. 4, p. 388.

Wang Tieya, ed. *International Law*, Law Press China, 1995, p. 272.

Wu Shicun, *The Origin and Development of the Dispute of the Nansha Islands*, China Ocean Press, 1999, p. 30.

Zhang Aining: Theory and Cases of International Law, People's Court Press. 2000, pp. 208–281.

Zou Keyuan, "Chinese Traditional Marine Boundary Line of the South China Sea and Its Legislative Effects in the Dispute Settlement of the Spratly Islands", *International Journal of marine and Coastal Law*, Vol. 1 1997, p. 48.

Chapter 4
Jurisprudential Grounds for China's Claim for Rights Over the Nansha Islands and Surrounding Sea Areas

4.1 China Has Indisputable Sovereignty Over the Nansha Islands According to Intertemporal International Law

4.1.1 Discussions and Resolutions of Intertemporal International Law

Intertemporal law, existed in Roman law, was firstly proposed by the Roman Emperor Theodosius II in A.D 440. One of his decrees pointed out that "laws and rescripts are published for future action modes rather than past facts", from which jurists drew a famous legal principle, namely, "the Principle of law of non-retroactivity". In other words, the principle is "to determine which law to apply with respect to the applicable issues attributed by law changes."[1] Law of non-retroactivity is widely incorporated in national laws currently, such as Article 9(3) of the United States Constitutions and Article 2 of the Napoleonic Code. Article 12 of Criminal Law of the People's Republic of China provides that "if an act is committed after the founding of the PRC and before the implementation of this law when it was not deemed a crime under the laws at that time, the laws at that time are to be applicable. If the act was deemed a crime under the laws at that time, and if under the provisions of Chapter IV, Section 8 of the general provisions of this law it should be prosecuted, criminal responsibility is to be investigated according to the laws at that time. However, if this law does not deem it a crime or imposes a lighter punishment, this law is to be applicable. The effective judgments that were made according to the laws at that time before the implementation of this law will continue to be in force." Article 3 of Interpretation I of the Supreme People's Court of Several Issues concerning the Application of the Contract Law of the People's Republic of China provides that "The people's court shall, when confirming the validity of a contract, apply the Contract Law if the contract is formed before the implementation of the Contract Law is void under the

[1] Li (1989, p. 97).

C. Yang and Q. Zhang, *Legal Study on China's Sovereignty over the Nansha Islands*,
https://doi.org/10.1007/978-981-15-8715-3_4

law at that time but valid under the Contract Law. Similar rules could also be found in the constitutions, civil laws and criminal laws of some other states.

In the Island of Palmas arbitration case (United States v. the Netherlands), Judge Huber introduced intertemporal law into international law for the first time. He insisted that the effectiveness of Spain's exploration should be judged in accordance with the international law in the first half of 16th century. In the Western Sahara case, the International Court of Justice also held that the answer to the dispute should be consistent with contemporary effective legal views. In 1970, a French international law scholar Paul Tavernier wrote a book *Application dans le Temps des Actes et des règles en droit International Public (Problemes de droit Intertemporel ou de droit Transitoire)*, and a German international law scholar Wolf-Dietrich Krause-AblaB published a book *Intertemporales Volkerrecht-Der zeitliche Anwendungsbereich von Volkerrchtsnormen* to discuss intertemporal law in international law. Moreover, *The Intertemporal Problem in Public International Law* was published by the Institut de droit International in August, 1975.

According to Wolf-Dietrich Krause-AblaB, international law is are changing. Existing norms become invalid when new norms come into effect, with a problem created: which one of these consecutive norms applies to one particular fact. In this regard, conflicts arise between these consecutive international norms in the judgement of a past fact. And it is necessary to clarify the time range of application of the old and new norms so as to resolve the conflicts. Intertemporal law, including intertemporal private law, intertemporal criminal law etc., refers to rules for resolving time conflict of laws. Likewise, intertemporal international law is the time conflict of international legal norms.[2] G. Schwarzenberger notes that intertemporal international law is the application of sorts of international legal norms in specific cases in consecutive different time periods.[3] Both French Dictionnair De La Terminologie Du Droit International and Paul Tavernier made the explanation on the intertemporal law that the term is often used for determining all principles of the applicability of restated laws and regulations with temporal continuality to a certain specific case,[4] while Japanese International Relation Law Dictionary made the statement on the intertemporal law in the International Law that "(o)n the ground that Countries as the law subject in the International Law survive for long time, but the law regulations are constantly changed as the time passes, the issues that which law the acts or facts before the change are subject to arise. Therefore, the intertemporal law is regarded as the principles to address such temporal law contradictions".[5]

International law scholars from the above countries defined intertemporal international law from their perspectives. Views from some famous international law scholars are studied for a further discussion on the application of intertemporal international law in the sovereignty dispute on the Nansha Islands.

---

[2]Wolf-Dietrich (1970). Cited from Huang (2000, p. 75).

[3]Schwarzenberger (1967, p. 635). Cited from Huang (2000, p. 75).

[4]Basdevant (1960, p. 237). Cited from Huang (2000, p. 75).

[5]Law Dictionary of International Relations (1995, p. 379). Cited from Huang (2000, p. 75).

The UK international law scholar Gerald Fitzmaurice held that interpretation of judgment and treaty should be made in accordance with the international legal norm *ratione temporis* rather than that of today. The principle of *ratione temporis* in international law has already been widely acknowledged. As for territory acquisition, a country's rights of the land discovered in the 16th century should be judged according to international legal norms in the 16th century rather than more refined and clearer views three centuries later.[6] Another UK international law scholar, also once a judge in the International Court of Justice, Robert Jennings regarded it as an elementary and fundamental principle that a conduct should be defined according to the laws *ratione temprois*, instead of contemporary laws.[7] A country's rights over territory, discovered in the 16th century, should be judged through international legal norms *ratione temprois*, rather than clearer norms developed after 300 years.[8] The effect of conducts giving rise to rights…such as discovery, preoccupation etc., is judged according to the legal norms when rights were created instead of the norms when the question was proposed.[9] The interpretation of rights should be based on the concrete situations when the incident happened rather than the country's modern laws.[10]

The above opinions of scholars and judges were also confirmed in the annual meeting of the Wiesbaden Resolution made by the Institute of International Law in 1975. The Wiesbaden Resolution explicitly pointed out that: "1. Unless otherwise indicated, the temporal sphere of application of any norm of public international law would be determined in accordance with the general principle of law by which any fact, action or situation must be assessed in the light of the rules of law that are contemporaneous with it. 2. In the application of this principle: (a) any rule which relates to a single fact shall apply to facts that occur while the rule is in force; (b) any rule which relates to the repetition or succession of identical facts shall apply even though only one or some of such facts should occur after the entry into force of the rule; (c) any rule which relates to an actual situation shall apply to situations existing while the rule is in force, even if these situations have been created previously."[11]

Anthony D'amato held that the principle of non-retroactivity in international law is also called intertemporal jurisprudence.[12] Here Anthony D'amato regarded intertemporal law as an equal to the important principle of non-retroactivity. This interpretation is a very strong support to China in terms of the sovereignty dispute over the Nansha Islands.

The International Law Volume of China Law Dictionary defines intertemporal law as contemporary legal norms among varies of legal norms developed with time that apply to a specific situation.[13]

[6] Evance (1922, p. 132, p. 283).

[7] Jenning (1963, p. 28).

[8] Moore (1906, p. 259).

[9] Kittichaisaree (1987, p. 141).

[10] Choon-Ho (1979, p. 183).

[11] Yearbook of *the Institute of International Law*, (French version), 1975 edition, p. 537.

[12] D'amato (1986, p. 192). Cited from Huang (2000, p. 83).

[13] *China Law Dictionary, International Law Volume*. China Procuratorate Press, 1996 edition, p. 516.

Matin Dixon regards intertemporal law as legal norms that should be applied to a key date. The whole content of intertemporal law, in essence, is legal norms that should be applied to a specific dispute.... In this regard, the dispute should be judged according to the international law norms that existed in 1898, if it is the key date....For example, as we see later, it was already illegal to acquire territory by force in 1945, but legal before 1945. Consequently, the rights acquired by conquest before 1945, though illegal under current international law, remains valid according to intertemporal law jurisprudence.

The view of Matin Dixon is very clear. First of all, it is crucial to define the key date. From the context of his argument, the key date may not be the date of the disputed settlement. Besides, if the key date is the date of the disputed settlement, the applicable law to settle the dispute would be contemporaneous laws. Subject to the rule of intertemporal law, the laws applicable to settle the dispute should be that of the key date rather than contemporaneous laws. Secondly, after the key date is confirmed, the right is defined in accordance with the key date not subject to afterwards judgment, which may result in confusion, especially in areas where a state's power may not exercise extensively or frequently with regard to a state's territorial acquisition. We should pay special attention to this point. It is also somehow difficult for China to exercise its sovereignty over the Nansha Island which is far away from the continent, but the fact does not influence China's sovereignty over the Nansha Islands according to Dixon's view.

Dixon holds that, unfortunately, Judge Huber interpreted intertemporal law jurisprudence in a ineffective and unacceptable way in the Island of Palmas arbitration case. In light of Judge Huber's interpretation, the creation of rights is different from the existence of rights. Accordingly, the existence of territorial rights acquired on the basis of the key date international legal norms (e.g., 1898) has to be decided by contemporaneous (e.g., 1990) international legal norms. In other words, states' sovereignty over their territories should be (continually) re-defined because of the change of international law. This is obviously not acceptable if it is indeed what Judge Huber meant. The effect of such jurisprudence would inevitably give rise to some false arguments, as well as a widespread instability of territorial rights. Moreover, severe problems may arise in regions where states have acquired (territorial rights) legally, but do not exercise states' power that extensively or frequently.[14]

4.1.2 Cases Related to Intertemporal International Law

International law cases concerning the rule of intertemporal law are primarily the Islands of Palmas Arbitration Case and the Grisbadarna case between Norway and Sweden in 1909.

Palmas Island lies between the Philippines and the Netherlands East Indies. The Spanish discovered Palmas Island which was part of the Netherlands East Indies in

[14]Dixon (1990, p. 83). Cited from Huang (2000, pp. 83–84).

1677. The United States signed the Treaty of Paris with Spain in 1898, in which Spain ceded Palmas Island to the United States. The United States notified the Treaty of Paris to the Netherlands and the Netherlands did not raise any objection. Afterwards, the United States found the Netherlands' flag hanging in the Palmas Islands and thus negotiated with the Netherlands without reaching an agreement. Both countries agreed to submit the case to the Permanent Court of Arbitration on January 23, 1925. Max Huber, the president of the Permanent Court of International Justice as well as a Swiss legal scholar, was the sole arbitrator in this case. The award was made on April 4, 1928, which decided the Island of Palmas forms in its entirety part of the Netherlands territory. Huber acknowledged, however, that Spain held an inchoate title when Spain "discovered" Palmas in the 16th century.

In the analysis of why Spain could not grant what it did not hold to the United States, Huber, the sole arbitrator, pointed out that it was admitted by both sides that international law underwent profound modifications between the end of the Middle-Ages and the end of the 19th century, as regards the rights of discovery and acquisition of uninhabited regions or regions inhabited by aboriginals. Both parties also agreed that a juridical fact must be appreciated in the light of the law contemporary with it, not the law in force at the time when a dispute in regard to it arises or falls. The effect of discovery by Spain was therefore to be determined by the rules of international law in force in the first half of the 16th century.[15] In the application of intertemporal law, Huber noted again that "(a)s regards to the question which of different legal systems prevailing at successive periods is to be applied in a particular case (the so-called intertemporal law), a distinction must be made between the creation of rights and the existence of rights. The creation of rights is dominated by the law in force at the time when the rights are created. According to the same principle, the existence of the rights or its further development shall follow the conditions required by the evolution of law."[16] Put it another way, a distinction must be made between "the creation of rights" and "the existence of rights", which means the valid laws when rights are created must be applied to the creation of rights, while the existence of rights follows requirements of developed laws. Since *terra nullius* did not exist in the 19th century, international law has required an effective occupation to acquire territory through discovery. Discovery creates only an "inchoate" title. An inchoate title of discovery must be completed within a reasonable period by an effective occupation of the region. In this sense, Spain held an inchoate title when Spain "discovered" Palmas, but did not exercise effective occupation, and thus did not exercise sovereignty over the island. Therefore, Spain could not grant Palmas to the United States. Finally, Huber decided the Island of Palmas forms in its entirety part of the Netherlands territory. Another international law scholar A. G. Roche commented on Huber's view in the analysis of the Minquiers and Ecrehos Case that the intertemporal law covers two parts: the first is the principle that the acts shall be judged according to the applicable law at the same time when the rights are established; the second is that if the regulations are not changed along with the changes of international laws,

---

[15] Award of The Island of Palmas Section 3. Cited from Cheng, ed. (1998, p. 121).

[16] Award of The Island of Palmas, AJIL, 22, 1928, p. 883.

the validity of the right enjoyed effectively based on the applicable law at the same time when the rights are established may be eliminated.[17]

Another case involving intertemporal international law is the Grisbadarna maritime boundary delimitation arbitration case between Norway and Sweden in 1909. Norway claimed to apply a median-line principle to delimitate the maritime boundary. The tribunal found, however, the international law in the 17th century rather than 20th century when a median-line principle was proposed should be applied to the boundary treaty signed between Norway and Sweden in 1661. Consequently, the tribunal rejected Norway's claim and endorsed Sweden's claim on the basis of the 17th century international law.

Both the arbitration case of the Island of Palmas and the Grisbadarna maritime boundary delimitation between Norway and Sweden shed important light on the discussion of China's territorial sovereignty over the Nansha Islands, which is shown as follows.

4.1.3 The Application of Intertemporal Law in the Sovereignty Dispute Over the Nansha Islands

China discovered the Nansha Islands around the Christian Era, and exercised administrative jurisdiction over the Nansha Islands as early as in the Song Dynasty. Other countries such as Vietnam, the Philippines, Malaysia and Brunei had not claimed sovereignty over the Nansha Islands or occupied it by military force until 1950s.

Evidently, China's "discovery", "pre-occupation" and "exercise of administrative jurisdiction" could only be judged according to the international law in the Han Dynasty (from 206 B.C to 220 B.C) or the Song Dynasty (from 960 A.D to 1279 A.D). Both the Han Dynasty and the Song Dynasty were before the 18th century, when a sole discovery or symbolized occupation could grant a state's territorial sovereignty in accordance with the contemporaneous law. In this regard, the dispute of the Nansha Islands should be decided and judged in line with the principle of intertemporal law.[18] In other words, only international laws before the 18th century, rather than modern international maritime law, should be applied to the dispute on the Nansha Islands. Alternatively, China's existence of rights over the Nansha Islands accords with the development of international law, which require new administrative or judicial jurisdictional actions, because China's sovereignty over the Nansha Islands has been even more complete and comprehensive since the 19th century, especially in the 1940s. A discussion of China's state actions of exercising sovereignty over the Nansha Islands is to be made in the followings.

After the 1950s, Vietnam, the Philippines, Malaysia and Brunei claimed sovereignty over the Nansha Islands, and occupied these islands by military means. According to intertemporal international law in the 1950s, states are allowed neither

---

[17]Roche (1959, p. 79).

[18]Choon-Ho (1983, p. 220).

to use military force illegally, nor to take military force as a tool to implement national policies. *The Declaration on Principles of International Law concerning Friendly Relations and Co-operation among States in accordance with the Charter of the United Nations*, adopted by the United Nations convention on 24th October 1970 stipulates that "all States shall refrain in their international relations from the threat or use of force against the territorial integrity or political independence of any State, or in any other manners inconsistent with the purpose of the United Nations;" "the territory of a State shall not be the object of military occupation resulting from the use of force in contravention of the provision of the Charter; the territory of a State shall not be the object of acquisition by another State resulting from the threat or use of force shall be recognized as legal."[19] Therefore, these countries that illegally occupied the Nansha Islands by military means after the 1950s have violated the Charter and relevant legal documents of the UN, as well as other principles of international law.

4.1.4 The Key Date and the Dispute on Sovereignty Over the Nansha Islands

In the arbitration case of the Island of Palmas, Judge Huber points out that "If a dispute arises as to the sovereignty over a portion of territory, it is customary to examine which of the States claiming sovereignty possesses a title—cession, conquest, occupation, etc.—superior to that which the other State might possibly bring forward against it. However, if the contestation is based on the fact that the other Party has actually displayed sovereignty, it cannot be sufficient to establish the title by which territorial sovereignty was validly acquired at a certain moment; it must also be shown that the territorial sovereignty has continued to exist and did exist at the moment which for the decision of the dispute must be considered as critical. This demonstration consists in the actual display of State activities, such as belongs only to the territorial sovereign."

Gerald Fitzmaurice also believes that key date theory includes that the status remains the same no matter what the status has been determined at the key date; the title of each party remains no matter how the title of theirs was. If one of the parties had the title in the past, now it still has the title, or should be deemed to have the title. If none of the parties has the title, now the fact remains. The whole rule of the key date theory and why it exists is that time is regarded to froze on such a date. Nothing happens afterwards could change the status of the title. No matter what the situation was, the title is deemed to legally exist and be binding on all the parties. Fitzmuarice also points out that such a date "must exist in all disputes if such a date cannot exist after the start of legal procedures". Oppenheim agrees that "the choice of the key date is substantive rather than procedural".[20] The dispute should be settled based on

[19] Wang and Ding (eds.) (1994, pp. 3–4).

[20] Jennings and Watts (Revised) (1995, p. 92).

the key date after it is determined. Evidence before the date could be accepted by the court, and all evidence after the date should be inadmissible.[21]

Many international boarder or territorial disputes cases involve the issue of key date. In the *Eastern Greenland* case, the court held that "the sovereignty of Denmark must exist before the key date, July 10th, 1931", in order to invalidate the occupation of Norway. In the 1988 *Tapah Arbitration* case, arbitral tribunal had to determine "a key period", instead of a key date. And the court further held that any events happened after the key period could be relevant in principle. Such events will reveal or demonstrate the condition of what took place during the key period rather than according to changed circumstances.[22]

According to discussions by international law scholars and the international arbitral and judicial practice, the key date should also be determined in the disputes on sovereignty over the Nansha Islands. Otherwise it would be more difficult to find out what period of international law should be applied in dispute settlement since the rule of international law varies at different times. Professor Zhao Guocai, from National Chengchi University, said that China's exercise of sovereignty over historic water in the South China Sea could be found from the evidence before 1946. Therefore, the beginning date of disputes determined by China is on December 30th, 1946.[23]

4.2 China Has the First Discovery Right Over the Nansha Islands

4.2.1 *Discussions on Discovery from Worldwide Authoritative Public International Law Scholars and States' Practice*

With respect to the source of international law, it is widely recognized that authoritative writings of international law scholars who can represent the highest level are the auxiliary source of international law. According to the Statute of the International Court of Justice, Article 38.1.4, states that judicial decisions and the teachings of the most highly qualified publicists from various nations are subsidiary means to the determination of rules of law.[24] The reason is that opinions of the most highly recognized publicists always play significant roles in the formation of certain vital legal rules, principles and mechanisms in both international law and municipal laws. The results of scholars' research are likely to be accepted and become part of the law. "Indeed, early international law scholars such as Hugo Grotius, Samuel Pufendorf, Cornelius van Bynkershoek, Ememerich von Vattel etc. have substantial impact

[21] Jennings (1963, pp. 31–35).

[22] Jennings and Watts (Revised) (1995, p. 150, Annotation 364, 365).

[23] Zhao Guocai, *Analysis on Sovereign Dispute of Nansha Island from Present International Law.*

[24] *Statute of the International Court of Justice*, Article 38, Refer to Wang and Ding (eds.) (1994 p. 464).

on international jurisprudence. Their works are quoted in diplomatic documents and have drawn great attention in courts' judgments."[25] According to Dickinson's statistic, the number of times when the above four jurists had been quoted from 1789 to 1820 is 142 in argumentative proses, 69 in courts' citations and 34 in courts' quotations in America.[26] When the Supreme Court of the United States and the Privy Council of the United Kingdom deal with relevant cases, they also quote the teaching of publicists, which are even cited by the Permanent Court of International Justice and International Court of Justice in the S.S. Wimbledon case,Advisory Opinion of German Settlers in Poland, Certain German Interests in Polish Upper Silesia case, the *Lotus* case (France v. Turkey), the Nottebohm Case, etc.[27] Works of scholars continue to play significant roles in accordance with its scientific values, impartiality per se and the legal principle followed to state practice with the extent of determination to exam.[28] Liu Binghua, an oriental international law scholar, holds that the theories of scholars are necessary at anytime because international law is developing continuously. Jurists have great impact on legislators and judges although they do not have the power to create positive laws. Moreover, international law, largely composed of customary laws, have much room to improve, compared with municipal law. The theories of scholars are more important for international law than for municipal laws.[29] Hence, it is inevitable to study the discussions from authoritative worldwide international law scholars on the significance of "discovery" of a territory to acquisition with respect to China's first discovery right over the Nansha Islands.

It is generally believed that "discovery" means "the natural discovery or the pure sight view" or "the pure sight view" whether you reach or not in person".[30] There have been many discussions on acquisition of territory through "discovery" in international law academics. Ememerich von Vattel (1714—1768), a famous Swiss jurist on positive law, holds that everyone has equal rights to a thing that has not been occupied by anyone. Such a thing belongs to the first person who occupies it. Therefore, when a state discoveries a *terra nullius*, the state can occupy it legally. And this right cannot be deprived by others when the state fully expresses such an intention. Voyagers entrusted by sovereign discover ranges, islands and other *terra nullius* occasionally, and occupy them in the name of the sovereign. Usually the right should be respected assuming they are actually occupied subsequently.[31] Jennings, a British international law scholar and the judge of the International Court for Justice, explicitly points out that a simple discovery without occupation could be entitled in the past. Before the 16th century, it is indisputable that a simple discovery with the intention of preoccupation would be sufficient to create rights.[32] Nowadays, occupation

[25]Wang (1998, p. 104).

[26]Nussbaum, p. 158, Quoted in Wang (1998, p. 104).

[27]Wang (1998, p. 105).

[28]Jennings and Watts (Revised) (1995, pp. 25–26).

[29]Yu (1997, p. 236).

[30]Orent and Reinsch (1994, p. 443).

[31]de Vatel (1906, p. 207).

[32]Jennings (1963).

and administrative management are two requirements for an effective occupation, but were not deemed as necessary for an acquisition of territory through occupation in the past. In Age of Discovery, states did not claim that the discovery of scarcely known land means the state engaged in exploration has acquired the land through occupation. Rather, such an occupation is merely symbolic. Nevertheless, a real occupation is regarded as necessary subsequently. International law scholars regarded such a real occupation as indispensable in the 18th century, and states practice had not been consistent with the theory until the 19th century. So far, although states cannot acquire sovereignty through a discovery of territory, discovery is still of significance. It is widely recognized that the state which discovered the territory has an inchoate title. And such a title could temporally prevent other states' occupation during a reasonable period of time required for an effective occupation over the discovered territory.[33] O'Connell, a Professor from Oxford University, also points out that discovery, which may have been used as the basis of claims for a title during the expanding age, is an effective basis for other claimant.[34] Hill, an American international law scholar, holds the same opinion that the practice that claims for right over islets normally inconvenient or impossible to be occupied on the basis of symbolic occupations has been followed since early 15th or 16th century. In recent years, the United States and the United Kingdom also actively claimed sovereignty in the Pacific on the basis of symbolic occupation. Since a simple discovery is regarded as an adequate basis for sovereignty claim over t*erra nullius*, any practice that could be treated as real occupation or symbolic occupation has been well developed.[35] Simsarian, an American international law scholar, holds that the standpoint held by countries before the 20th century differed from the attitude after the late 18th century. In the early stage, symbolic occupation could be deemed by many big countries as sufficient for legal rights over *terra nullius* in North America.[36] Heydte also fully discusses that states' governmental practice has showed the inclination to admitting rights for the symbolic consolidation as the occupation of a newly discovered land since the 15th century. Symbolic conducts could be interpreted as means to show the world that the state acquires the preliminary right of the land. The conducts, as for other countries, indicate the discovered land cannot be occupied, yet the state does not have complete control and discretion over the land.[37]

The above discussions from distinguished international law scholars and judges of the International Court of Justice sufficiently elaborate the significance of "discovery" in territorial acquisition. An illustration concerning territorial acquisition through discovery in state practice is as follows.

The records of acquisition of territory through discovery are mainly the wide adoption by western colonizers who expanded oversea colonies from the 15th to the 16th century. From the end of 15th century to the end of 19th century, western

[33] Jennings and Watts (Revised) (1995, pp. 75–76).

[34] O'Connell (1970, p. 408).

[35] Hill (1945, p. 149). Cited from Zhao (1992).

[36] Simsarian (1938). Cited from Zhao (1992).

[37] Heydte (1935). Cited from Zhao (1992).

countries still acquired territories by such means. Spain, for instance, holds that Spanish discovered Florida in North America in 1489, and landed on the coast of Florida in 1513. Therefore, Spain claimed its sovereignty over the northern region of Gulf of Mexico. Portugal claimed its sovereignty over Brazil and Trinidad based on the theory of "discovery". Additionally, the Netherlands turned to the theory of "discovery" as the legal base to claim its territorial sovereignty in North America.[38] The United Kingdom has made even more full use of the theory. In 1496, King of the United Kingdom drafted a wide horizontal document "John Kabotto", and conferred John Cabot exclusive rights to explore and conquer the lands unknown to Christian in the name of the King. Two years later in 1498, Cabot voyaged and discovered the North America with the King's authorization, and sailed ahead south to Virginia along the coast. Hereby the United Kingdom claimed its sovereignty over the North America continent. France also claimed its sovereignty over large North America land according to the theory of "discovery". In the island dispute among France, the United Kingdom and Canada, France and the United Kingdom claimed that symbolic occupation could be the legal base for acquisition of *terra nullius*. Accordingly, all countries that acquired territories in America not only put forward their propositions but also reciprocally admitted the discoverers' absolute rights.[39] Even the United States claimed its title through discovery on the Palmas Island in Island of Palmas case.

The acquisition of territory through discovery is also involved in some well-known cases, such as Island of Palmas case and the Clippton Island case.

In the Island of Palmas case, Judge Huber agreed on the Spanish's title over the island through "discovery" in the 16th century.

In the Clippton Island case, Mexico argued that the Clippton Island was firstly found by the British at the beginning of 18th century and was just taken as a refuge harbor, so it belonged to Spain in accordance with temporal laws after the Spanish discovered it later. The Italian King Emmanuel III, the sole arbitrator of this case, pointed out that "as for an inhospitable land, occupation should be regarded as complete and entire once the discoverers initially appeared and this land was under absolute and indisputable status ever since."[40]

4.2.2 *The Significance of Teachings of Worldwide Authoritative Publicists and State Practice on China's Discovery Over the Nansha Island*

The Nansha Islands is far away from continent, and only a few islands with large area are habitable. Most of the islands are inhospitable. Therefore, acquisition of

[38] Evans (1922).

[39] Evans (1922, p. 284).

[40] The Clipperton Island Case (France—Mexico), A. J. L., 1932, Vol. 26. No. 2.

the Nansha Islands should be original acquisition, which means discovery is of vital significance to China for acquiring sovereignty over the Nansha Islands.

China is the first country that discovered the Nansha Islands. When Vietnam, the Philippine, Malaysia, Brunei and other countries involved in the Nansha Island dispute, were in the age of barbarism, there were already records of the Nansha Islands in Chinese history books, and Chinese people were already conducting activities such as sailing, fishing, collecting spats, hunting turtles, dragging shrimps and hunting snails in the Nansha Islands and its nearby waters.

The records of Chinese people and kings' discovering, exploring and managing the Nansha Islands have been abundant and complex. Such records last thousands of years in documents. The main documents are briefly described as follows to demonstrate that Chinese people and the Chinese government are the first to discover the Nansha Islands.

Shi Jing, the earliest collection of Chinese poetry, which was complied during China's Spring and Autumn Period (770 B.C.–476 B.C.), recorded that "the boundary expands to the South China Sea when administrates the border land and runs the King's land". Some records in Y*u Gong*, the masterpiece in the Zhou Dynasty (1066 B.C.–221 B.C.), also proves the tight relationship between mainland China and the islands in the South China Sea, including the Nansha Islands. The First Emperor of Qin (259 B.C.–210 B.C.) established Xiang county, which may imply that the Emperor had conducted some activities in the South China Sea. Several months before the Emperor died, he had attempted to sail with an expectation to reach the three god-living mountains, which has left many stories and legends.[41] Such stories and legends show that it is pioneering that the Emperor tried to develop the channels of the South China Sea in order to explore and administrate islands there.

The records of the Nansha Islands in Chinese historical books are more plentiful and authentic with details after the Qin Dynasty. *Yi Wuzhi*, written by Yang Fu in the Easter Han Dynasty (25 A.D.–220 A.D.), recorded that "water is shallow with a lot of reef flats in the South China Sea.[42] When boats are sailing here, they are usually trapped as if being attracted by a magnet."[43]

There are six types of records on the Nansha Islands in the Three Kingdoms Age (220 A.D.–280 A.D.) and the periods of the Western and Easter Jin Dynasties (265 A.D.–420 A.D.), namely, *Nanzhou Yi Wuzhi*, written by Wanzhen (from Wu state in Three Kingdoms Age.), *Record of Cambodia* and *Foreign Miscellanea* by Kangtai (from Wu state in Three Kingdoms Age.), *Record of Wu State* by Zhangbo (Jin Dynasty), *Record of Guangzhou* by Peiyuan (Jin Dynasty), and *Annotation on*

[41] Han Zhenhua, "The South China Sea Islands have been under China's sovereignty in accordance with Chinese ancient books", refer to Han (1996, p. 52).

[42] According to Han Zhenhua's explanation, *Zhang Hai was the name of the South China Sea in ancient time. It includes the Dongsha Islands, the Xisha Islands, the Zhongsha Islands and the Nansha Islands and their waters. Qi Tou was the name of the reefs and shoals in the Nansha Islands in antient time. Zhanghai Qitou refers to the reefs and shoals in all the islands, including the Nansha Islands.*

[43] Yangfu, *Yi Wu Zhi*, in Tangzhou (1964, p. 14), copied in Shanghai Ancient Book Store. Cited from Han (eds.) (1998, p. 23).

Erya by Guopu (Jin Dynasty). In *Nanzhou Yi Wuzhi*, the islands in the South China Sea, including the Nansha Islands, are called "*Zhang Hai*" or "*Qi Tou*". In *Record of Cambodia*, the Nansha Islands and the Xisha Island are called "*Coral Shoal*". The islands in the South China Sea are named "*Zhanghai*" in the *Foreign Miscellanea*, the *Record of state Wu*, and the *Annotation on Erya*. And the islands are called "*Coral Shoal*" in the *Record of Guangzhou*.[44]

It is notable that Kangtai, titled Zhonglang General of State Wu in the Three Kingdom Age, had personally been to Funan (Cambodia), and the South China sea is the route that he had to pass by. He authentically and lively described that "sailing to the South China Sea and reaching *Coral Shoal*, massive rocks are under the shoal and coralline grows on the rocks." As the Zhonglang General, he apparently served as an envoy of State Wu to Cambodia. The meaning of his "discovery" of the Nansha Islands is much more than that of the civilians. The claim that the Philippines "discovered" the Nansha Islands by Cloma in the middle and late 20th century is incomparable with China's argument. State Wu in the Three Kingdom Age lasted from 222 A.D to 280 A.D, which is 1700 years earlier than Cloma's so-called "discovery" of the Nansha Islands.

According to historical records, non-government communications with south China was increasing during the Western Jin and Eastern Jin Dynasties. Monk Fa Xian who went to India for Buddhist scriptures knew that he should take water route through the South China Sea. He started from "Ye Poti" (the Java Island) and on the way back to Guangzhou, he lost his way at somewhere which is still unclear.

In the Northern and Southern Dynasties (420A.D.–581A.D.), the records on the islands in South China Sea were in the *Record of Nanyue* by Shen Huaiyuan, the *Eulogy of Emperor Wu* by Xie Lingyun and the *Song of Wucheng* by Bao Zhao. Such records describe the communication between mainland China and the Nansha Islands, and the fact that the navy of State Song cruised in the South China Sea area in the Southern Dynasty.

In the Sui and Tang dynasties(581A.D.–907A.D.), there were four kinds of historical documents that recorded the islands in the South China Sea, namely, the *History of Sui Dynasty*, the *Tong Dian*, the *New History of the Tang Dynasty*, and the *Merits and Drawbacks of All the Provinces and Counties in China.*

In the Sui Dynasty, the records that Emperor Yang of Sui sent Chang Jun, Wang Junzheng, etc. to Chitu Country to get tribute were collected in the *Book of Su* which was compiled by Wei Zheng, Zhangsun Wuji, etc. There are different views on the current location of Chitu Country. In *An Assembly of Materials Concerning the Islands in Southern China Sea*, it is said that Chitu Country refers to the place in the west of Malay Peninsula.

In the Tang Dynasty, there was an article titled *Guangzhou Tong Hai Yi Dao* which was edited by Jia Dan, the chancellor of Emperor De Zong, who finished the article by asking diplomatic envoys and envoys sent to foreign countries about the geography, national conditions, cultures and products. Jia Dan compiled a ten-volume book called *Huang Hua Si Da Ji, which* served as China's geographical records with its

---

[44]Han (eds.) (1998, pp. 25–27).

neighbors. The book seemed to be lost in early Ming Dynasty, but was copied in *Xin Tang Shu* (*New Book of Tang*) which was written by Ouyang Xiu. There are records of seven roads which connected China with other states in the Tang Dynasty, as well as records of Guangzhou Tong Hai Yi Dao in *Hua Hua Si Da Ji*. A description of Guangzhou Tong Hai Yi Dao can be found in *Xin Tang Shu* (New Book of Tang): It is around 200 miles to Tunmen Mountain starting from Guangzhou and taking the sea roads by heading to the southeast. And it took another two days to arrive at Jiuzhoushi by sailing to west with wind. Then it took another two days to arrive at Xiangshi by sailing to south. It took another three days to arrive at CulaoCham, in the sea centre 200 miles away from the Champa Kingdom by sailing to southwest.[45]

The *Guangzhou Tong Hai Yi Dao* records the whole channels from Guangzhou, into the Indian Ocean through Malacca by water, then into the Tigris, Euphrates in the Persian Gulf from the Indian Ocean, and finally Bagdad. Moreover, the directions and distances of the states, urban cities as well as nearby areas are also included.

China's historical records of the Nansha Islands were numerous in the Song Dynasty (960A.D–1279A.D), the Yuan Dynasty (1279A.D–1368A.D), the Ming Dynasty (1368A.D–1644A.D) and the Qing Dynasty (1644A.D–1911A.D). In the Song Dynasty, the Nansha Islands was named Wanli Shitang. There are following records in historical books: "It is already the end of land and top of sea when arriving at Jiyang. If you step further, there are shoals called Wu Li and Su Ji Lang in the sea. These shoals face Zhan Cheng southwards, Zhen La westwards, Qianli Changsha and Wanli Shitan eastwards. A wide expanse of mist-covered waters and the horizon where the sky meets the water make the boundary invisible. The ships can only rely on the guidance of compass and focus on its direction when shipping around these areas. No mistake is allowed because it matters the safety of both ships and crews.[46] In addition, according to the collections by Han Zhenhua, in the Song Dynasty alone, there were 14 types of historical records about the Nansha Islands and other islands, such as *General Geography Records* by Wang Xiangzhi with the quotation in *Hainan Administration Records* in the Song Dynasty, *Hainan Geography Records* by Cai Wei, *Qiongtai Records* by Tang Zhou, *Guangzhou Records, Qiongshan County Records, General Guangdong Records, Wanzhou Records, Ancient and Modern Books Collection, Lingwai Daida, Fangyu Shenglan, Song Dynasty History, Song Dynasty Proposals,* and *Menglianglu,* in which there is the description of "QianLi Changsha" and "Wanli Shitang".[47] Here, "QianLi Changsha" refers to the Xisha Islands, and "Wanli Shitang" refers to the Nansha Islands. And even if we take the Song Dynasty as the period when the Nansha Islands were discovered, it is earlier than the discovery time of the Philippines by more than 700 years.

There are more documents about the Nansha Islands in three China's dynasties: Yuan, Ming, and Qing, such as *Seas beyond the Continent Records Simplification* by Wang Dayuan, *Yuan Dynasty History, New Yuan Dynasty History,*

---

[45] Jia Dan, *Guangdong Tong Hai Yi Dao,* in Ouyang Xiu, ed., *New Book of Tang,* Vol. 43, Geographical Records, Kaiming Book Company, p. 110. Refer to Han (eds.) (1998, p. 30).

[46] (Song Dynasty) Zhao Rushi, *Chorography of All Provinces*, Vol. 2 Hanhai Edition.

[47] Han (eds.) (1998, pp. 33–44).

and *Chenla Customs Documents* in the Yuan Dynasty; *Zhenghe Navigation Map, Qiongtai Customs Documents, Sea Merchants' Notes, Zhengde Qiongtai Records, General Guangzhou Records, Siyi Guangji, Navigation Sightseeing, Shouxichangyu Compilation, Zhenze Records, Different Adjacent Regions Records, Shunfeng Xiangsong, Haichayulu, Seas Beyond the Continent Investigation, Ancient and Modern Books Collection, Xianbinglu, Sea Sightseeing Poem, Quanzhou County Records, Tong'an County Records* in the Ming Dynasty; *Yue Customs, Development of Trades Among Various Countries, Compass Navigation, Foreign Countries Records, Xiamen Records, Overview of Qing Dynasty Literatures, General Provisions of Qing Dynasty and Foreign Countries Records Simplification* in the Qing Dynasty. Therefore, if we take the Yuan, Ming or Qing Dynasty as the period when the Nansha Islands were discovered, it is earlier than the so-called "discovery" time of the Philippines by several or almost hundred years.

Since the Song dynasty, Chinese central government has been exercising effective jurisdiction over the Nansha Islands. Therefore, the next discussion will be from the perspective of China's exercise of jurisdiction over the Nansha Islands.

According to above-mentioned theories of discovery from worldwide publicists, as well as the practice of the European and American countries, a conclusion could be drawn as follows with the analysis of Chinese historical documents.

First, in the 15th to 16th century, some authoritative public law scholars argued or some cases (late in 18th century) showed that the title of *terra nullius* can be acquired simply through discovery in international law. China discovered the Nansha Islands in around the Han Dynasty (206A.D.–220A.D.), 1800 to 2000 years earlier than western countries. Vietnam, the Philippines and even the United States who are totally irrelevant to the Nansha Islands rampantly criticize and intervene in China's sovereignty over the Nansha Islands. They illegally arrested Chinese fishermen in the water sea in the Nansha Islands. These facts indicate that either they are not clear about China's history and ignore China's legal rights, or they have some ulterior motivations.

Second, the Nansha Islands is far away from mainland China, and there are only a few habitable islands. Thus, territorial sovereignty can be acquired through simple discovery or symbolic conduct for these islands. Symbolic conducts could be various, such as naming these islands (the Nansha Islands was named "*Zhang Hai Qi Tou*", and the South China Sea was named "*Zhang Hai*"), fishing, navy cruising, etc.

Third, the islands could be discovered within the range of vision, with or without landing. Before the Song dynasty, Chinese people and Chinese officials not only discovered the Nansha Islands within the range of vision, but also landed on the islands. There were records that Chinese people fished on the islands, and Chinese navy cruised around these islands.

Fourth, before the Song dynasty (960 A.D. or even earlier), China acquired the preliminary right, namely "right of discovery", over the Nansha Islands, which conferred China an inchoate title that could effectively prevent other surrounding countries such as Vietnam, the Philippines, Malaysia, etc. from claiming territorial sovereignty over the Nansha Islands. In other words, the Nansha Islands cannot be territories of any other countries except China. Besides, China subsequently exercised effective administrative jurisdiction over the Nansha Islands within "a reasonable period of time", which meets the requirement of "preoccupation".

Fifth, now that the teachings of authoritative public law scholars are the auxiliary information to determine principles of international law, and of great importance to formation of principles, rules and systems of international law, the arguments on discovery made by British, American and French publicists undoubtedly can be the legal basis for China to solve the Nansha dispute. It is beyond doubt that China has sovereignty over the Nansha Islands with sufficient evidence to prove China that has the "right of discovery" of the Nansha Islands.

4.2.3 China Has the Right of Preoccupation Over the Nansha Islands

4.2.3.1 Rules on "Preoccupation" and "Effective Occupation" in International Law

Preoccupation means a state intentionally acquires a territory which has not been under the sovereignty of other states. Preoccupation must be made by a state and in the name of such state. The object of preoccupation is *terra nullius* which is a land that does not belong to any state. *Terra nullius* includes uninhabited land and barren islands, but not state where aborigines live, or lands that once belonged to a state but were abandoned afterwards.

There are two requirements to constitute a preoccupation, one is subjective and the other objective. The subjective one requires an intention of occupation, such as making declaration or statement in the name of a state; expressing an intention to control the *terra nullius* in the way of domestic legislations and administrative measures; delimiting the *terra nullius* in a state's map. The objective one requires the state's effectively control over the land through legislative, judicial or administrative measures, such as hanging national flags, establishing administrative institutes, building sovereignty steles, and establishing housing settlements, etc. Once preoccupation is finished, the occupied land becomes part of the territory of the occupants.

In relations to "effective occupation", the Permanent Count of International Justice pointed out in the *Legal Status of Eastern Green Land case* that "two elements should be demonstrated for a state to claim sovereignty based not upon some particular acts or titles (e.g., a treaty of cession) but merely upon continued displaying of authority: the intention and will to act as sovereign, and some actual exercise or display of such authority."[48] Here Henkin indicates that an effective occupation is the basis for preoccupation. According to the discussions from publicists, arbitral decisions and decisions of the Permanent Count of International Justice, the following actions

[48]Louis (1980, pp. 263–264).

could be taken as an "effective occupation": an administrative management,[49] legislations (e.g., promulgation of decree),[50] judicial activities (e.g., taxation, establishment of customs station and autopsy),[51] landing and issuing sovereign statements in newspaper,[52] declaration of official occupation or rising national flags.[53]

According to the rules of "preoccupation" and "effective occupation" in international law, China meets both the subjective and objective requirements of "preoccupation." This point is further elaborated as follows.

4.2.4 Claims of Sovereignty

There are various forms of sovereign claims, including the statement or proclamation made by the Chinese government, and specific administrative activities such as building sovereignty steles and navy cruising, etc.

In the Three Kingdoms Age, Kang Tai, titled Zhonglang General of State Wu, and Zhu Ying, titled Congshi in Xuanhua County, cruised around waters of the Nansha islands during 225A.D.–230A.D.,[54] which is a sort of sovereign claim per se. Afterwards, in the Southern and Northern, the Eastern and Western Jin, the Sui and the Tang Dynasties, Chinese officials and Chinese armies had been to and cruised in the waters of the Nansha Islands.

Since the Song Dynasty, including later in the Yuan, Ming, Qing Dynasties and the Republic of China period, Chinese government entrusted Hainan authority to exercise administrative jurisdiction over the Nansha Islands.[55] There was the Nansha Islands in maps of China in the Ming and Qing Dynasties,[56] and Chinese central government exercised administrative jurisdiction over the Nansha Islands. Hence, such activities were no longer a simple claim of sovereignty.

In the Republic of China period, a review committee of maps of land and water was established by the Chinese central government to publish the locations and names of the Nansha Islands, sent navies to exercise jurisdiction over the Nansha Islands,

---

[49] Jennings and Watts (Revised) (1995, p. 75).

[50] Legal Status of Eastern Green Land (Denmark – Norway), Schwarzenberger (1945, Appendix 4, p. 534).

[51] Liu and Chen (eds.) (1998, pp. 133–136).

[52] An arbitrator pointed out in the Clipperton Island Case that it was sufficient to support the submissions from France according to geographical observations, the sailors' landing by going through many difficulties, as well as the sovereignty statement published in the *Polynesia*. Refer to Greig (1976, p. 162).

[53] Tandon and Tandon (1974, p. 199).

[54] Han (eds.) (1988, pp. 25–26).

[55] (Song Dynasty) Zhao Rushi, *Chorography of All Provinces*, vol. 2, Hanhai Edition.

[56] There are a number of maps that demonstrate Qing government's administrative jurisdiction over the Nansha Islands, such as the official map of Qing Dynasty in 1800, Summary of Coast Defense in 1838 etc.

protest against the occupation from France over nine islands, and conduct investigations in the Nansha Islands, etc. All of these activities are Chinese government's sovereign claims. In December, 1946, government of the Republic China took over the Nansha Islands from Japanese invaders and built sovereignty steles in Taiping Islands and some other islands in the Nansha Islands in order to demonstrate China's sovereignty over the Nansha Islands. In 1947, government of the Republic China published the map of locations of the islands in the South China Sea, used the dotted lines as China's boundary, and published numerous Chinese maps that included the Nansha Islands. These actions are sovereign claims in light of modern international laws.

Since the establishment of the People's Republic of China, Chinese government has repeatedly made sovereign statements on the Nansha Islands. Moreover, China has declared its sovereignty over the Nansha islands to foreign countries though legislative, judicial and administrative meansures.

After the establishment of the People's Republic of China, China published corresponding maps which included the Nansha Islands by administrative measures.

In May, 1950, Chinese government made the statement that the People's Republic of China would never allow the Tuansha Islands and other islands belong to China in South China Sea to be illegally seized by any states.[57]

In response to the draft treaty between Anglo-America and Japan, Zhou Enlai, the then Chinese Premier, announced that islands in the South China Sea were under the jurisdiction of Guangdong Province on 15 August 1951. He also stated on the same day that the draft treaty between Anglo-America and Japan was the outcome that America and its satellite states separately made peace with Japan. With respect to the territorial issue, Zhou Enlai stated that the United States of America and the United Kingdom published the draft of Peace Treaty with Japan simultaneously in Washington D.C and London on 12 July 1951, and prepared to sign the draft in the Peace Conference in San Francisco on July, 20th.[58] In response to this, Chinese government delegated me to make such a statement.

With respect to articles concerning territory, the Peace Treaty completely accorded with the U.S government's intention of expansion and invasion. In the Draft, the United States would gain the trusteeship over the Ryukyu Islands, Bonin Islands, Iwo Jima, Nishiro-shima Island, Okinotori Island and Marcus Island. The Taiping

[57] *People's Daily*, the front page on 20 May 1950.

[58] Treaty of Peace with Japan (also called Treaty of San Francisco or Peace Treaty of San Francisco), is the peace treaty signed between The Central Powers and Japan, a major member of The Allies. On 8 September 1951, representatives from 48 countries, including Japan, signed this treaty in the War Memorial Opera House in San Francisco in the United States. And the treaty officially came into force on 28 April 1952 (10:30 pm in Japan time). One of the drafts of the Treaty of Peace with Japan was Dulles, the United States Secretary of State. This treaty was meant to solve the international law issues of Japan's legal status and clarify the responsibilities of each state after the Second World War. The second statement in the Treaty of Pease with Japan states that Japan acknowledges the independence of North Korea, and abandon its rights to Taiwan, Penghu, Kuril Islands, the south Sakhalin, the Nansha Islands, the Xisha Islands etc. In article 3, Japan agrees that the United States exercises trust management over the Ryukyu Islands.

Islands, once trusted by Japan, was trusted by the United Nations. All of the above-mentioned islands had never been regarded as independent islands separated from Japan in any international treaties until then.[59]

On the other hand, the Draft is a violation of the Cairo Declaration, the Yalta Agreement and the Potsdam Proclamation. The Draft only stated Japan's obligation to abandon all its rights to Taiwan, Penghu, Kuril Islands, the south Sakhal and the nearby islands. Nevertheless, the Draft did not mention about Japan's obligation to give Taiwan, Penghu, Kuril Islands, the south Sakhal and the nearby islands back to the People's Republic of China, and territories back to the Soviet Union. The purpose of the drafter was to intensify relations with the Soviet Union so as to cover up for the United States' expansion and occupation, and to render a long-time occupation on Taiwan, which was indeed China's territory, by the United States. Also United States attempt to occupy Taiwan in long term. Nevertheless, such an invasion is never allowed by Chinese. The holy responsibilities to liberalize Taiwan and the Penghu Islands have never been abandoned by Chinese as well. The draft deliberately stated that Japan had to give up its rights to the Nanwei and Xisha Islands, but did not mention the sovereign retrocession of these islands. In fact, the Xisha Islands, the Nanwei Islands, as same as the Nansha, the Zhongsha and the Dongsha Islands, all have been part of China's territories since ancient times, were seized and occupied temporarily by invaders because of Japanese invasion. The Chinese government took over these islands after surrender of Japan. Right now, the Chinese government made the following statement: Central government of the People's Republic of China has the imprescriptible sovereignty over the Nanwei Islands and the Xisha Islands.

[59]The government of the People's Republic of China pointed out that the Treaty of Peace with Japan, proposed by Anglo American, was a draft that violated the spirit in international agreements and therefore was unacceptable in principle. Moreover, the San Francisco Conference, which was going to be compulsorily held on September 4th by the U.S government and where the Chinese government was openly excluded, was a violation of states' obligations under international laws. The standpoint of the government of the People's Republic of China was indisputable in accordance with the articles in the Treaty of Peace with Japan between Anglo America and Japan. Article 2 of the Treaty of Peace with Japan between Anglo America and Japan concerning territory accorded well with the U.S government's intention of expansion and invasion. On one hand, the draft of the treaty conferred the U.S government trust rights to the Taiping Islands, trusted by the former League of Nations to Japan and to the Ryukyu Islands, the Bonin Islands, the Volcano Islands, the Nishino-shima Island, the Okinotorishima and the Minamitorishima etc. In fact, Japan's right to occupy these islands were therefore maintained. And all of the above-mentioned islands had never been regarded as independent islands separated from Japan in any international treaties until then. On the other hand, the Draft is a violation of Cairo Declaration, Yalta Agreement and the Potsdam Proclamation. The Draft only stated Japan's obligation to abandon all its rights to Taiwan, Penghu, Kuril Islands, the south Sakhal and nearby islands. Nevertheless, the Draft did not mention about Japan's obligation to give Taiwan, Penghu, Kuril Islands, the south Sakhal and nearby islands back to the People's Republic of China, and territories back to the Soviet Union. The purpose of the second point was to intense relations with the Soviet Union so as to cover up the United States' expansion and occupation. The purpose of the first point was to render a long time occupation on Taiwan, which was indeed China's territory, by the United States. Nevertheless, such an invasion is never allowed by Chinese. The holy responsibilities to liberalize Taiwan and the Penghu Islands have never been abandoned by Chinese as well.

China's exercise of its sovereignty over these islands would not be interfered by what is contained in the draft of the Peace Treaty.[60]

On 29 May 1956, Chinese government made another statement that China would defend its sovereignty over the Nansha Islands.[61]

In 1958, the Chinese government issued *A Statement of government of the People's Republic of China on the Territorial Sea*. Article 1 of the statement stipulates: "Territorial waters of the People's Republic of China extend for 12 nautical miles. This rule applies to mainland China and its coastal islands, to Taiwan that was separated by high seas from mainland China and other coastal islands, and to the surrounding islands including the Penghu, the Dongsha, the Xisha, the Zhongsha, and the Nansha islands that belong to China. With respect to straight baseline and passage of foreign aircrafts and ships, Article 4 "also applies to Taiwan and its nearby islands, the Penghu, the Dongsh, the Xisha, the Zhongsha, the Nansha Islands and other islands that belong to China.[62]

On 16 July 1971, Chief of the General Staff of the People's Liberation Army made the following statement: the Nansha and the Xisha Islands have been China's territories since it was in the ancient time. China has the indisputable legal sovereignty over these islands. China will never allow any countries to encroach upon the territorial integrity of China by any excuses or means.[63]

On 11 January 1974, the Ministry of Foreign Affairs of the People's Republic of China made the following statement: the Nansha, the Xisha, the Zhongsha and the Dongsha Islands are China's territories. The People's Republic of China has the indisputable sovereignty over these islands. Resources in the nearby waters of these islands also belong to China.[64]

On 20 January 1974, the Ministry of Foreign Affairs of the People's Republic of China made the following statement: It is well-known and indisputable that the Xisha, the Nansha, the Zhongsha and the Dongsha Islands belong to China since very ancient times. After World War II, the Xisha Islands, the same as other islands in the South China Sea, had been officially taken over by Chinese government.[65]

On 4 February 1974, Chinese government condemned and pretested Saigon authority's building of the so-called "sovereignty steles" on the Nanzi Islands in the Nansha Islands by stating that "the Chinese government had already made the statements for many times that the Nansha, the Xisha, the Zhongsha and the Dongsha Islands are China's territories. The People's Republic of China has incontestable sovereignty over these islands and its nearby waters. China will never allow Saigon

---

[60] *Compile of Foreign Relations Files of the People's Republic of China*. World Affairs Press, 1958. Vol. 2, pp. 30–32.

[61] *Compile of Foreign Relations Files of the People's Republic of China*. World Affairs Press, 1958. Vol. 4, pp. 61–62.

[62] *A Statement of government of the People"s Republic of China on the Territorial Sea* (1958), refer to the State Oceanic Administration People's Republic of China (eds.) (1998, p. 1).

[63] *People's Daily*, the second page on 17 July 1971.

[64] *People's Daily*, the front page on 12 January 1974.

[65] *People's Daily*, 21 January 1974.

authority to violate China's sovereignty by any excuses. This standpoint of Chinese government is unalterable.[66]

On 30 March 1974, the People's Republic of China stated in the 30th session of the United Nations Economic Commission for Asia and Far East, held in Colombo, that "the Xisha and the Nansha Islands are the inseparable parts of China's territories since ancient time. China has incontestable sovereignty over these islands and its nearby waters."

On 5 May 1974, with respect to "international cooperation of mapping", representatives of the Chinese government pointed out that "the Nansha Islands, together with the Xisha, the Dongsha and the Zhongsha Islands, belong to China all along. The People's Republic of China has indisputable sovereignty over these islands and its nearby waters. Chinese delegations requested authorities concerned to take measures to cease relevant hydrographic planning by the so-called "South China Sea Hydrographic Committee", and ensure similar circumstances would never happen again.[67]

In the United Nations Conference on the Law of the Sea, the People's Republic of China pointed out "the Chinese government has solemnly stated several times that the Nansha and the Xisha Islands are an inseparable part of China's territories. Chinese people and the Chinese government would never allow the Saigon authority to violate the territorial integrity of China by any excuses."[68]

On 14 June 1976, in response to the Philippine's claim for a joint-exploitation with foreign petroleum companies in the Reed Bank areas, the People's Republic of China made the statement that "the Nansha Islands, same as the Xisha, the Zhongsha and the Dongsha Islands, are China's territories since ancient time. The Chinese government declared more than once that China has an indisputable sovereignty over these islands and its nearby waters, whose resources also belong to China. It is a violation of the integrity of China's territorial sovereignty and China would never allow any state to send troops to seize and occupy the Nansha Islands or explore and exploit oil and other resources in the Nansha Islands areas. It is illegal and invalid for any other state to claim sovereignty over the Nansha Islands."[69]

In the conversation memo with Pham Van Dong, the former Prime Minister of Vietnam, Li Xiannian, the former Vice Premier of China, pointed out that it is incontestable that China has the sovereignty over the Nansha Islands. The Vietnamese governments had always admitted the fact before 1974.[70]

On 29 December 1978, the Chinese Foreign Ministry spokesman declared in terms of the issue of sovereignty over the Nansha Islands that "the Nansha Islands, same as the Xisha, the Zhongsha and the Dongsha Islands, is China's territories since it was in the ancient time. The Chinese government declared more than once that China has an indisputable sovereignty over these islands and its nearby waters, whose resources

[66] *People's Daily*, the front page on 5 February 1974.

[67] *People's Daily*, the sixth page on 8 May 1974.

[68] *People's Daily*, 3 July 1974.

[69] *People's Daily*, 15 June 1976.

[70] *People's Daily*, 23 March 1979. Cited from Wu ed. (2001, p. 76).

also belong to China. It is a violation of the integrity of China's territorial sovereignty and China would never allow any state to send troops to seize and occupy the Nansha Islands or explore and exploit oil and other resources in the Nansha Islands areas. It is illegal and invalid for any state to claim sovereignty over the Nansha Islands."[71]

On 26 April 1979, in the negotiations between China and Vietnam, representatives of the Chinese government pointed out that "the Xisha and the Nansha Islands have been China's inseparable territories through the ages. Vietnam shall acknowledge the fact as before, respect China's sovereignty over the two islands, and evacuate all personnel from occupied islands in the Nansha Islands."[72] China's head of delegation also made the same point in the fifth of the eight principles in dealing with relationship between China and Vietnam.

On 13 May 1979, in the speech titled "Clarifications on the Territorial Disputes between China and Vietnam", the head of Chinese government's delegation pointed out that "the Xisha and the Nansha islands are China's territories since it was in the ancient time. In view of this fact, we require the Democratic Republic of Vietnam to acknowledge and respect China's sovereignty, no matter in official documents including consultations, statements, or in Vietnamese newspapers, textbooks and officially published maps as well as in conference of heads." The spokesman also enumerated relevant documents, letters and conversations in which Vietnam acknowledged China's sovereignty over the Nansha Islands, and pointed out that "all these evidences are iron-clad facts that cannot be denied by anyone."[73]

On 26 September 1979, the Ministry of Foreign Affairs of the People's Republic of China reiterated that the Nansha Islands, as well as the Xisha, the Zhongsha and the Dongsha Islands, are China's territory all along. The Chinese government declared more than once that China has an indisputable sovereignty over these islands and its nearby waters, whose resources also belong to China. Any activity that encroaches on the Nansha Islands or exploites in this area would constitute a violation of China's territorial integrity and sovereignty, which is never allowed. It is illegal and invalid for any state to claim sovereignty over the Nansha Islands.[74]

On 30 January 1980, the Ministry of Foreign Affairs of the People's Republic of China issued a document titled "China Has An Indisputable Sovereignty over the Xisha and the Nansha Islands",[75] which pithily denounced outrageous lies and capricious position of Vietnam.

On 21 July 1980, in response to the agreement between Vietnam and the Soviet Union on cooperative exploration and exploitation of oil and natural gas in the so-called "Southern Continental Shelf of Vietnam", the Ministry of Foreign Affairs of the People's Republic of China pointed out that the Nansha islands and three other archipelagos in the South China Sea "are China's territories through ages. China has an incontestable sovereignty over these islands and its nearby waters. Resources in

[71] *People's Daily*, 29 December 1978.

[72] *People's Daily*, 27 April 1979.

[73] *People's Daily*, 13 May 1979.

[74] *People's Daily*, 27 September 1979.

[75] *People's Daily*, 31 January 1980.

the above regions also belong to China as a matter of course. It is illegal for any state to enter into the above regions and conduct exploration, exploitation or any other activities without China's permission. In addition, any contracts signed to explore, exploit or carry out any other activities in this region are invalid."[76]

On 28 November 1982, the spokesman of the Ministry of Foreign Affairs of the People's Republic of China issued a statement that "Gulf of Tonkin boundary line claimed by the government of Vietnam is illegal and invalid. It is reiterated that the Xisha Islands and the Nansha Islands are an inseparable and sacred part of China's territories."[77]

On 14 September 1983, the spokesman of the Ministry of Foreign Affairs of the People's Republic of China pointed out "China has an indisputable sovereignty over the Nansha Islands, whose resources belong to China. China's sovereignty over the Nansha Islands is never allowed to be violated by any countries with any excuses. Any states' occupation of the Nansha Islands and activities in this region are illegal and not allowed."[78]

On 15 April 1987, the People's Republic of China strongly condemned Vietnam's illegal occupation of parts of the Nansha Islands. The spokesman pointed out that the Xisha and the Nansha Islands are inseparable parts of China's territories all along. China has an indisputable sovereignty over these islands and its nearby waters. China would never allow any countries to infringe China's sovereignty with any excuses. China required Vietnam to evacuate from these illegally-occupied Nansha islands. Moreover, the spokesman especially pointed out that the Chinese government reserved the right to reoccupy these islands at appropriate time.[79] In the same year on June 17th, the spokesman of Ministry of Foreign affairs of the People's Republic of China stated that "the Nansha and the Xisha Islands are sacred parts of China's territories through ages. China has an indisputable sovereignty over these islands, and such solemn standpoint of China is well-known." "Vietnam illegally occupied some of the Nansha Islands. Vietnam shall evacuate from these islands and it has no rights to accuse China's exercise of legal rights over China's territories."[80] On December 2nd, the spokesman of Ministry of Foreign affairs of the People's Republic of China restated that "China has an indisputable sovereignty over these islands and its nearby waters. It is illegal and invalid for any state to occupy the Nansha Islands by encroaching, legislative or delimiting means."[81]

In 1988, the Chinese government successively made 9 announcements, and pointed out that the Nansha islands is an inherent part of China's territory. It is China's sovereignty rights to send vessels to the Nansha Islands and its nearby waters to conduct research and cruise. Vietnam has no right to interfere. Furthermore, it is Vietnam that illegally occupied some of the Nansha Islands and shall

[76] *People's Daily*, 22 July 1980.

[77] *People's Daily*, 29 November 1982.

[78] *People's Daily*, 15 September 1983.

[79] *People's Daily*, 16 April 1987.

[80] *People's Daily*, 18 June 1987.

[81] *People's Daily*, 28 December 1987.

evacuate from these islands. If Vietnam ignores the consistent standpoint of China, and impedes China's legal activities in the Nansha region, Vietnam shall bear all consequences caused by their activities. On March 14th, in response to Vietnam's attack to the Chinese ships that were conducting research and cruising, the Ministry of Foreign Affairs of the People's Republic of China protested to the Vietnamese Embassy by stating that "Vietnam shall immediately stop provoking China in the South China Sea by force, and evacuate from China's islands and its nearby waters. Otherwise, Vietnam shall bear all the responsibilities caused by such activities." On March 16th, in response to Vietnamese military ships' attack and fire to Chinese ships that were conducting research, the spokesman of Ministry of Foreign Affairs of the People's Republic of China stated that Nansha Islands are China's territory. Their research activities are China's sovereignty rights. China's retaliation is totally deliberately provoked by Vietnam. On April 5th, the spokesman gave a speech to warn that Vietnam shall immediately stop illegally occupying the Nansha Islands. Vietnam continued to seize Collins Reef, Qiong Reef, Daxian Reef, Alison Reef, Tennent Reef, Cornwallis South Reef, Bolan Jiao, South Reef and other islands and reefs by using rescue as an excuse. Vietnam's above activities, by using rescue as an excuse, severely violated *the 1949 Geneva Convention* which stipulates that rescuing ships shall not be used for military purpose, and is a flagrant breach of international law. Vietnam shall stop occupying the Nansha Islands by any means, and evacuate from the seized territories. Otherwise, Vietnam shall bear all consequences caused by its illegal activities. On April 6th, the Deputy Foreign Minister of Ministry of Foreign Affairs of the People's Republic of China gave a speech and pointed out that Vietnam had acknowledged China's sovereignty over the Nansha Islands for many times, but Vietnam changed their position very quickly. The change was resulted from Vietnam's ambition of territorial expansion. On April 20th, the spokesman of Ministry of Foreign Affairs of the People's Republic of China pointed out that Vietnam should return to its correct standpoint before 1975, stop occupying China's Nansha islands, and evacuate from illegally occupied islands. On May 11th, the spokesman of Ministry of Foreign Affairs of the People's Republic of China pointed out that Vietnam had illegally occupied more than 20 of China's reefs in the Nansha Islands. The conflict between China and Vietnam can be avoided as long as Vietnam stops provoking and occupying the Nansha Islands, and evacuate from these islands. On May 12th, in *the Memorandum on the Nansha and the Xisha Islands*, the Chinese government reviewed the detailed historical facts of Vietnam's acknowledgment of China's sovereignty over the Nansha Islands, and illustrated facts to prove that the Chinese government had been exercising jurisdiction over the Nansha Islands and Chinese people had been engaging in productive activities in the Nansha Islands. The Chinese government required Vietnam to stop occupying China's territory, stop creating tension, and evacuate from illegally occupied islands in order to restore peace in this region. On November 24th, the spokesman of Ministry of Foreign Affairs of the People's Republic of China pointed out again that China has an indisputable sovereignty over the Nansha Islands and its nearby waters.[82]

On 28 September 1989, in response to Vietnam's illegal occupation of Vibrant Reef, Vanguard Bank and Prince of Wales Bank, the spokesman of Ministry of Foreign Affairs of the People's Republic of China pointed out that "such activities are flagrant infringement of China's sovereignty." The Chinese government strongly condemned Vietnam's illegal occupation of part of the Nansha islands, and firmly demanded Vietnam to evacuate from these illegally occupied islands.[83]

On 13 and 15 December 1990, Li Peng, the then Chinese Premier, gave speeches in Manila and Kuala Lumpur and pointed out that "it is indisputable that the Nansha Islands is part of China's territory."[84]

On 14 September 1991, the spokesman of Ministry of Foreign Affairs of the People's Republic of China reiterated that China has an indisputable sovereignty over the Nansha and its nearby waters.

On 25 February 1992, the 7th National People's Congress standing committee passed the *Law of the People's Republic of China on the Territorial Sea and the Contiguous Zone*, in which Article 2 stipulates that "The territorial sea of the People's Republic of China is the sea belt adjacent to the land territory and the internal waters of the People's Republic of China. The land territory of the People's Republic of China includes the mainland of the People's Republic of China and its coastal islands; Taiwan and all islands appertaining there, which include the Diaoyu Islands, the Penghu Islands, the Dongsha Islands, the Xisha Islands, the Zhongsha Islands and the Nansha Islands, as well as all the other islands belonging to the People's Republic of China. The waters on the landward side of the baselines of the territorial sea of the People's Republic of China constitute the internal waters of the People's Republic of China."[85] Hereby China has declared its sovereignty over the Nansha Islands in the form of legislation.

On 16 July 1992, the spokesman of Ministry of Foreign Affairs of the People's Republic of China pointed out that "the Nansha Islands has belonged to China since it was in the ancient time."[86]

On 16 June and 17 July in 1994, the spokesman of Ministry of Foreign Affairs of the People's Republic of China pointed out that "China has an indisputable sovereignty over the Xisha and the Nansha Islands and its nearby waters. The Chinese government will never allow above sovereign requirements of Vietnam."

On January 21, April 20, May 16, and November 10 in 1995, the spokesman of Ministry of Foreign Affairs of the People's Republic of China repeatedly pointed out that "China has an indisputable sovereignty over the Nansha Islands and its nearby

---

[82] *People's Daily*, 23 February 1988, 15 March 1988, 17 March 1988, 6 April 1988, 7 April 1988, 21 April 1988, 12 May 1988, 13 May 1988, 24 November 1988.

[83] *People's Daily*, 28 September 1989.

[84] *People's Daily*, 14 December 1990, 16 December 1990.

[85] *Law of the People's Republic of China on the Territorial Sea and the Contiguous Zone*, China Ocean Press, 1998, p. 4.

[86] People's Daily, 17 July 1992.

waters. No country shall conduct exploration, exploitation and research without Chinese government's permission."

The Chinese Taiwan government has also adopted relevant measures to defend China's sovereignty over the Nansha Islands besides the Chinese central government's sovereign claims. The Taiwan government's sovereign claims comprise of protests and negotiations to Vietnam, the Philippine and Malaysia concerning their invading activities.

As for the Philippines, in 1973, the Taiwan authority for many times negotiated with the Philippine in order to defend China's sovereignty over the Nansha Islands. On 11 February 1974, Taiwan's representatives in the Philippines made the note to the Philippine government and reiterated China's sovereignty over the Nansha Islands. On 9 March 1978, the Taiwan authority strongly protested that the Philippines garrisoned on the Nansha Islands, and reiterated that China's sovereignty over the Nansha Islands "would never be affected by any measures taken by any states".

As for Vietnam, on 14 February 1975, the Taiwan authority made a statement to denounce the so-called white papers about the Nansha and the Xisha islands published by Vietnam, and defended China's "indisputable and inviolable" sovereignty over the Nansha Islands. On 27 May 1977, the Taiwan authority protested Vietnam's violation of China's sovereign over the Nansha Islands, and reiterated that China has an indisputable sovereignty over the Nansha water sea. On 26 November 1983, the Taiwan authority objected Vietnam's drawing the Nansha Islands into Vietnam's territorial waters. On 30 May 1983, the Taiwan authority strongly protested that Vietnam garrisoned in Amboyna Cay, and stated that China has an incontestable sovereignty over the Nansha Islands.

As for Malaysia, in response to Malaysia's drawing two islands into their maps, the Taiwan authority solemnly stated on 25 April 1980 that China has an exclusive sovereignty over the Nansha Islands. "Such standpoint would never be changed by any activities or measures taken by any countries."

On 21 January 1998, the Taiwan authority promulgated the *Law on Territorial Waters and Contiguous Zone* and the *Law on Exclusive Economic Zone and Continental Shelf* in order to protect China's sovereignty over the Nansha Islands.

On 14 April 2004, the spokesman of the Ministry of Foreign Affairs of the People's Republic of China pointed out that China has an indisputable sovereignty over the Nansha Islands and its nearby waters. Vietnam's activities violated China's territorial sovereignty.

On 10 April 2007, the spokesman of the Ministry of Foreign Affairs of the People's Republic of China reiterated China's sovereignty over the Nansha Islands. He pointed out that "any activities unilaterally adopted any states within the waters is a violation of China's territorial sovereignty, sovereignty rights and jurisdiction. Such acticvities are invalid and illegal."

On 3 February 2009, the spokesman of the Ministry of Foreign Affairs of the People's Republic of China stated that China has an indisputable sovereignty over the Scarborough Reef and the Nansha Islands. The situation of the South China Sea remains stable by joint effort. We hope relevant countries realistically comply with the *Declaration on the Code of Conduct on the South China Sea*, and do not take any measures that would make the dispute complicated and worse, and jointly maintain peace and stability in the South China Sea.

On 10 May 2011, in response to Vietnam's standpoint concerning China's Nansha Islands made in the so-called "congressman" election, Jiang Yu, the spokesman of Ministry of Foreign Affairs of the People's Republic of China, stated that China has an indisputable sovereignty over the Nansha Islands and its nearby waters. She stressed that any activities unilaterally taken by any countries are a violation of China's territorial sovereignty, which are invalid and illegal. Such actions do not accord with the *Declaration on the Code of Conduct on the South China Sea.*

On 28 February 2012, Hong Lei, the spokesman of Ministry of Foreign Affairs of the People's Republic of China, stated that China has an indisputable sovereignty over the Nansha Islands and its nearby waters. It is illegal for any state or any company to conduct oil and gas exploitation within waters in China's jurisdiction without the Chinese government's permissions.

On 23 January 2013, the spokesman of Ministry of Foreign Affairs of the People's Republic of China stated that there are sufficient historical and legal bases to demonstrate China has an indisputable sovereignty over the Nansha Islands and its nearby waters. The root and core of the conflict between China and the Philippines on the South China Sea is the territorial dispute resulted from Philippine's illegal occupation of the partial Nansha Islands. China has always strongly opposed such illegal occupations.

The continual sovereign claims by the Chinese government are sufficient for China to have sovereignty over the Nansha Islands and its nearby water. Since China has been exercising sovereign power over the Nansha islands and its nearby waters, the Chinese government has never abandoned and will never abandon its sovereignty claims over the Nansha Islands and its nearby waters.

4.2.5 Incorporation of the Nansha Islands into Maps; Implementation of the Administrative Jurisdiction

In the ancient China, the Nansha Islands was named "Wan Li Chang Sha" or "Wanli Shitang." Such a naming behavior is an implementation of administrative jurisdiction.

The Nansha Islands has been under China's administrative jurisdiction since the Northern Song Dynasty.

In *Chorography of All Provinces*, it is documented that Hainan is Zhuya prefecture and Daner Prefecture in the Han Dynasty. Emperor Wu of Han pacified the south Guangdong, and sent envoys to Zhuya Prefecture and Daner Prefecture to manage the operation and delimit the boundaries of the lands from Xuwen County by taking ships. Daner Prefecture was dissolved and incorporated into Zhuya Prefecture by Emperor Zhao of Han. Later, Emperor Yuan of Han dissolved Zhuya Prefecture under the suggestions from Jiajuan. Until in the periods between Liang in the Nan Dynasty (A.D 502–557) to the Sui Dynasty (A.D 581–618), Zhuya Prefecture was re-established. In the first year of Zhenguan period in the Tang Dynasty (A.D 627), Zhuya Prefecture was divided into Yazhou, Danzhou and Zhenzhou, which belonged to south Guangdong Provinces. In the fifth year of Zhenguan Period (A.D 631), Qiongshan, which was part of Yazhou, was separated as a prefecture. And County Wanan was upgraded as a city to Wanan City today (Song Dynasty). Danzhou and Zhenzhou are today's (Song Dynasty) Changhua City in Jiyang. In the fifth year of Zhenyuan Period in the Tang Dynasty (A.D 789), Qiongzhou Governorer was established, and such structure has been kept until now...It is already the end of land and top of sea when you reach Jiyang (Sanya City in Hainan Province today). There is no land any more if you step further, but shoals are called Wuli, Sulilang in the sea. Zhancheng is in the south of the shoals; Zhenla is in the west of the shoals; and Qianli Changsha and Wanli Shitang are in the east of the shoals......Eleven counties in total are governed by four cities, and all of them belong to Guangnanxilu.[87] It can be seen that the Nansha Islands has been under China's administrative jurisdiction since 789 A.D. In the Song Dynasty, the Nansha islands were administrated by Guangana Xilu Qiong[88] which was within the jurisdiction of Hainan Sizhou Army.

In the Ming Dynasty, in Annals of *Qionghai's Territory* of *Annals of Qionghai*, "territory" was "bounded by the sea, adjacent to Wuli, Sumi, Jilang and among others. Zhancheng is in the south while Zhenla and Jiaozhi are in the west. Qianli Changsha and Wanli Shitang are in the east, while Leizhou and Xuwen areas are in the north.[89]

The documents about territories are noticeable. It can be seen that China has knowledge about the Nansha Islands territories. In the Yuan Dynasty, Annals of *Dao Yi* and *Customs of Cambodia* also recorded territories of the South China Sea besides the *History of Yuan Dynasty*. *Annals of Dao Yi*, complied by Wang Dayuan on the basis of his personal experience, described the locations of Kunlun and Wangli Shitang in details.[90]

Urano Tatseo, a Japanese legal scholar, confirmes that China has exercised jurisdiction over the Nansha Islands. After a comprehensive analysis of the documents and files, he holds that the earlist records that prove China's jurisdiction over the Nansha Islands is in the *General Annals of Guangdong*, which stated that "Qiong is bounded by the sea with abundant resources. Li nationality is living there and there are several counties and cities surrounding it. Qiali Changsha and Wanli Shitang are there with mists and waves partly visible and partly hidden."[91] "Qiong is the capital of the province, and is in the north. Dan is in the west, Ya is in the west and Wan is in the south. Li Natinality is living there in the high and steep mountains.

[87] (Song Dynasty) Zhao Rushi, *Chorography of All Provinces*,Vol.2 Hanhai Edition.

[88] (Song Dynasty) *Qiong Guan Zhi*. It has been lost but records can be found in *General Geography Records*.

[89] (Ming)Tangzhou, Zheng De *Qiong Tai Zhi*, Vol. 4, cited from Han (eds.) (1998, p. 34).

[90] (Yuan) Wang Dayuan, *Dao Yi Zhi Lue*, Wanli Shitang, p.93. Xue Tangcong printed edition. Cited from Han (eds.) (1998, p. 49).

[91] (Qing Dynasty) Hao Yulin, General Guangdong Records. Volume 4, Qiongzhou County, Scenic spots, Territory documents, p. 52. Cited from Han (eds.) (1998, p. 66).

It is bounded by the sea and adjacent to other countries."[92] "It is 1700 miles from Qiongzhou Province to the capital city. Most of the province is covered by sea. The length is 970 miles while the width is 975 miles. It takes only one day to go from Leizhou to Qiong by sea. Qiong is the capital of the province, and is in the north. Dan is in the west, Ya is in the west and Wan is in the south. Li Natinality is living there in the high and steep mountains. It is bounded by the sea and adjacent to other countries."[93]

In the late Qing Dynasty, the fact that the Chinese government incorporated the Nansha Islands into coast defense system was documented in the *Annals of Qiongzhou* by Ming Yi, *Annals of Ya* by Zhong Yuandi, *Annals of Ganen County* by Zhou Wenhai, *Records and Maps of Guangdong* by Mao Hongbin, Y*ang Fang Shuo Lue* by Xu Jiagan and *General Map of Guangdong Province* by Liao Tingxiang.

To conclude, in the Ming and Qing Dynasties, local annals compiled by the Chinese government have recorded in the parts of "Boundary", "Mountains and Rivers", "Sea Territories" and "Cultures and Views" that "Qianli Changsha and Wanli Shitang are located in Wanzhou". "Wanli Shitang" represents today's Nansha Islands which is under the jurisdiction of Lingshui Country, Hainan Province.

The Nansha Islands were included into China's territory in the *Qing Dynasty Global Map* (formulated in 1716), *Qing Dynasty Provincial Division Map* (formulated in 1724), *Qing Dynasty Provincial Division Map* (formulated in 1755), *Qing Dynasty Map for the Territory with the Sovereignty* (formulated in 1767), *Qing Dynasty National Map* (formulated in 1800), *Qing Dynasty Map for the Territory with the Sovereignty* (formulated in 1817) and *Overall Map of Provincial Seas in Seas Protection Overview*.

In 1911, Guangdong Government determined that the islands in the South China Sea were under the jurisdiction of Ya County of Hainan Province. Meanwhile, the central government set up a Territorial Department to be in charge of the affairs of the South China Sea. In 1921, the Southern military government reiterated this decree.

In 1933, government of the Republic of China directed staff and navy department to hold a conference of consultation to investigate the Nansha Islands.[94] In August, the Guangdong government sent two warships to conduct investigations in the Nansha Islands.[95] Such activities is the evidence to prove government of the Republic of China had exercised administrative jurisdiction. Moreover, such administrative jurisdiction activities were far earlier than sovereignty claims by the Philippines, Vietnam and Malaysia. In any case, it is an undoubted fact that China has territorial sovereignty over the Nansha Islands and its nearby waters.

---

[92](Qing Dyansty) Jin Guangzu, *General Guangdong Records*. Volume 2, Territory, Block-printed edition in the 36th year of Kangxi (1697). Cited from Han (eds.) (1998, p. 34).

[93](Qing Dynasty) Hao Yulin,. *General Guangdong Records*. Volume 4, territory documents, p. 48. Cited from Han (eds.) (1998, p. 35).

[94]"The Central Leadership's Attaching Importance to the Case of France's Invasion in Nine Islands", printed in *Shen Bao*, July 31, 1933.

[95]"Chen Jitang's Investigation for the Nansha Islands through the Ships", printed in *Shen Bao*: August 2, 1933.

In 1935, the Amphibious Map Review Committee of the Chinese government published the names of 103 islands of the Nansha islands.[96]

After Anti-Japanese War, government of the Republic of China continued to exercise administrative jurisdiction over the Nansha Islands. On 2 August 1946, the Cantonese government determined to investigate prewar and current situations of the Dongsha and the Xisha Islands in response to the applications from the Interior Ministry and Kaohsiuing city government. At the same time, departments of the central government were discussing the time to garrison the Xisha and the Nansha Islands. On September 13, the Ministry of Interior, the Department of Defense and the Ministry of Foreign Affairs convened a meeting of taking over the Nansha Islands. The Department of Defense and the Cantonese government suggested the central government follow the scheme of the Ministry of Interior to take over the Tuansha Islands (the Nansha Islands) as soon as possible. The Ministry of Interior made a map which recorded details about names and locations of each archipelago. The Ministry of Interior, the Department of Defense and the Commander Department of the Navy delivered the documents to the Ministry of Foreign Affairs for the record to prevent interferences from foreign states. Eventually, the Commander Department of Navy was required to send warships, and the Ministry of Interior, the Department of Defense and the Air Commander were required to send representatives in the take-over. Additionally, the Cantonese government dispatched officers to participate in taking over these islands. Lin Zun held the post of commander of warships, and Yao Ruyu was appointed as the deputy commander to take over the Xisha and the Nansha Islands. They went to the Xisha and the Nansha Islands with four warships, namely Tai Ping, Yong Xing, Zhong Jian and Zhong Ye. After the French army retreated in September 1946, the four warships sailed from Nanjing on October 2. On November 29, Yong Xing and Zhong Jian arrived at Yongxing Islands and garrisoned there. In the Nansha areas, France sent warships to Taiping and Spratly Islands and built steles there on October 5. Two warships, Tai Ping and Zhong Ye, arrived in the Nansha Islands on December 9, and landed 3 days later. On December 15, the Tai Ping warship cruised around the Thitu Island, the Shuangzi Island and the nearby islands. Each warship parked a nautical mile away and sent military forces to land on the islands by boats. After ensuring there was no enemy, they led crews to land on the islands with goods and materials, rise national flags, salute fires, perform taking-over ceremony, rename the islands and build sovereign steles. The taking-over process lasted until 4 February 1947.

In 1947, the Ministry of Interior published a comparison table of the new and old names of the Nansha islands in order to aviod confusion in applications. Publishing the names of the Nansha Islands and determining the specific locations and areas of the islands can be per se regarded as the Chinese government's exercise of administrative jurisdiction.

---

[96]In 1935, *the South China Sea Islands Map* by the Committee for Reviewing Map of Land and Water in the Republic of China indicated specific names of all the South China Sea islands including the Nansha Islands in detail.

On 16 January 1947, the Chinese Department of Defense convened a conference concerning construction on the Xisha and the Nansha Islands. The conference determined to establish Hainan Special Administrative Region (HNSAR) to exercise jurisdiction over the Xisha and the Nansha Islands, which was issued in No.1117 Decree by Executive Yuan on January 27. In response to the actions of France and the Philippines, Chiang Kai-shek, President of the Republic of China, promulgated the *Organizational Regulations of HNSAR*, in which Article 1 stipulates that "HNSAR includes the Dongsha, the Xisha, the Zhongsha, the Nansha islands and other islands, shoals, cays, sands or submerged rocks."

No.442 Decree issued by the Interior OPublication Bureau of the Ministry of Interior of the People's Republic of China states: Before the establishment of HNSAR, the provisional administrative power of Tibet Autonomous Region and the South China Sea temporarily belongs to the Navy. After the establishment of HNSAR on April 1, the administrative power shall be retroceded to HNSAR, and two islands should be merged into Hainan administrative division.

On 1 April 1947, under the Commander Department of Navy's permission, the Ministry of Interior renamed the biggest islands of the Nansha as "Taiping Islands", in the name of taking-over warships. On April 14, the Ministry of Interior, together with the Department of Defense and Department of Navy's participation, held "a meeting on determination of sovereignty over the Xisha and the Nansha Islands as well as publication of the locations." In this meeting, the southernmost point of China's territory in the South China Sea is determined as Zengmu reef. The Ministry of Interior also renamed the islands, shoals of the Nansha and the Xisha Islands, and announced China's sovereignty over the two islands to the whole country. In addition, the meeting also determined that navy shall send officers and soldiers to all islands as far as possible. In October, the Ministry of Interior submitted materials in which the southernmost point of China is referred to as Zengmu reef, 4°N, in the compilation of Republic of China Statistical Yearbook.

The Ministry of Interior organized manpower and material resources to conduct investigations in the Nansha Islands again. In 1949, Dr. Ma Yanying,[97] the head of Geological Department of National Taiwan University, led and coordinated an investigating group with participation of Guo Lingzhi,[98] associate professor of the Geological Department of National Taiwan University. They went to the Nansha

---

[97]Ma Yanying (1899–1979), a paleontologists, marine geologist, and marine biologist, is an important pioneer on the China marine geology. Over his earlier years, he was engaged in studies on the coral growth rhythm, who was the first investor of the "paleontological clock"; in addition, he was devoted to and made contributions to studies on the "palaeoclimate and continental drift". Great achievements were obtained for his investigation and research on Taiwan Strait petroleum resources. He led Taiwan University and Culture University Departments of Geology to cultivate plenty of talents.

[98]Guo Lingzhi (1915–), born in Anlu, Hubei and a geologist, was one of important pioneers on China plate tectonics and terrane tectonics studies, who has served as Vice-president of Nanjing University, Acting President, Director of University Administration Committee and Vice-chairman of Geological Society of China successively.

Islands by taking Zhongye Warship, and conducted general geological, maritime and other investigations there.

After the investigation, the Cantonese government and the Recorder Compilation Committee of the Xisha and the Nansha Islands held a product exhibition concerning the Nansha and the Xisha Islands in Guangdong Literature Libary in order to enhance public awareness to the south border of Guangdong province. About 40,000 people visited this exhibition.

On September 4, the Ministry of Interior officially declared in No. 080 Decree that Guangdong has jurisdiction over the Xisha Islands, the Nansha Islands, the Dongsha Islands and the Zhongsha Islands. The names of affiliated islands, shoals and cays were also published, against which no state protested. On December 1, the government published a comparison table of old and new names of islands in the South China Sea.

After taking over the islands in the South China Sea, the Chinese government established administrative offices of the Dongsha Islands, the Xisha Islands and the Nansha Islands, determined to deliver food to these islands twice a year, and replace the guards annually.

On 24 March 1948, in order to replace the islands' guards, the Commander Department of Navy sent warships to the Nansha Islands. The warships carried Major Zhang Junran, the head of the Administrative Office of Xisha Islands, Major Peng Yunsheng,[99] the head of the Administrative Office of the Nansha Islands, Captain Pan Ziteng, the member of Legal Committee of Commander Department of Navy, and other 104 soldiers.

In response to the new actions including France and the Philippines's dispatch of armies and shelling of Chinese fishing ships, on 6 June 1949, President Chiang Kai-shek promulgated the *Organizational Regulations of HNSAR*, in which Article 1 stipulates that "Hainan Special Administrative Region includes the Dongsha, the Xisha, the Zhongsha, the Nansha and other islands, shoals, sands and submerged rocks."

It should be specially noted that the fishermen who fished in the Nansha Islands had to pay taxes to the Hainan local government. The fishermen who fished in the Nansha Islands were "mostly employed by the fishery owners. Besides, a few fishermen voluntarily organized and borrowed money and fishing ships from fishery owners. The owners set up shops in town, and applied business license and paid taxes to local government. …. The fishermen who went to the Xisha and the Nansha Islands had compact organization, and signed contracts in units of ships."[100] The Hainan local government levied taxes on the fisherman who fished in the Nansha Islands, which proves that the Chinese government had exercised administrative jurisdiction over the Nansha Islands. In the Minquiers and Ecrehos Case (France/United Kingdom),

---

[99] Peng Yunsheng was born in Huangpo Taergang Qili Village in 1918. During the period under the rule of the Nationalist Party, he graduated from Qingdao Naval Officer College Stage V Class B navigation division and served as Capital of Yongjia Vessel in Taiwan. In 1959, he was appointed as Chief Officer and Vice-marshal in College for Naval Sergeancy and was then arranged to deal with the local affairs.

[100] He (1981, p. 49).

the United Kingdom turned to the evidence that the United Kingdom had levied taxes, registered estate, built customs inspection post, and conducted autopsy in the two archipelagos to demonstrate that the United Kingdom exercised sovereign power over the two archipelagos. And the court's judgment supported this claim.

Therefore, in the period of Republic of China, China exercised administrative jurisdiction in the sense of modern international law over the Nansha Islands, which can sufficiently prove China has territorial sovereignty over the islands.

After the establishment of the People's Republic of China, the islands of the South China Sea have been under the jurisdiction of Guangdong province. In March 1959, Hainan Administrative Region of Guangdong Province officially established county government institutions titled "Working Committee of Communist Party of China in the Xisha Islands, the Nansha Islands and the Zhongsha Islands" and "the Xisha, the Nansha and the Zhongsha Islands Office" in Yongxing Island. In March 1963, the institutions were renamed as "Revolutionary Committee of Guangdong Province in the Xisha Islands, the Zhongsha Islands and the Nansha Islands". In 1984, the Second Session of the Sixth National People's Congress examined and adopted a proposal of establishing People's Government of Hainan Administrative Region. The Congress decided to establish Hainan Administrative Region which administrates the islands and waters of the Xisha Islands, the Nansha Islands and the Zhongsha Islands. On 12 April 1988, the First Session of Seventh National People's Congress adopted a proposal of establishing Hainan Province. The jurisdiction of Hainan Province includes the islands and waters of the Xisha Islands, the Nansha Islands and the Zhongsha Islands. The central government has enhanced its jurisdiction over islands in the South China Sea by establishing Hainan Province.

In addition, we have to notice that local government of Chinese Taiwan also adopted effective measures to protect China's sovereign integrity of Nansha Islands.

The main measures adopted by the Taiwan authority are: escrowing islands of the South China Sea to the government of Kaohsiung city; establishing district town halls; dispatching local officers to the Taiping Islands to build sovereign steles; making plans of defending, developing and constructing the Nansha Islands; organizing scientific missions to collect resources and data of the Nansha Islands; assigning Chinese Petroleum Corporation to explore resources in the Nansha Islands. Until the beginning of 1990 s', Taiwan authority set specialized institution titled "Mission of the South China Sea", whose main task was to draw up plans to maintain, construct and develop the South China Sea.

Administrative jurisdiction is the most important aspect of territorial administrative jurisdiction, as well as an vital part of sovereignty. The main function of administrative jurisdiction is to build administrative institutes in the territory of a state, to exercise administrative power and other administrative activities. Administrative jurisdiction has various forms such as establishment of administrative institutes, division of administrative areas, organization of producing activities, exercise of administrative jurisdiction over people and objectives within the territory etc. Implementations of administrative measures including entrusting, depriving, ordering, licensing, absolution, accepting cases, accreditation, rejection, approval, testifying, confirming, informing etc. are ways for a state to exercise administrative jurisdiction.

China has been constantly exercising administrative jurisdiction over the Nansha Islands in a long term. Such jurisdiction is acknowledged by nearby countries explicitly or tacitly, which sufficiently demonstrates that China has an indisputable sovereignty over the Nansha Islands.

4.2.6 Exploration, Management and Navigational Trade

There are abundant Chinese historical documents which record that the Chinese people have explored, managed and carried out navigational trade in the Nansha Islands. The relevant examples are as follows.

It is recorded in *Yi Zhou Shu·Wang Hui Jie* that Emperor Tang in the Shang Dynasty ordered his minister to make a "Order for Neighbourhoods". And the minister recommended that the southern states use pearls and hawksbills as tributes. This record indicates that the South China Sea citizens explored the sea and fished there as early as in the 18th century B.C. The *Geographical Records of Book of Han* also recorded that the fishermen in the South China Sea "lived by fishing and cutting woods."

Miscellaneous of Foreign Countries, written by Kang Tai who lived in the Wu State in the Three Kingdom Age, recorded that: "It is 700–800 miles to reach Shanhuzhou in the South Sea. There are huge stones at the bottom of Shanhuzhou, and people usually use iron nets to explore the stones.[101] *Records of Wu* stated that: "There are corals in the sea of Jiaozhou. People use iron nets to explore the corals.[102] It is noteworthy that the fact that "people use iron nets to explore" indicates that Chinese fishermen conducted productive activities in the Nansha Islands.

Meng Liang Lu, written by Wu Zimu in the Southern Song Dynasty, recorded that "People can start out from Quanzhou by sea if they would like to trade with foreign states. Then they struggle through Qizhou Ocean. Measured from the boat, the water depth is about more than 70 *zhang*. In Kunlun, Shelong, Wuzhu and other seas, some mythical creatures make rain by magic there. The body of Dragon is visible if it is cloudy. The eyes of the Dragon are shining, like a flash. The claws and horns are crooked. Only the tale of the Dragon is invisible. Suddenly, it will be horrible raining and winding heavily. Water is not deep in the ocean off the reefs and rocks. Boats are ruined if they hit the reefs. In this regard, compass is indispensable for shipping in this sea area. Anyone is likely to be lost in the sea and eaten by fish if he is not careful enough. Therefore, people who take boats usually say that they are afraid of passing Qizhou Sea when shipping out, and afraid of passing Kunlun Sea when shipping back. The depth of sea water in this area is also about more than 50 *zhang*…. Merchants who trade only in such areas as Taiwan, Wenzhou, Quanzhou and Fuzhou will not go through big seas like Qizhou Ocean and Kunlun Sea. If they ship out,

[101] (Tang Dynasty) Xu Jian. *Book for Beginners*, Volume VI, P6, Yunshizhai Series, Huang Family Collection Edition, refer to Han (eds.) (1998, p. 26).

[102] (Song Dynasty) Le Shi. *Geography History,* Volume 170, 14 States in Lingnadao: Jiaozhou, Local Product (Xylographic Edition), refer to Han (eds.) (1998, p. 26).

they start from the Quanzhou Harbor, go through Yueyu Gate, and then head to other states.[103]

There are also many historical materials that documented Chinese fishing and navigation activities in the Nansha Islands in the Yuan and Ming Dynasties, including the following documents.

Hai Guo Guang Ji, written by Shen Maoshang in the Ming Dynasty, recorded Wuhui's navigation as follows. "In the sixth year of Zhengtong Period (A.D 1441), a senior supervising secretary whose last name is Shu, together with a director whose name is Wuhui, sailed from Dongguan County on December 23rd, and went through Wuzhu Sea on December 24th. They reached Qizhou Sea on December 25th, and they could see Tonggu Mountain from there. They reached Duzhu Mountain on December 26th, when they could see Dazhou Mountain. They reached the boundary of Jiaozhi State on December 27th. At that time, they saw a huge island in the sea. The reefs in that island were very sharp. If there was heavy wind, the boat was very likely to hit those reefs and get ruined. In this regard, every crew was very worried and anxious, so they passed this area as quickly as possible by the heavy wind. They reached the Wailuo Sea in Zhancheng on December 28th." "In the sixth year of Zhengtong Period, the Kingdom of Zhancheng died. His son Mokeguiyou requested the Ming Emperor to allow him to inherit his father's title of nobility. The Ying Emperor of Ming issued an imperial edict, in which he sent a senior supervising secretary whose last name is Shu, together with a director whose name is Wuhui, to Zhancheng for investiture. They arrived in Zhancheng in the first month of the lunar year in the seventh year of Zhengtong Period (A.D 1442). One day on their way to Zhancheng, they enjoyed the green mountain views when sailing in the sea, but suddenly came across heavy wind and big sea waves. Their boat was blurring to the bottom of Langya Mountain. The rocks in the Mountain were as sharp as knives and swords. Many people died there. The Shu senior supervising secretary thought he was definitely going to lose his life here, but Wuhui was very calm. Afterwards, the heavy wind went away and all of them arrived in the sea safely. Wuhui wrote a poem to describe this experience: The huge sea waves can overturn the Mountain and even sky. The waves to the sky are constantly hitting the high mast. How dangerous this sea area is!"[104]

Shou Xi Chang Yu, written by Wang Ao in the Ming Dynasty, recorded navigation as follows: "Wuhui was born in Dongting in Hunan Province. In the seventh year of the Zhengtong Period (A.D 1441), he was appointed by the Emperor as an envoy abroad to confer titles of nobility in the city of Zhancheng. He started from Dongguan County in December, and went through Wuzhu Sea the next day. They reached Qizhou Sea the next day, and they could see Tonggu Mountainfrom there. Then they reached Duzhu Mountain the next day, when they could see Dazhou Mountain. After another day, they reached the boundary of Jiaozhi State. The reefs in that island were

[103](The Southern Song Dynasty) Wu Zimu. *Meng Liang Lu*, Volume 12, River and Vessel, Xuehai Leibian, pp. 15–160.

[104](Ming Dynasty) Shen Maoshang. *Haiguo Guangji*. Governed by Champa(Xuanlantang Series Sequel, Volume 14).

very sharp. If there was heavy wind, the boat was very likely to hit those reefs and get ruined. In this regard, all crews were very scared, so they passed this area as quickly as possible by the heavy wind. They reached the Wailuo Sea in Zhancheng on the next day. On May 6th, Wuhui and his group went back home. They came across a heavy wind when the ship was sailing in Qizhou Ocean. The ship was almost overturned then… On May 15th, mountains in the area of Guanghaiwei can be seen from far away. Therefore, the group started from the south and head to Guangdong Province."[105]

The navigation of the Chinese people in the South China Sea can be found from the above quoted documents of navigation records in the Ming Dynasty.

The geological book, *Dong Xi Yang Kao* written by Zhang Xie, has twelve volumes. In this book, the main navigational routes have been divided into "route to east (Dongyang Zhenlu)" and "rout to west (Xiyang Zhenlu)". The locations of objectives are determined by taking mountains, islands, shoals and other navigational target as reference subjects.

It can be concluded that China has been exercising sovereignty over the Nansha Islands since the Ming Dynasty and the South China Sea was dangerous waters that sailors would avoid according to the above historical documents.[106]

During the Daoguang period (A.D 1821–1850) in the Qing Dynasty, fishermen from Wenchang came to the Nansha Islands to fish in the waters. "The nine coral islands are situated in the Southeast of Xisha Islands. Because of poverty, the fishermen from Wenchang come to other places to fish during the Daoguang period. In the later time, many fishermen from various counties migrated to other places, built houses and 'fraternal temples'."[107]

Some foreign books even recorded activities of Chinese fishermen's exploration and management of the Nansha Islands. In 1868, the *Guide of the South China Sea*, published in the United Kingdom, recorded a fishing village in the Nansha Islands "Sin Cowe", which was located 30 nautical miles south to Namyit.[108] It was recorded in the *Guideline of China Sea* (1923 version) that "Amboyna Cay (7°51′N, 112°55′E)… According to the Wonderer's report in 1889, relics of some simple houses have been found in the islands. In Tizard Banks (Zheng He Reefs), the fishermen from Hainan lived on catching trepang and shells. In majorities of the islands, the fishermen left their living trails. Some fishermen have stayed in the islands for a very long time. Each year, there were boats sailing from Hainan to the islands with grains and other necessities, so as to trade for trepangs and shells with the fishermen. In December or January every year, the boats sail from Hainan and will not return until the first southwest monsoon in this year. In Itu Aba Island (Taiping

---

[105](Ming Dynasty) Wang Ao, *Shouxichangyu Compilation*, see (Ming Dynasty) Gao Mingfeng, *Jinxian Collected Works VI—Shouxichangyu Compilation*, Shanghaihanfenlou, p. 26, Jingming Block-printed edition; Cited from Han, *Historical Data Compilation of the the Islands in Southern China Sea*. p. 55.

[106]Urano Tatseo said so.

[107]Xu (1937, p. 270).

[108]*Guidance for China Seas: 1868, Main Routes to China.*

Island), spring water was better than the water in other islands. … In North Danger Reefs (Shuangzi Reefs), the fishermen from Hainan usually inhabited, caught sea cucumbers and shells."[109] A British ship "Lifeman", recorded after conducting some surveys on the Nansha Islands that "living traces of the fishermen from Hainan can be found in each island. People lived on catching sea cucumbers and shells. Therefore, these fishermen stayed in the islands throughout the year. Thus, the residents from Hainan sail boats to provide grains and foods in order to exchange for sea cucumbers and shells at the beginning of every year."[110] The *Times*, a British newspaper, published an editorial by stating that "At all events, such sovereignty claim proposed by China is 1000 years earlier than the maps published in western countries."[111]

Even the French with improper thoughts on the territorial sovereignty of the Nansha Islands have to admit the fact that Chinese fishermen had conducted producing and exploring activities in the Nansha Islands. In 1933, when French warships went to the Thitu Islands, they saw 5 Chinese people living on this island. "There was a fresh water well, which could support 5 people's daily drinking. They excavated phoshorite besides fishing, planting coconuts, banana and pumpkin."[112] In the Twin Islands, the French met 7 Chinese people who came from Hainan, including 2 children. In the Nanwei Island, they met another 4 Chinese people. These Chinese people mainly lived on fishing, catching sea cucumbers, hunting turtles and planting coconuts, bananas, pumpkins and other vegetables. On Taiping Island, the biggest one of the Nansha Islands, the French found cottages where the Chinese lived in and other living traces. "There is a cottage built with twigs and leaves, a well-maintained area planted with sweat potatoes, a small shrine in which a tea pot was placed in the middle, and some sacrifice urns. Those are penates of the Chinese. In the middle of this cottage, there was a small wood board, in which some Chinese characters were engraved. The characters generally mean that 'I'm the ship-owner Demao. I was coming to deliver food to you in mid-March, but did not see anybody. Now, I drop the rice here and am leaving.'"[113]

Sankei Shimbun, a Japanese newspaper, also pointed out that "from historical perspective, China's sovereignty claims over the Nansha and the Xisha Islands can date back to years before the Han Dynasty. In the 15th century, Chinese traveler had been there."[114] In 1917, Matsuji Hirata, a Japanese "explorer" to the Nansha Islands, reported that "around 500 Chinese families were settled in these islands. They lived on fishing."[115] On 14 July 1933, The National Press reported in Manila that "Only a few fishermen live on the islands (the Nansha Islands). The fishing ships from

[109]Bureau of Surveying and Mapping of English Navy (eds.) (1923). Refer to *Review of the Ministry of Foreign Affairs*: 1933(9), Volume 2, Period 9, pp. 16–19.

[110]Lin (1934).

[111][U.K] *Time*, June, 16, 1976.

[112]Lin (1934).

[113](France) *Illustration*: No. 4715, P382, July 15, 1933. Cited from Zhang (1982, p. 19).

[114]Sankei Shimbun (1974).

[115]"Nine Islands in the South Hainan". Printed in *Shen Bao Monthly*: Volume 2, Period 9, September 1933.

Hainan also stay in the islands." On August 18, Mainichi Shinbum News Agency, in Osaka, Japan, sent a sailing vessel with 2 sailors to the Nansha Islands conducting investigations, and recorded that "on August 25, we reached our destination, Parala Island....2 Chinese people from Hainan waved their hands to welcome us. We left for Southwest Cay .... There were houses in the southern part of the islands, where 3 Chinese people lived."[116]

The archaeological findings in the archaeology of the Nansha Islands have characteristics of China's central plain culture, which could reflect the situation of Chinese people's living and producing activities.

4.2.7 Geng Lu Bu

Since Chinese fishermen have been living in the waters of the Nansha Islands for a very long time, they accumulated extensive producing experiences. Furthermore, they explicitly documented names and locations of these islands, navigating routes and fisheries in the Nansha Islands. All of the experiences are recoded in *Geng Lu Bu.*[117]

Geng Lu Bu is a book of navigational guidance for Chinese fishermen from Hainan to catch fish, shrimps and turtles, and to conduct other productive activities. It has recorded the voyages of fishermen who sailed from Qinglan Harbor in Wenchang County or from Tanmen Harbor in Qionghai County to the Nansha Islands and the Xisha Islands. There are 200 records of voyages to the Nansha Islands and 72 geographic names in this book. It records and narrates the voyages from the Xisha Islands to the Nansha Islands and round trips among the islands of the Nansha Islands. Routes to the Nansha Islands usually start from the second round of Xisha (Yuzhu Reef), third round of Xisha (Langhua Reef), Baizhi Zi (Passu Keah), and Banlu Zhi, and sail to Shuang Zhi (North Danger Reefs) or Luokong (Lawak Island) and other islands. The sailing routes among the Nansha Islands can be divided into the middle, the east and the west. The middle route is from Shuang Zhi to south, by the way of Tie Zhi (Thitu Island), Disan Zhi (Loaita Island), Huangshan Mazhi (Itu Aba Island), Nanyi Zhi (Namyit Island), Pinggou Zhi (Sin Cowe Island), and then by the way of Wumie Xian, Mujing, Shen Quan (Investigator Shoal), Boji, Tongzhong, Guangxing Zi, ZhiShi Gongli (Swallow Reef), Wubaier (Royal Charlotte Reef), Danjie Xian (Louisa Reef), and Moguang Xian. Ships to the Nansha Islands usually start from the Xisha Second Round (Yuzhu Reef), Third Round (Langhua Reef), Baizhi Zi (Passu Keah), and Banlu Zhi. Ships sail to Shuang Zhi (North Danger Reefs) or Luo Kong (Lawak Island) and other islands. There are three routes to sail to the Nansha Islands: the middle one, the east one and the west one. The middle route starts from Shuang Zhi to south, and goes through Tie Zhi (Thitu Island), the Third Zhi (Loaita Island), Huang Shan Ma Zhi (Itu Aba Island), Nan Yi Zhi (Namyit Island), and

[116]RuoLin et al. (1939).

[117]Refer the types, names and detailed contents of *Geng Lu Bu* to Han (eds.) (1988, pp. 366–369).

Ping Gou Zhi (Sin Cowe Island). Then ships go by Wumie Line, Mu Jing, Shen Quan (Investigator Shoal), Bo Ji, Tong Zhong, and Guang Xing Zi to Shi Gong Li (Swallow Reef), Wu Bai Er (Royal Charlotte Reef), Dan Jie Line (Louisa Reef), Mo Gua Line and others. The east route and the west route can be divided into top lane and bottom lane. The top lane of the east route starts from Shuang Zhi, and goes through Hong Cao Xian Pai, Hong Cao Zhi, Luo Kong, Wu Feng, Ban Lu Xian Yu Lin (Xianbin Shoal), and to Dong Tou Yi Xin. The bottom lane of the east route starts from Shuang Zhi, by the way of Tie Zhi, Ku Dang, Sanjiao, Shuang Men, Duan Jie (Second Thomas Reef), Niu Che Ying, Jiao Po, and to Shilong (Royal Captain Reef) and Hai Gong (Half Moon Shoal). In sunny days, filmy image of Palawan can be seen from Dong Tou Yi Xin and Shi Long. The top lane of the west route starts from Huangshan Mazhi, goes through Lao Niu Lao (Da Xia Island), Shang Wu (Fiery Cross Island), Tong Chong Zi (Cuateron Reef), Da Tong Chong, Long Bi and Niao Zi Zhi (Spratly Island) to Xi Tou Yi Xin (Ladd Reef). The bottom lane of the west route starts from Cheng Gou Zhi, goes through Liu Men and Shi Pan (Pearson Reef) to Tong Chong Zhi, and then joins with the top lane of then west route. Besides, there are some routes that are not frequently taken.[118] In the waters of the Nansha Islands, navigational routes are crisscross, as intensive as nets. The routes reflect that there are frequent producing activities of Chinese fishermen in the waters. Without long-term practice, there cannot be such detailed documents.

During the late Qing Dynasty, fishery products from the Nansha Islands were sold to Singapore. Hence the fishermen working in the waters have explored the navigational routes to Singapore. There are three routes that start from the Nansha Islands to foreign states: from Xi Tou Yi Xin, through Luo Han Bay of Vietnam, to the south; from Dan Jie Line and Mo Gua Line, past the edge of Natuna Island of Indonesia, to the south, from Niao Zi Zhi and Xi Tou Yi Xin, through Chao Man Island, Dong Xi Zhu and Bai Shi He Deng of east coast of southern Malaya Peninsula to the harbor of Singapore.[119]

Both Geng Lu Bu and such location names are still in use today. Genglu Bu is firstly written in the Ming Dynasty. Since then, the records are more complete by the fishermen. There are several versions of handwritten copies, which clearly record producing, trade and navigational activities by Chinese fishermen in the Nansha Islands.

Besides Genglu Bu, the Sketch of the Geological Location of Xisha Islands (this map is currently collected in Guangdong Provincial Museum) can also serve as evidence. This map is drawn by Fu Hongguang, a fisherman who had been carrying producing activities in the Nansha Islands for a long term. This maritime sketch is of 107 cm length and 79 cm width, in which names and geological locations of 63 islands of the Nansha Islands have been illustrated.

Considering the fact that the concept of territorial sovereignty was not developed in ancient time, it is especially important to refer to the Chinese people's exploration and management in the region to understand China's sovereignty over the Nansha

[118]He (1981, pp. 52–53).

[119]He (1981, p. 53).

Islands. As an international law scholar, Ian Brownlie, wrote in his book *International Law* that "Differences of interests between states and individuals in traditional agricultural economy cannot be certain as what could be expected in modern industrial economy. Grazing and other economic activities carried by private land owners can be regarded as the evidence of acquisition of territorial sovereignty."[120] In the Minquiers and Ecrehos case, Judge Levi Carneiro of International Court of Justice held that "the presence of a private person as the citizen of a certain state may signify or entail occupation by that State. Therefore, such an individual's activities are particularly important as to areas situated at the border of two countries and are claimed sovereignty by the two states."[121] In the Rann of Kutch Arbitration case which involves an area of up to 7,000 square miles between India and Pakistan, president of the arbitral tribunal pointed out in the judgement that "the territorial boundary under different territories is the strict boundary of economic rights, as it is the boundary of governmental power."[122] Since the Rann of Kutch was drowned more than half a year, the undrowned areas can only be used for grazing. The Pakistani residents in Sindh province grazed, fished and reclaimed in the area that is close to Pakistan. Therefore, the President held in the judgement that "Residents of Sindh who have been publicly using the pasture for over 100 years. The authority of Sindh apparently takes Dhara Banni and Chhad Bet as the territory of Sindh."[123]

From the management and exploration of the Chinese people in the Nansha Islands, and a combination with international law rules and relevant international law cases, China has in incontestable sovereignty over the Nansha Islands. Considering that the Nansha Islands are far from the continent, the producing activities of Chinese fisherman has constituted an actual occupation of the Nansha Islands for China, a country with a long history in agriculture and fishing. The activities indirectly proved that China exercised the administrative jurisdiction and had the sovereignty over the Nansha Islands from this perspective.

4.2.8 Patrolling Activities of Chinese Navy in Each Dynasty (Since the Three Kingdoms Age)

Army is the military force of a state, and also is the representative and sign of a state power to defense and protect sovereignty integrity. Therefore, military activities not only represent state actions, but also have significance in terms of international law.

From the Wu State of the Three Kingdom Age to the South Dynasty, the South China Sea had been the trade center of the Chinese government all along. Moreover, the south of the Five Ridges was a strategically important area. Therefore, armed forces including the navy were used to secure peace in the sea. *Wu Di Lei*, written by

[120] *Ian Brownlie, International Law*, 1973, p. 146.
[121] D.P.O' Connell, *International Law,* V. 1, p. 482.
[122] *International Legal Materials*, 1968, P. 674.
[123] *International Legal Materials*, 1968, P. 689.

Xie Lingyun, recorded as follows: "The cavalrymen are running in wet lands, while the navy is taking battles in the South Sea." In this regard, the South Sea Islands have already been under Chinese navy's jurisdiction since the South Dynasty and Jin Dynasty.

Wu Jing Zong Yao, edited by Zeng Gongliang, Ding Du and among others in the Northern Song Dynasty, recorded the patrolling facts towards the navy in ancient times of the Northern Song government in the South Sea. The records are as follows: "Guangnandonglu, where some aboriginal people were living, is the City of South Sea in Guangzhou Province, in the Northen Guangdong in ancient times. This area was under the central government's jurisdiction ever since from the Han Dynasty, when counties were established, and under the navy's jurisdiction in the Tang Dynasty. After the regime of Liu Chang in the Southern Han was put down in Song Dynasty,Guangdongnanlu was re-established as a city which administrated armies and peace of 16 counties. Besides, profits of maritime trading were possible by controlling other maritime states. Because the Han and minority groups co-habited here, the central government sent armed forces to garrison here and organized a navy patrolling the sea areas. The place where the navy were settled was in the east and west side of sea entrance. And the width is 280 *zhang* of length, about 200 miles from Tunmen Mountain. The navy was equipped with boats like warships. The distance of South Sea County of Guangzhou Province is 40 miles from southeast to the sea, 420 miles to Huizhou in the east, 240 miles to Duangzhou in the west, 750 miles to Enzhou in the south, 250 miles to Shaozhou in the north, 400 miles to sea lands in the southeast, and 20 miles to Tunmen Moutain. The water was very shallow all along. It was about 200 miles in total, and people can march forward about 50 miles one day. Starting from Tunmen Mountain, it took seven days to head southwest by east wind to arrive in Jiuruluo Sea. It took another three days to arrive at Bulao Mountain. It took three days to head south to arrive in east Ling Mountain. You can go to Dashi, Fushizi, Tianzhu and some other countries from Ling Mountain by heading southwest, but the distance was hard to calculate. In the period of Tai Ping Xing State, the central government sent three army officers to suppress Jiaozhou. The army took water routes to attack. The military force station of Guangnandonglu was established here, and was administrated by Jiaozhou.[124]

In the Yuan Dynasty (A.D 1277), an army officer Liu Shen took a battle with Zhao Shi, Emperor Rui of Song, in Qianwang. Zhang Shijie lost that battle, and thus hid the Emperor in Xiu Mountain, subsequently to Jingao. At that time, Chen Yizhong ran away to Zhancheng and never came back. In December, the Emperor Rui came

[124](Song Dynasty) Zeng Gongliang, The Outline of the Military Classics, Part I, Volume 20, Guangnan North Road, P15-16. Completed in the fourth year of Song Dynasty Qingli (1044), and photocopied by Shanghai Editing Office, Chung Hwa Book Company in 1959 based on the publication in Ming Dynasty Zhengde. According to related annotation of documents of the Ministry of Foreign Affairs of China, The Outline of the Military Classics is the authoritative document on the military systems and national defense affairs in Song Dynasty, which was compiled through the collaboration of Ding Du, the Chinese assistant administrator, Deputy minister of the Ministry of Industry, equivalent to Deputy prime minister (in feudal China) and Zeng Gongliang, a "Tianzhangge Scholar", equivalent to the Emperor consultant.

to Jingao. The sea wind was blowing heavily and ruined his boat, so he was almost lost in the sea. The Emperor of Rui was so scared that he was ill. After more than 10 days, soldiers who survived began to gather. More than half of the soldiers died in the accident. Liu Shen quickly caught up with the Emperor and took another battle in Jingao. The Emperor had to escape to Xienv Strait, and entered the South Sea to the Qizhou Sea from here. He intended to go to Zhancheng, but failed.

It can be seen from above documents that the territory controlled by the army of the Yuan Dynasty extended to Qixing Yang (Seven Zhou Yang). So far, the army of the Yuan Dynasty defeated the fleet of the South Song Dynasty.

Besides, according to records concerning Potamic and Maritime Vessel Volume 12 of Meng Liang Lu, written by Wu Zimu, circuitous routes are necessary for security because Seven Zhou Yang is very dangerous for sailing. Thus, there is a saying that "people are afraid of going through Qizhou, and coming back through Kunlung."

There are records about inspection tours of Wu Sheng who was the deputy commander of navy in the *Annals of Quanzhou*, revised by Huang Ren and Guo Gengwu.

What are worth being quoted from from the writings of Yuan Dynasty are biographical history books as the *History of Yuan, the Biography of Shi Mi*, and the Java part of *New History of Yuan Dynasty* which were revised in early Qing Dynasty. Because Java has refused to pay tributes to Yuan Emperor for three times, Kubla Khan decided in December 1292 to dispatch Shi Mi, the chief commander, to go on a punitive expedition of Java. According to China's Compilation of Historic Documents of the Nansha Islands, Shi Mi's army set out from Quanzhou, went through the Xisha Islands, Qizhou Yang, and Champa Kingdom (a small kingdom of Vietnam) to Java. Records of Biography of Shi Mi can be found in Volume 162, *Collected Biographies* No. 49 in the *History of Yuan*, written by Song Lian, as follows:

> In December of 1292, 5000 people led by Shibi, together with some other soldiers and staffs, started from Quanzhou. The sea wind was so heavy and the wave was so huge that the boats were jolting heavily. Soldiers on the boats could not take diets for more than several days. The army passed Qizhou Sea and Wanli Shitang, and then to the boundary of Liu and Chen [125]

There is no doubt that Wanli Shitang refers to the Nansha Islands. Qiu Hongda, a famous publicist, also held that Qizhou Sea is the seven Islands in east Xisha Islands, and Wanli Shitang is the Nansha Islands.

New History of Yuan recorded the history of Shi Bi's sending forces to Zhuawa as follows: "In February, the Emperor of Yuan honored Shi Bi, Gao Xing, Yi Hei, Mi Shi and some other people as government directors of Fujian. They ruled armies of more than 20,000 people coming from Fujian, Jiangxi, Huguang Provinces and more than one thousand army ships…. The army gathered in Quanzhou and started from there. The sea wind was so heavy and the wave was so huge that the boats were jolting heavily. Soldiers on the boats could not take diets for more than several

[125](Ming) Song Lian. *Yuan Dynasty History*. Vol. 162, Collected biography 49, Shi Bi. See *Twenty-five Dynastic Histories*, New Yuan Dynasty History, Collected biography, p. 382. Cited from Han Zhenhua (eds.) *Historical Data Compilation of the the Islands in Southern China Sea* [M]. p. 45.

days. The army went through Qizhou Sea, Wanlishitang, and then to the boundary of Jiaozhi and Zhancheng. In the first month of the next lunar year, the army arrived in Dongdong Mountain, Xidong Mountain, Niuqi Island, and then got into Hundun Sea, Ganlan Island,[126] Jialimada,[127] Goulan Mountain and some other mountains. The army garrisoned there, cut woods and made boats to enter into Java."[128] Obviously, the Nansha Islands are still where the Chinese armies were taking activities in Yuan Dynasty.

In the Ming Dynasty, the inspection tours in Wu Sheng, the deputy commander of navy, was also recorded in the *Annals of Quanzhou*, edited by Huang Ren and Guo Gengwu.

In the Qing Dynasty, the Chinese government still took the Nansha Islands as ranges where the navy cruised around. For example, *Annals of Qiongzhou* written by Ming Yi, *Annals of Yazhou* written by Zhong Yuandi, *Annals of Gan En County* by Zhou Wenhai, *Recoreds and Maps of Guangdong* by Mao Hongbin, and *Yang Fang Shuo Lue* by Xu Jiagan all included "Qiong Yang" of "Qianli Shitang, Wanli Changsha" in the coastal defense system of Wanzhou.

In the Republic of China, Chinese navy patrolled in the Nansha Islands for many times. In 1937, the Cantonese government sent warships to patrol in the South China Sea. In 1946, government of the Republic of China took over the islands in the South China Sea. The government sent warships including "Taiping" and "Zhongye" to carry out the mission. Some steles had been built with names such as "Taiping Island", "Taiping Island in the Nansha Islands", "Nanwei Island" and "Xiyue Island." Chinese armies garrisoned in the Nansha Islands after the completion of the take-over. The Chinese government also sent warships to convoy the fishermen in the Nansha Islands.

After the establishment of the People's Republic of China, the Taiwan authority still adopted military measures to maintain China's sovereignty over the Nansha Islands, such as garrison in the Nansha Islands and regularly patrolling in the Nansha Islands. On 2 June 1956, the Taiwan authority dispatched Yao Ruyu to lead two warships to garrison Taiping Island, and established garrison district of the Nansha Islands. On June 11, the army landed in West York Island, built sovereign steles and raised national flag. On June 29, they patrolled in the Nansha Islands. On September 24, they patrolled in the waters of the Nansha Islands again. Ever since that, navy of the Taiwan authority patrolled in the Nansha Islands every three or four months. Furthermore, the Taiwan authority sent officials to inspect the Nansha Islands and comforted the defenders. In 1966, the Taiwan authority sent warships to the Southwest Cay, the Northwest Cay, the Thitu Islands and the Loaita Islands and built

[126]Today's Tambelan Islands in Indonesia.

[127]Today's Karimata Islands in Indonesia.

[128](the Republic of China) Ke Shaowen Vol 253, Collected biography 150, Foreign Country V, Java. see *Twenty-five Dynastic Histories*, New Yuan Dynasty History, Collected biography, Kaiming Press, p. 479, Kaiming edition. Cited from Han Zhenhua (eds.) *Historical Data Compilation of the the Islands in Southern China Sea*, p. 45.

sovereign steles in these islands. On 20 April 1994, it was the first time for the Taiwan authority to have dispatched policemen patrolling in the Nansha Islands.

After the establishment of People's Republic of China, the Chinese navy irregularly cruised in the Nansha Islands to protect maritime warships that were conducting Chinese scientific investigations in the Nansha Islands. On 8 January 1988, the Chinese navy entered and garrisoned in the Fiery Cross Reef. In February, the navy successively garrisoned in the Cuarteron Reef, the Gaven Reef, the Hugh Reef, the Johnson South Reef, and the Subi Reef.

4.2.9 Anti-Piracy Operation and Exercising of Jurisdiction

In the Ming Dynasty, because of rampant piracy, the government sent out navy. Hence there have been records about navy's cruise. There have been records of cruising and striking piracy during the period from 1397 to 1518 in *Kangxi Qiongzhou Documents*.

"On the way of delivering the tributes from Tibetan Regime in ancient China to the central government, some officers were employed to guard them when passing Qiongzhou. The Siam sent its local delicacies as tributes in 1397, 1445 and 1459. Zhancheng sent its local delicacies as tributes in 1429 and 1437. They paid elephants as tributes in 1447, local delicacies in 1449, white and black elephants in 1463, elephants and tigers in 1471, tigers in 1480, elephants in 1504, and other tributes in 1518. Mancijia State paid five-colour parrots as tributes in 1505. On every way to pay the tributes, the Ming government sent officers to guard the ministers and tributes to Beijing."[129] The above records indicate that the Ming government once sent nany to neighbor states in the South Sea so as to guard their people who came to Beijing to pay the tributes, in case of being attacked by pirates. The navy in the Ming Dynasty already took activities in the whole South Sea areas.

In the *Haiyu* Chapter of *Annals of Guangdong* written by Wang Zuo, there were records of "Niaochu, Duchu and Qizhou" and some other names of places. It can be inferred that these places were under patrolling, and China was conducting sea patrolling and anti-pirate activities in the South China Sea.

Professor Fu Kuncheng had a spendid analysis about "the punishment of pirates in the South Sea." He cited the documents in *Qing Shi Lu*, which recorded in details that the Chinese government strengthened its sea guard forces and punished the pirates in the South China Sea in the Gao Emperor period in the Qing Dynasty and the De Emperor period in the Qing Dynasty from the middle of the 16th century to the end of the 19th century. The citations are as follows: "Strengthen the sea guard forces. Treat them with leniency to the boats of Annan and waive them from being deprived of weapons. Request the Siam King in necessity to help the central government defeat Burmese bandits. Request the Siam King to look for Burmese bandits. Study the cost

---

[129](Qing Dynasty) Niu Tiansu and Zhu Zixu. *Kangxi Qiongzhou Documents*(revised), Vol 8, Coast foreign countries, Block-printed edition in Kangxi Period, pp. 25–26.

and effect of attacking Burmese bandits by water armed forces. Prevent the turbulence of Annan but do not interfer in its affairs. Request Annan to help the central government to catch pirates. Award the Annan King of his help with catching pirates. Doubt about the Annan King's hiding facts for pirates. Encourage the Annan King to catch pirates seriously. Award the Annan officers for their contributions to catching pirates. Deal with the Annan pirates who surrendered. Some famous surrendered pirates verified that the Annan King had harbored pirates. Hand over to the government departments to deal with the failure of catching pirates. China caught 14 pirate ships. Award the Vietnam King for his help with catching pirates in the sea. The Chinese Lu Kun caught pirates. Order the Vietnam King to send the caught Chinese pirates by lands. The Vietnam King sent officers to bring pirates to Guangdong to be judged. The Vietnam King understood the important principles thoroughly, so the central government decided to honor the King when his ministers came to Beijing to send their tributes next year. Advocate catching pirates by Chinese water army forces rather than the Vietnam forces. Being robbed on the way of guarding the Vietnam army forces and ships back to Vietnam. Award the Vietnam King for his saving of the Chinese who caught pirates and their ships in heavy wind. Honor the Vietnam King again for his saving of the Chinese who caught pirates and their ships in heavy wind. The Chinese water army forces patrolled in the Vietnam sea areas to maintain peace and safety. Strengthen the sea armed forces and never loose the attention."[130] Professor Fu Kuncheng listed altogether 27 kinds of activities of catching pirates in this period in the Qing Dynasty. All of these actions clearly prove that the Qing government exercised jurisdiction and judicially cooperated with Vietnamese government. It has been mentioned above that a state's exercise of jurisdiction can be taken as an "effective occupation". Therefore, it is sufficient to conclude that China has an "effective occupation" over the South China Sea, including Nansha Islands, merely by the Qing government's exercise of jurisdiction. The main reason is that jurisdiction is an important part of a state's territorial and personal jurisdiction, and is the embodiment of state's territorial sovereignty. And territorial sovereignty is an important part of state sovereignty. If Vietnam, the Philippines, Malaysia or other states ignore the historical facts and legal basics, the principle of state sovereignty that support the systems of international relationship and international law would definitely be ruined.

4.2.10 Protest and Prevention of Illegal Activities by Foreign States on the Nansha Islands

Protest and prevention of illegal activities by foreign states is a way to exercise territorial sovereignty.

In 1883, when German survey vessels went to the Xisha and the Nansha Islands and conducted measuring and surveying activities, the Chinese government strongly

[130] Fu (1995, pp. 62–85).

protested against it to the German government. Then Germany had no choice but to stop such activities.[131]

In 1930, French soldiers landed on the Nanwei Island, and raised the French flag. Nevertheless, the flag was torn by Chinese fisherman, Fu Hongguang, who raised the Chinese national flag bought from Hainan. In 1933, flagpoles used to hang French flags in the Southwest Cay and the Northwest Cay were cut by Chinese fiershman, Ke Jiayu, who used these timbers to make a bed board. On the Zhongye Islands, a Chinese fisherman Wang Anrong, dug and destroyed the "memo" sealed in a glass bottle, which was buried by the French. A Fisherman Zheng Landian tore up the French flag.[132] The French flagpole hung in the Taiping Island was cut down by the Chinese fishermen and they used it as masts. The series of actions taken by the Chinese fishermen expressed protests of the Chinese fishermen to the French invaders. The Chinese people and the Chinese government strongly protested against the invasion of France. Social groups, including Qiongya Association in Beijing, fishery organizations, General Union of Nanjing, General Union of Shanghai, Peasant Union of Ninghai County, Shaoxing Chamber of Commerce, and Shanghai Union of Filature, all successively rallied and protested. They asked the government to take effective measures to ensure the integrity of China's sovereignty over the Nansha Islands.

In July, 1933, spokesman of the Ministry of Foreign Affairs of the Republic of China made a statement that only Chinese people lived in the Nansha Islands. The international community also acknowledged the Nansha Islands are China's territory and they are illegally occupied by the French. The Ministry of Foreign Affairs and the Admiralty of the Chinese government planed counter measurements and made strong protests to the French government. In August, the Guangdong government lodged a protest to France, and attempted to maintain China's sovereignty over the Nansha Islands. At that time, a resolution had been reached in the Southwest Politic Session: report the information and evidence of locations, as well as longitude and latitude of the nine islands occupied by France in Guangdong to the Kuomintang government. Request the government strongly to protest against France in order to maintain the integration of China's territory. The Guangdong government discussed with Gan Jiehou about collecting documents and arranging for fishermen who live in the nine islands. Then protests were lodged to France Consulate in Guangdong.

The Chinese government and Chinese people have protested against France and adopted specific administrative and judicial means to protect China's sovereignty over the Nansha Islands. The protest is a form of sovereign declaration which has significance in international law. The protest not only excludes the possibilities of acquiesce, recognition and other legal activities (however, such activities express the attitudes adopted by the Philippine government when France occupied the nine islands) that China admits that France enjoys the sovereignty of the nine islands, but also demonstrated the determination that the Chinese government and Chinese people protect China's sovereignty of the Nansha Islands. Meanwhile, it is highlighted that

---

[131]Chen (1982).

[132]He (1981, p. 61).

no matter when and what government it is, the Chinese government and Chinese people have continuous and effective occupations over the Nansha Islands.

4.3 China Determined Its Territorial Sovereignty Over the Nansha Islands in the Form of "Dotted Boundary Lines"

4.3.1 The Generation and Evolution of "Dotted Boundary Lines" of the South China Sea

After taking over the islands in the South China Sea from Japanese invaders, the Chinese government hoped to determine the sovereign range of inlands in the South China Sea through publishing dotted boundary lines in order to strengthen its sovereignty over the Nansha Islands, and to avoid recurrence of the painful histories e.g., France's seizing of the nine islands in the southern Hainan in 1933 and the Japanese invasion that encroached Chinese territory during 1930s to 1940s. Publishing dotted boundary lines is also the continuation of sovereign maintenance of islands in the South China Sea before the Anti-Japanese War, and was effected by the Declaration of Continental Shelf made by President Truman and announcement of 200 nautical miles maritime administrative power by Latin-American Countries. Hence, publishing dotted boundary lines played an important role because it was the first time for the Chinese people and the Chinese government to completely defeat foreign invaders, arouse national dignity and the resolution to protect territorial sovereignty.

After more than ten years' plan, consultation and preparation, the dotted boundary line of the South China Sea was finally decided. Early in the 1930 s, the Chinese government published the *Rules on Review of Amphibious Map*. The reason for publishing these rules was that there had not been any maps with detailed reconnaissance in China. Besides, there were many errors in published maps, which resulted in "significant consequences that foreigners could pass the Chinese boundaries at will." Therefore, the General Staff and the Admiralty of the Republic of China discussed and passed the *Rules on Review of Amphibious Maps*. In June 1931, the Interior Department convened the General Staff, the Ministry of Foreign Affairs, the Admiralty, the Ministry of Education and the Mongolian and Tibetan Affairs Commission to hold a conference, and decided to publish the amended and expanded *Rules of Review on Amphibious Maps*. In May 1933, the Reviewing Committee of Amphibious Maps was officially established and came into force on June 7. The Committee was comprised of the representatives of the Interior Ministry, the Ministry of Foreign Affairs, the Ministry of Education, the Admiralty, the General Staff and the Mongolian and Tibetan Affairs Commission.

On 21 December 1934, the 25th session of the Committee approved resolutions on English and Chinese names of islands in the South China Sea. Afterwards, the

Committee broadly collected geographic and literal materials concerning the islands in the South China Sea, including the Nansha Islands. In March 1935, resolution of the 29th session of the Committee pointed out that "the administrative zones of the Dongsha islands, the Xisha Islands, the Nansha Islands and the Tuansha Islands, etc. must be explicitly drawn in the maps. The rest only needs to be included in the maps. If the islands exceed the map margin, they do not need to be drawn."[133] In January 1935, the first proceeding, which listed 96 names of islets of the Nansha Islands, was published by the Reviewing Committee of Amphibious Maps. The southernmost point was the Zengmu Reef; the westernmost point was Vanguard Bank; the easternmost point was Seahorse Shoal. This delimitation method was in conformity with the method taken in 1947, after the Anti-Japanese War.

The Chinese people and the Chinese government were busy with fighting back invasions by the Japanese imperialism, thus the map plotting work was laid aside. At the end of the Anti-Japanese War, China resumed the excise of sovereignty over the Nansha Islands from Japan, and sent navy and government officials to take over the Islands. After that, the Chinese government carried on the incomplete work. On 14 April 1947, the Interior Ministry invited the Ministry of National Defense, the Ministry of Foreign Affairs and the Commander Department of the Navy to hold a meeting on "determination and publication of the range and sovereignty over the Xisha Islands and the Nansha Islands". The conclusions of the meeting are: 1. The southernmost point of China's territory in the South China Sea shall be Zengmu Reef, which is the territorial criterion that was used in publications by governmental institutes, schools and press, and was recorded in the documents of the Interior Ministry, and it shall remain the same. 2. After being named by the Interior Ministry, the sovereign range of the Nansha Islands will be publicized, attached with maps and explanations. The Interior Ministry announces the maps to all nationals after it is recorded by the government of the Republic of China. Before the publication, the Commander Department of the Navy shall garrison in the islands of each archipelago as possible as they can. 3. The fishing season in the Xisha and the Nansha Islands is coming. Thus, the Commander Department of the Navy and the Cantonese government should convoy and offer convenience including transportation and communication to the fishermen who go to these waters.[134] In October, documents concerning boundaries submitted by the Interior Ministry to the Department of Budget, Accounting and Statistics included four poles of Chinese territory, their longitudes as well as latitudes. The easternmost point was the junction of Ussuri River and Amur River, 135°4' E; the Westernmost point was Panj River in Pamir 71° E; the southernmost point was the Zengmu Reef, 4°N; the northernmost point was Sayan Mountain in Tannu Uriankhai, 53°57'.[135] Subsequently, the Department

[133] *Publication of Committee for Reviewing Map of Land and Water*, Vol. 3, September 1935, pp. 79–80.

[134] *A Measurement of the Boundary Stone of Sha Tau Kok in the Xi'sha and the Nansha Islands*, Guandong Province Government Archive.

[135] *Compiled by Department of Statistics, the Ministry of Domestic Affairs in accordance with information provided by the Local Administration Bureau,* refer to Han (eds.) (1988, p. 184).

of Boundary of the Interior Ministry timely printed the *Map of Locations of Islands in the South China Sea.* The map included the Nansha Islands into China's territory by 11 dotted national boundary lines. Ever since then, published maps demarcated dotted national boundary at around 4°N according to the rules made by the government. The map printed by the Department of Boundary included the Nansha Islands and three other archipelagos in the South China Sea, and determined the southernmost point of China's territory to be at 4°N by national boundary lines, 11 lines in all. The 11 dotted national boundary lines were called "U-type lines" by some scholars. In the beginning of 1948, the Department of Boundary included *Map of Locations of Islands in the South China Sea* into *Map of Administrative Region of Republic of China,* and published it. The publication announced China's sovereignty over the Nansha Islands and the territorial range of the South China Sea to the world.

After the establishment of People's Republic of China, the Chinese government continued using the dotted national boundary line in published maps. In 1953, the Chinese government approved removing two dotted national boundary lines within Gulf of Tonkin. The dotted national boundary lines in subsequently published maps became 9 lines until now. The continual use of the dotted national boundary lines indicate that the Chinese government still insist that the southernmost point of China's territory to be at 4°N, including the Zengmu Reef. China's sovereignty includes the Nansha Islands.

Since the 1930s, according to the range of exercised sovereignty by successive central government, the Chinese government re-defined the sovereign range of the Nansha Islands. It is obviously several decades earlier than the 1960s, when Vietnam, the Philippines, Malaysia and other states claimed sovereignty over the Nansha Islands. Moreover, Chinese government determined its sovereign range of the Nansha Islands and published it in forms of government decree and maps. After the Chinese government published the territorial sovereign range of the Nansha Islands, countries surrounding the Nansha Islands had not raised any objection for a long while, which showed that these states explicitly or implicitly acknowledged China's sovereignty over the Nansha Islands. Since re-confirmation of China's territorial sovereign range of the Nansha islands in the 1930s, China's standpoint has been consistent all the time.

4.3.2 Legitimacy of the Government of the Republic of China's Demarcation Through Dotted National Boundary Lines

On 14 April 1947, the Interior Ministry held an ad hoc meeting to discuss the sovereign range of the Xisha Islands and the Nansha Islands as well as its publication. This meeting confirmed the keynote and the range of China's sovereignty over the South China Sea as follows: 1. The southernmost point of China's territory in the South China Sea is the Zengmu Reef; 2. After the Xisha Islands and the Nansha

Islands are named by the Interior Ministry, the publication of sovereignty over the islands is recorded in the national government. Then the Interior Ministry announces it to the whole nation. Before the publication, the Commander Department of Navy shall garrison in each island as much as they can. After this meeting, the Department of Boundary printed *Maps of Locations of Islands in the South China Sea* in order to specify the sovereign range of the Xisha Islands and the Nansha Islands. This map served as a significant blueprint of modern map of the South China Sea. It is important in the following ways: 1. The southernmost point of China's boundary is at around 4°N; 2. The locations and names of the Dongsha, the Xisha, the Zhongsha and the Nansha Islands have been clearly marked in the South China Sea waters. 3. In this map, China's territory in the South China Sea has been determined by 11 dotted lines, which became a solid evidence for China to verify its sovereignty over the South China Sea. The 11 dotted lines are also called the "traditional boundary lines". Additionally, the line resembles a "U-shape", so those lines are also called "U-type lines". So far, China's territorial range of the South China Sea had been specified in Chinese maps. In February 1948, the Interior Ministry of the Republic of China published the *Maps of Administrative Regions of Republic of China*, and announced China's sovereignty and jurisdictional range of islands in the South China Sea and nearby waters to the international community. The attached map to *Maps of Administrative Regions of Republic of China* is the *Map of Locations of Islands in the South China Sea*. Therefore, the government of the Republic of China's demarcation through dotted lines at that time is legitimate.

4.3.2.1 The Government of the Republic of China's Demarcation Is a Preoccupation According to the Independent Time of Vietnam, the Philippines and Malaysia

In term of subject, the government of the Republic of China was China's legal government, and therefore had rights to exercise jurisdiction over China's territory. From subjective aspect, the Chinese government had the will to incorporate islands of the South China Sea into China's administrative regions. From objective aspect, islands in the South China Sea were not part of territories of the Philippines, Vietnam or other countries that were newly independent states. And Malaysia was not an independent state yet. From aspect of actions, the government of the Republic of China intended to specify China's territorial range of the South China Sea. Furthermore, activities, such as announcement of demarcation, publication of the *Map of Locations of Islands in the South China Sea*, plotting 11 dotted national boundary lines around four archipelagos did not violate relative international laws and regulations. Vietnam was independent on 2 September 1945, the Philippines on 4 July 1946, Malaysia on 31 August 1957, and Brunei on 1 January 1984. At the independent timing of involving states, viewing from their domestic laws and policies before and after their independence, the states adopted no actions as China did to claim territorial sovereignty over islands in the South China Sea.

4.3.2.2 Conformity with International Treaties Related to Sovereignty of Islands in the South China Sea After World War II

Japan was defeated in World War II. First of all, *Cairo Declaration* stipulates that "The Three Great Allies are fighting this war to restrain and punish the aggression of Japan. They covet no gain for themselves and have no thought of territorial expansion. It is their purpose that Japan shall be stripped of all the islands in the Pacific which she has seized or occupied since the beginning of the first World War in 1914, and that all the territories Japan has stolen from the Chinese, such as Manchuria, Taiwan, and The Pescadores, shall be restored to the Republic of China." Furthermore, the *Treaty of San Francisco* stipulates that "Japan renounces all right, title and claim to Taiwan and the Pescadores. Japan renounces all right, title and claim to Taiwan and the Pescadores. Japan renounces all right, title and claim to the Spratly Islands and to the Paracel Islands. Japan renounces all right, title and claim to the Spratly Islands and to the Paracel Islands." Moreover, Article 2 of the *Peace Treaty between Republic of China and Japan* stipulates that "Japan has renounced all right, title and claim to Taiwan and the Penghu." (During this period, activities of the government of the Republic of China deserved attention. The succession of the government of the People's Republic of China from the government of the Republic of China was a gradual process. Succession timing could be the time when Resolution 2758 of the United Nations General Assembly was adopted. It was on that day that representatives of the Republic of China withdrew from the United Nations.)

According to above international treaties and resolutions, the Government of the Republic of China had sovereignty over islands in the South China Sea in that period. The *Treaty of San Francisco* only stipulates that "Japan renounces all right, title and claim to Taiwan and the Penghu. Japan renounces all right, title and claim to the Nanwei Islands and the Xisha Islands.", rather than clarifying who is the successor of the rights and titles. However, it could be indicated from the resumption of the sovereignty over Taiwan and Penghu by the government of the Republic of China that Japan's renounced rights and titles of the South China Sea was taken over by the government of the Republic of China. Moreover, the *Peace Treaty between Republic of China and Japan* specifies the transfer of the rights and titles.

4.3.2.3 No Objections from Surrounding States

On 21 December 1934, the Chinese government held the 25th session of the Amphibious Map Review Committee Conference. The conference examined and approved Chinese and English names of Chinese islands in the South China Sea. In January 1935, the first phase of the *Proceeding of Amphibious Map Review Committee* published names of islands and archipelagos after examination and approval. In April 1935, the Amphibious Map Review Committee published the *Map of Islands in the South China Sea.* It is the first time that the Chinese government has published an official map of the South China Sea. In 1948, the Department of Boundary of the government of the Republic of China officially published the *Map of Administrative Regions of Republic of China*, edited by Fu Jiaojin, and compiled by Wang Xiguang. The attached map is *Map of Location of Islands in the South China Sea*.

First of all, for a long time no surrounding states have raised any objections since the official publication of China's sovereign range in the South China Sea. Even in the next decade after the adoption of convention in the first United Nations Conferences on the Law of the Sea in 1958, Vietnam had not raised any objections to China's exercise of sovereignty over the South China Sea. Moreover, the majority of other states published maps in which they admitted the Chinese government's demarcation in the South China Sea.

Secondly, the principle of estoppels should be noted. The main content of this principle is that if anyone who can represent a state, such as the head of a state, chiefs of government or foreign ministers, etc. has made a statement, formal speech or declaration in other forms concerning some important issues or issues related to major interests of other states, this statements, speeches or declarations would have legal effects that could not be regretted or denied because of the changes of circumstances. On 4 September 1958, the Chinese government issued a Statement on Territorial Sea in which the Chinese government reiterated that islands including the Xisha Islands and the Nansha Islands were part of China's territories. Besides, the statement confirmed that China's territorial sea was 12-nautical-miles in breadth measured from the baselines. The Vietnamese premier, Pham Van Dong, sent an official letter to Zhou Enlai, the then Chinese premier. In the letter, Pham Van Dong agreed and supported China's statement. Besides, Vietnamese officials in the Ministry of Foreign Affairs publicly admitted in 1956 that the Xisha Islands and the Nansha Islands had belonged to China since the Song dynasty.

4.3.2.4 Delimitation by the Government of the Republic of China Did not Violate International Laws

Before further development and establishment of modern marine legal system, represented by *United Nations Convention on the Law of the Sea*, legal status of China's dotted lines has already been generated and been universally accepted. The establishment of new marine legal system cannot deny a state's existing rights and titles. The government of the Republic of China's demarcation of 11 dotted lines was earlier than the *United Nations Convention on the Law of the Sea*. Therefore, according to the principle of non-retroactivity, the Convention cannot change the established titles of the South China Sea.

Modern marine legal system had not been established when the Chinese government demarcated dotted lines. During the period, it was the age when independent national states were emerging, determining territorial ranges in sea and claiming maritime rights and titles. Even states such as the United States or Latin American countries that had been independent since long ago did not make unilateral claims to marine rights and titles until then. For instance, the Truman Proclamation of United

States in 1945, and maritime sovereignty claim of 200-nautical-mile by South American states (these states did not claim maritime right until this time, not to mention colonial or semi-colonial surrounding states the in South China Sea). These unilateral claims have been incorporated into *the United Nations Convention on the Law of the Sea* and have been established as universally recognized maritime legal rules. Therefore, according to the international laws at the end of 1940s, China's 11 dotted lines in the South China Sea should be regarded as the precedent like the legal rules of continental shelf, as well as a component of regional international laws in the South China Sea.

I suggest we persist in the validity of dotted national boundary lines of the South China Sea in the upcoming negotiations. The reasons are as follows:

First, the dotted lines have legitimacy no matter from the perspective of international laws or domestic laws.

Second, from a political perspective, we should persist in the validity of the dotted line. As the legal successor of the government of the Republic of China, the government of the People's Republic of China has the responsibility and obligation to guard its South China Sea. Otherwise, infamy will label on the Chinese government.

4.3.3 Legal Status of "Dotted Lines" of the South China Sea

Chinese scholars have their own interpretations on the legal status of the South China Sea.

Scholars from Taiwan regard that the "U-type lines", demarcated by China in the South China Sea, is the "response to the world after the publication of the Truman Proclamation." "Islands, rocks and low-tide elevations within the U-type lines are the parts of China's territory. Therefore, the U-type lines should be at least regarded as the lines that determine China's sovereignty over these islands." "Waters within the U-type lines are special historic waters. The basis to claim rights and titles in the waters is China's 'historical interests'." "There are two types of waters with different qualities within the U-type lines: one is 'archipelagic waters' formed by a straight baseline; the other is 'historic waters' based on traditional interests of rights and titles." "The function of the U-type lines is to distinguish space of interest between China and its surrounding countries in the South China Sea." "The U-type boundary lines have not been fully developed to a detailed boundary line in historic waters."[136] "Historic waters" in the South China Sea has been lined out via the U-type boundary lines by the Interior Ministry of China. The U-type lines share similarities with "archipelagic waters" of archipelagic states mentioned in the *United Nation Convention on Law of the Sea.*

Scholars from mainland China hold that the dotted boundary lines of the South China Sea illustrate the following points: 1. the lines have determined China's territory in the South China Sea. The legal nature of the lines is "sovereignty". This

[136]Fu (1995, p. 45).

territory includes islands, reefs, and underwater reef-flat, as well as waters. 2. The Chinese government sent armies to garrison the Taiping Islands, which demonstrates that China has effective control over the Nansha Islands. 3. The Chinese Central government demands navy and Guangdong government convoy and protect fishing and other economic activities of Chinese fishermen, which embodies China's jurisdiction over the waters. 4. The Chinese government has not imposed any restrictions on ships that pass through the Xisha Islands and the Nansha Islands. It could be concluded from above that the connotation of dotted boundary lines is very clear. Dotted boundary lines are located between the middle of China's islands and neighboring states' lands, which is fair and equitable according to temporal international laws. The Chinese government has adopted the form of dotted national boundary lines to demarcate boundary, which not only demonstrates the division of waters, but also leaves room for an actual boundary settlement. Legal status of the regions within dotted national boundary lines is equivalent to continental shelf or exclusive economic zone.[137] Legal status of the "9 dotted lines" of the South China Sea is that "islands, reefs within the lines and nearby waters constitute parts of China's territory. China has historic titles over the islands, reefs, shoals and cays within the lines." "Original international navigational routes remain open. The rights for freedom of navigation should be respected."[138]

Thus, scholars from mainland China and Chinese Taiwan have elaborated on the dotted national boundary lines of the South China Sea. Among these, the most significant common ground is that China has territorial sovereignty over the islands, shoals, reefs and rocks including the Nansha Islands within the dotted lines. And China has other sovereign rights over the waters near the islands, shoals, reefs and rocks. The lines distinguish the rights and interests in the South China Sea between China and Vietnam, the Philippines, Malaysia and other states. China has historic titles within the dotted national boundary lines. International navigational routes within dotted boundary lines remain open. And other foreign states have rights to pass through the navigational routes. Dotted national boundary lines provide the legal basis for China's sovereignty over the Nansha Islands and future delimitation of territorial waters, contiguous zones, exclusive economic zones and continental shelves of the Nansha Islands. The dotted national boundary lines are not only recognized by international community, but also explicitly or implicitly acknowledged by involving states. Therefore, the Chinese government must insist on the legal sense of the dotted lines.

---

[137]Xu Sen'an, *Connotation of the South China Sea Intermittent Border*.

[138]Li (2001, p. 16).

4.4 China Has "Historic Titles" Over the Nansha Islands

4.4.1 "Historic Titles" in International Laws

Rule of historic titles in international laws is a pivotal legal basis for China to enjoy territorial sovereignty over the Nansha Islands. Therefore, it is necessary to discuss this issue.

On the issue of determination of territorial sovereignty, historic title has been stated in the *Convention on the Territorial Sea and the Contiguous Zone* in 1958 and the *United Nations Convention on the Law of the Sea* in 1982. It has also been proved in international practices.

In 1958, the first United Nations Conference on the Law of the Sea passed *the Convention on the Territorial Sea and the Contiguous Zone* in which "historic title" and "historic bay" has been stated. Article 7.6 states "the foregoing provisions shall not apply to the so-called 'historic' bays, or in any case where the straight baseline system provided for in Article 4 is applied." The Article 12.1 states that "where the coasts of two States are opposite or adjacent to each other, neither of the two States is entitled, failing agreement between them to the contrary, to extend its territorial sea beyond the median line every point of which is equidistant from the nearest points on the baselines from which the breadth of the territorial seas of each of the two States is measured. The provisions of this paragraph shall not apply, however, where it is necessary by reason of historic title or other special circumstances to delimit the territorial seas of the two States in a way which is at variance with this provision." The Convention regards historic title as an exception in delimitating territorial sea, which shows that the Convention confirms that relevant states could have historic titles over certain waters in accordance with certain circumstances.

Many provisions in *the United Nations Convention on the Law of the Sea* of 1982 involve historic title. Article 10.6 "Bays" of Section 2 "Limits of the Territorial Sea" in Part II "Territorial Sea and Contiguous Zone" states "the foregoing provisions do not apply to so-called 'historic' bays, or in any case where the system of straight baselines provided for in article 7 is applied." Article 15 "delimitation of the territorial sea between states with opposite or adjacent coasts" stipulates that "Where the coasts of two States are opposite or adjacent to each other, neither of the two States is entitled, without any agreements between them in the contrary, to extend its territorial sea beyond the median line every point of which is equidistant from the nearest points on the baselines from which the breadth of the territorial seas of each of the two States is measured. The above provision does not apply, however, where it is necessary by reason of historic title or other special circumstances to delimit the territorial seas of the two States in a way which is at variance therewith." In Part XV "dispute settlement", Article 298.1.(a) (1) of Section 3 states that "disputes concerning the interpretation or application of articles 15, 74 and 83[139] relating to sea boundary delimitations, or those involving historic bays or titles, provided that a State having made such a declaration shall, when such a dispute arises subsequent to the entry into force of this Convention and where no agreement within a reasonable period of time is reached in negotiations between the parties, at the request of any party to the dispute, accept submission of the matter to conciliation under Annex V, Section 2; and provided further that any dispute that necessarily involves the concurrent consideration of any unsettled dispute concerning sovereignty or other rights over continental or insular land territory shall be excluded from such submission."

In the conference and documents of specialized institutes of the United Nations such as the International Law Commission and United Nations Secretariat, legal status of "historic title" in delimitating maritime or terrestrial territory has been affirmed. Provisions on the Law of the Sea were passed in the 8th session of the United Nations International Law Commission, in which Article 7.4 stipulates the legal status of "historic bay". In 1957 and 1962, the United Nation Secretariat put forward two documents on the legal rule of "historic bay" and "historic waters" (including historic bay) respectively. It is clearly stated in the documents that states have rights to enjoy "historic title" over a "historic bay" and "historic waters". There are three conditions that constitute a "historic title": a state has been exercising power over the sea; the power is continuously exercised; the power has acquired *patientia* by foreign states.

In the practices of international community, there are many cases that are involved with historic interests and historic rights in delimitation agreements or treaties. In the case concerning continental shelf (Tunisia/Libyan Arab Jamahiriya) in 1982, the International Court of Justice holds the opinion that "'historic titles' should be respected and be preserved as they have always been by long usage. This could be recalled by the adoption of a resolution entitled 'Régime of historic waters' in the 1958 Conference on the Law of the Sea in dealing with this issue. The resolution was attached to the Final Act, referred to the General Assembly for further study. In 1959, the Assembly adopted a resolution which requires the International Law Commission to do research about juridical régime of 'historic waters', including historic bays. The International Law Commission has not yet done so. Nor does the draft Convention of the Third Conference on the Law of the Sea contain any detailed provisions on the 'régime' of historic waters: neither a clear definition of the concept nor detailed elaborations of the juridical régime of 'historic' waters" or 'historic bays'. There are, however, references to 'historic bays', or 'historic titles', or historic reasons in a way of reservation of rules set forth therein. It is clear that the issue of historic title is still dictated by general international laws. There are no independent regimes of 'historic waters' or 'historic bays' in general international laws, but there are rules in each concrete and recognized cases involving 'historic waters' or 'historic bays'. Clearly,

[139] Article 74. "Special Economic Border Division among Countries with Coast Opposite or Adjacent" and Article 83. "Limits Division of the Continental Shelf with Coast Opposite or Adjacent" or other contents. the United Nations Convention on the Law of the Sea (both Chinese and English). China Ocean Press, 1996.

the fact is that the notion of historic rights or waters and that of the continental shelf are basically dictated by distinct legal régimes in customary international law. The first régime is based on acquisition and occupation, while the second is based on the existence of rights '*ipso facto and ab initio*'. No doubt that both régimes may sometimes partly or wholly coincide, but such a coincidence could only be fortuitous. For example, in the case of Tunisia, Tunisian fishing areas cover the access to its continental shelf. Though it is possible that Tunisian historic rights and historic titles are more closely related to the concept of exclusive economic zones, Tunisia has not made claims on the basis of the concept."[140] From the above elaboration by the International Court, it is clear to see that the International Court does acknowledge 'historic titles' or 'historic rights'. According to Article 38 in International laws, it is no doubt that China can cite the elaboration of 'historic titles' by the International Court when maintaining its territorial sovereignty over the Nasha Islands.

The Eritrea-Yemen Conflict Over the Hanish Islands in the Red Sea Arbitration Case in 1998 is involved with the issue of "historic title". The sovereign claim by Yemen over the territorial sovereignty of islands in dispute can be dated back to the 6th century A.D, namely, the Mninquiy the period of Ancient Yemen. Since then, Yemen has been exercising administrative jurisdiction and actual occupation over the islands. Thus, Yemen enjoys the "primitive", "historic" and "traditional" title over the islands. On the other hand, Eritrea argued that since Italy colonized Eritrea in the late 19th century, both parties in dispute have claimed historic rights over the islands. After examining both parties' submissions and evidence, the arbitral tribunal held the opinion that "there can be no doubt that the concept of historic title has special resonance in situations that may exist even in the contemporary world." "A different situation exists with regard to uninhabited islands which are not claimed to be falling within the limits of historic waters". Therefore, "as long as that colonial situation prevailed, neither Ethiopia nore Yemen was in a position to demonstrate any kind of historic title that could serve as a sufficient basis to confirm sovereignty over any the disputed islands." "In the first place, the conditions that have prevailed during many centuries with regard to the traditional openness of southern Red Sea marine resources for fishing, its role as means for unrestricted traffic from one side of both coasts, are all important elements capable of creating certain 'historic rights' which were beneficial for both parties through a process of historical consolidation as sort of '*servitude internationale*' falling short of territorial sovereignty."[141] From the award of the case, the arbitral tribunal acknowledged the existence of "historic title" in international laws.

In addition, there are many cases concerning "historic title" in international community, such as Land, Islands and Maritime Frontier Dispute (El Salvador v. Honduras: Nicaragua intervening) in 1917, Fisheries Case (United Kingdom *v.* Norway) in 1951, The 1974 Agreement regarding historic waters between Sri Lanka and India in the Palk Strait and the Palk Bay, The Minquiers and Ecrehos Case (France/United Kingdom) in 1977. Also, France, United Kingdom, Canada, United

[140] Xu Sen'an, *Connotation of the South China Sea Intermittent Border.*

[141] *Eritrea -Yemen, Permanent Arbitration Award*, para. 123, para. 126.

State, Former Soviet Union, Tango and other states have claimed "historic bay", "historic waters" and "historic title" to different extent.

Some well-known publicists also expounded "historic rights" in their articles. Charles de Visscher pointed out in the article titled "Consolidation of Historic Rights" that "it has been proved in long-term practice that the basis of historic rights is the integration of various interests and relations, which per se have the effect that a land or water can be regarded as the part of a State. It is the different interests and relations under different circumstances, rather than the lapse of time, which should be taken into consideration by the judges to find out whether the historic rights exist or not. Further, the lapse of time is whatever not stated by international law." "In the important research concerning the courts' application of rules in deciding territorial disputes, Muckermann list economic and historical factors as related issues."[142] Hyde, a United States publicist, thinks it is important that historic waters should be adjacent to states which claim their rights. Scholars from the Former Soviet Union hold that "a State has been exercising powers over the water for a long term, and most states have raised no objection on the any regions within the claimed historic waters", which is the unique element of historic waters. Gary Knight holds that on the contrary to the application of international laws and rules, historic waters is where the states has been explicitly, effectively, continuously and chronically exercising sovereignty, and which is acquiesced by international community. The United States Department of State points out in the statement of the standing of the United States on Historic Bay that "in order to be consistent with the international standards that make the claim, a state shall explain that a coastal State's exercising rights is open, well-known, effective and continuous; the activities of exercising rights acquire acquiesce of foreign states."[143] "'Historic title' is generated in a long term. The concept contains a series of long-term action, inaction and action state during the process. The integration, through its accumulative effects, can generate historic title and can be reinforced. The process can make the integration become effective rights in international law." In other words, "a state exercises the rights by effective means to one or more states, and acquired the rights due to concerning states' acquiesce."[144] It can be concluded that international law scholars have sufficiently realized the existence of "historic title", and have expounded how a state can possess the historic title.

4.5 China's Historic Rights Over the Nansha Islands

Provisions and articles related to "historic rights", "historic waters" and "historic titles" in the Convention on Territorial Sea and Contiguous Zone and the United Nations Convention on the Law of the Sea can be applied to China's Nansha Islands and nearby waters. Practices on "historic waters", "historic rights" and "historic

[142]Jennings and Watts (Revised) (1995, pp. 90–91).

[143]Knight (1980, pp. 5–90).

[144]Yehuda (1965, pp. 247–248).

titles" by international community and relevant discussions and analysis have further proved China's legitimate historic right and historic title over the Nansha Islands.

On the basis of the above international law rules and international practice, the Chinese government has confirmed the legal status of the Nansha Islands through relevant legislations. Early in 1958 when the Convention on Territorial Sea and Contiguous Zone was adopted, the Chinese government published the Statement on Territorial Sea, in which Article 4 stipulates that the above Article 2 and Article 3 shall also be applied to Taiwan and its nearby islands, Penghu, Dongsha Islands, Xisha Islands, Zhongsha Islands, Nansha Islands and other Islands which belong to China.[145]

In the 1990s, affected by the UN Convention on the Law of the Sea, the Chinese government promulgated the Law of the People's Republic of China on the Territorial Sea and the Contiguous Zone and the Law on the Exclusive Economic Zone and the Continental Shelf of the People's Republic of China, which reconfirmed that China has territorial sovereignty over the Nansha Islands.

On 25 February 1992, the 7th National People's Congress adopted and implemented the Law of the People's Republic of China on the Territorial Sea and the Contiguous Zone, in which Article 2 stipulates that the territorial sea of the People's Republic of China is the sea belt adjacent to the land territory and the internal waters of the People's Republic of China. The land territory of the People's Republic of China includes the mainland of the People's Republic of China and its coastal islands; Taiwan and all islands appertaining thereto including Diaoyu Islands, the Penghu Islands, the Dongsha Islands, the Xisha Islands, the Zhongsha Islands and the Nansha Islands, as well as the other islands belonging to the People's Republic of China.[146]

On 15 May 1995, the Standing Committee of Nansha People's Congress adopted the Decision concerning Ratifying the United Nations Convention on the Law of the Sea, in which the Article 1, 2 and 3 respectively stipulates that, "the People's Republic of China has sovereign rights over the exclusive economic zones and continental shelves of 200 nautical miles." "The People's Republic of China will consult with the states in opposite or adjacent directions, and delimitate the boundary of maritime jurisdiction based on equity principle on the basis of international laws." "The People's Republic of China reiterates its sovereignty over archipelagos and islands that are stipulated in Article 2 of the Law of the People's Republic of China on the Territorial Sea and the Contiguous Zone of 25 February 1992."[147] Meanwhile, the Statement of the Government of the People's Republic of China on the Territorial Baseline of the People's Republic of China, adopted at the same time, stipulates that "according to the Law of the People's Republic of China on the Territorial Sea and the Contiguous Zone of 25 February 1992, the government of the People's Republic of

[145] Wu (2001, p. 51).

[146] *Collection of the Sea Laws and Regulations of the People's Republic of China,* China Ocean Press, 1998, p. 4.

[147] *Collection of the Sea Laws and Regulations of the People's Republic of China,* China Ocean Press, 1998, p. 3.

China declares sovereignty over part of baselines of the People's Republic of China and baselines of the Xisha Islands." With regard to the baselines which have not been included, the statement particularly stipulates that "the government of the People's Republic of China is going to declare sovereignty over the rest of the territorial sea baselines of the People's Republic of China in other occasions."[148]

It should be noted that Article 14 in the Law on the Exclusive Economic Zone and the Continental Shelf of the People's Republic of China, adopted at the 3rd Meeting of the Standing Committee of the Ninth National People's Congress on June 26, 1998, stipulates that the provisions in this law shall not affect the historic rights of the People's Republic of China.[149]

In 1947, government of the Republic of China delimitated 11 dash boundary lines, aiming at determining China's historic rights in the South China Sea under the condition that the international boundary had not been determined. Professor Zhou Zhonghai, a famous Chinese expert in maritime law, by combining international laws and international customs with modern maritime law, held that the legal status of China's historic rights in the South China Sea contain the following points: all islands, shoals and cays within the dash boundary lines belong to China; waters inside of the straight baseline of all islands should be China's internal waters, subject to other states' rights of transit passage because the Nansha Islands are located in the crucial point of international navigational route; China has the sovereign rights over the biological and non-life resources in the waters, seabed and subsoil in the South China Sea; other states enjoy the freedom of sailing, flying, laying submarine cables and pipelines, and related international legal maritime applications beyond the line of internal water.[150]

4.6 International Community's Recognition of China's Territorial Sovereignty Over the Nansha Islands

4.6.1 The Recognition from International Treaties

In 1943, the Republic of China, the United Kingdom and the United States issued the Cairo Declaration, and explicitly declared that "It is their purpose that Japan shall be stripped of all the islands in the Pacific which she has seized or occupied since the beginning of the first World War in 1914, and that all the territorial Japan has stolen from the Chinese, such as Manchuria, Taiwan, and the Penghu, shall be restored to the Republic of China."[151] Since the first World War, Japan has encroached many

[148] *Collection of the Sea Laws and Regulations of the People's Republic of China*, China Ocean Press, 1998, p. 8, p. 10.

[149] Wu (2001, p. 187).

[150] Refer to Zhou Zhonghai, *Study on the "Historic Sovereignty" in the Sea Laws.*

[151] *Collected International Treaties* (1934–1944), World Affairs Press, 1966, p. 407.

Chinese territories, including the Nansha Islands. The Nansha Islands was renamed as "the Shinnan Islands" under the jurisdiction of Kaohsiung, Taiwan, after it was encroached by Japan. Therefore, "Manchuria, Taiwan, and the Penghu", mentioned in the Cairo Declaration, including the Nansha Islands, should be returned to China. In July 1947, China, the United States and the United Kingdom signed the Potsdam Proclamation which reiterated that the terms of the Cairo Declaration shall be carried out. In addition, Japanese sovereignty shall be limited to the islands of Honshu, Hokkaido, Kyushu, Shikoku and such minor islands as determined in the Cairo Declaration.[152]

On 8 September 1951, the Treaty of Peace with Japan was concluded in San Francisco. Article 2(10) of this treaty stipulates that Japan renounces all rights, titles and claims to the Spratly Islands and to the Paracel Islands.[153] The Treaty of Peace with Japan should be consistent with the Cairo Declaration and the Potsdam Proclamation because they all deal with issues of Japanese Aggressive War. Hence, all rights to Nansha Islands should be restored to China after Japan renounces its rights.

On 28 April 1952, Japan and the government of Chinese Taiwan signed a bilateral treaty, Article 2 of which stipulates that "According to the Treaty of Peace with Japan which was concluded in San Francisco, the United States on 8 September 1951, we acknowledge that Japan has renounced all rights, titles and claims to Taiwan, the Penghu, the Nansha Islands and the Xisha Islands." Taiwan, the Penghu, and islands in the South China Sea, including the Nansha Islands, had been occupied by Japan. The bilateral treaty signed between Chinese Taiwan and Japan stipulates that Japan renounces all rights, titles, and claims to these islands. Considering that the Republic of China was the leader in the anti-Japanese war, and the legal representative of China, and the governments of Japan and the People's Republic of China did not recognize each other at that time, Chinese Taiwan could legally take over these "rights, titles, and claims" after they were renounced by Japan. In addition, the takeover was in accordance with the provisions of the Cairo Declaration and the Potsdam Proclamation.

It is noteworthy that the Nansha Islands was renamed as "the Shinnan Islands" under the jurisdiction of Taiwan after it was encroached by Japan.

The Japanese government convened a cabinet meeting, and adopted a resolution that included the Nansha Islands in the imperial territory under the jurisdiction of Taiwan. No.31 Order of the Governor-General of Taiwan, issued on 21 July 1931, incorporated the Nansha Islands into Kaohsiung. In 1931, No. 32 Order of the Governor-General of Taiwan confirmed the ranges and names of the Nansha Islands: Bei Er Zi Island, Nan Er Zi Island, Xi Qing Island, San Jiao Island, Zhong Xiao Island, Gui Jia Island, Nan Yang Island, Long Island, Bei Zi Island, Nan Zi Island, Fei Niao Island, Xi Niao Island and Wan Island.

On 31 March 1939, the Japanese government completed the procedures of incorporating the Nansha Islands into Taiwan. Japan decided to officially exercise administrative jurisdiction over the Nansha Islands on 31 March 1939, and proclaimed it to

[152] *Collected International Treaties* (1945–1947), World Affairs Press, 1959, p. 77.

[153] *Collected International Treaties* (1950–1952), World Affairs Press, 1959, p. 335.

the world by the Japanese Ministry of Foreign Affairs. The Decision on Exercising Administrative Jurisdiction over the Nansha Islands is as follows: "the Nansha Islands is the islands and reefs at south China 7~12°N, 110°~117°E." "Nansha Islands is incorporated into the Governor-General of Taiwan." "The Kaohsiung government is responsible for managing the administrative and economic activities of the Nansha Islands. The Japanese Ministry of Foreign Affairs was going to proclaim the determination on exercising administrative jurisdiction to the Nansha Islands on 31 March 1939."

On 17 April, the Japanese Ministry of Foreign Affairs published an article titled "Location and current situation of Nansha Islands", which published the locations and names of major Nansha Islands. The article reads: "The Nansha Islands is well-know since ancient time. This archipelago is located in the South China Sea 7~12°N, 110°~117°E, between the French Indo-China and the Philippines archipelagoes. Most parts of the islands are dangerous navigational zone. The archipelago consists of shoals and islets 4.37–15.31 feet high above the water surface with an area of 165–364 km^2. The major islands mentioned include Bei Er Zi Island, Nan Er Zi Island, Xi Qing Island, San Jiao Island, Zhong Xiao Island, Gui Jia Island, Nan Yang Island, Long Island, Bei Zi Island, Nan Zi Island, Fei Niao Island, Xi Niao Island, Wan Island and among others.

The area of the archipelago is relatively small, with bushes, weeds, scarce willows and large forests. There are abundant minerals and phosphoric acid guano. The waters are teemed with tunas, voladors, sea turtles, shells and other marine products. Occasionally, Chinese fishermen drove ships of 20–30 tonnes to this water, and fished around the islands."

According to above names and information published by the Japanese government, documents of the Japanese government mentioned that "Chinese people ship here to fish and catch sea cucumbers," which indicates that Japan acknowledged that the development and exploitation conducted by Chinese people over the Nansha Islands. In order to occupy the Nansha Islands completely, Japan renamed the Nansha Islands according to their Chinese names. Obviously, Japan never mentioned the Vietnamese, the Filipinos, the Malaysians or the Indonesians had come there to fish or catch sea cucumbers. Neither did Japan rename the Nansha Islands according to Vietnamese.

On 21 July 1931, the No.31 Order of the Governor-General of Taiwan incorporated the Nansha Islands into Kaohsiung. In 1931, the No. 32 Order of the Governor-General of Taiwan stated ranges and locations of the Nansha Islands. It is clear from the published names that the names of Nansha Islands were borrowed from their Chinese names.

The Japanese government had conducted administrative investigations on the Nansha Islands since 23 May for strategic purposes. The Govenor-General of Taiwan and the police department of Kaohsiung sent officials and policemen to the Nansha Islands, and adopted necessary administrative management measures.

On 11 August, the Japanese government adopted the following rules and policies in the Nansha Islands.

① Rule the islands effectively in order to exercise an effective occupation,
② Accelerate the development of the islands,
③ Demand the nationals of a third party and of French Indo-China to evacuate. Those who do not evacuate have to obey the law of Taiwan.
④ Coordinate mining rights and monopolies with the Lhasa Joint-stock Company to expedite joint exploitation.

All activities by the Japanese invaders objectively strengthened the close relationship between Chinese Taiwan and the Nansha Islands, and can be regarded as the China's preparation to restore the Nansha Islands after the second World War.

When Germany was predicted to be defeated in November 1943, Theodore Roosevelt, the President of the United State, Winston Churchill, the Prime Minister of the United Kingdom, and Chiang Khai Shek, the President of the Republic of China, convened a meeting at Cairo, and proposed the Cairo Declaration. They stated in the meeting that "Japan shall be stripped of all the islands in the Pacific which it has seized or occupied since the beginning of the first World War in 1914. All the Chinese territories encroached by Japan, such as Manchuria, Taiwan, and the Penghu, shall be returned to the Republic of China." Though the Cairo Declaration only mentioned the sovereignty of the Nansha Islands in "all the Chinese territories encroached by Japan," these regions clearly included the Nansha Islands. Moreover, Japan incorporated the Nansha Islands into the jurisdiction of the Governor-General of Taiwan in March 30, 1933. Hence, "Taiwan" mentioned in the Cairo Declaration naturally included the Nansha islands.

The subsequent activities of the Japanese government verified the above points of view. In 1952, "Map of East Asia" of the Standard World Map,[154] signed and recommended by the Japanese Foreign Minister Okazako Katsuo, includes the Nansha Islands and other three archipelagos in the South China Sea in the boundaries of the People's Republic of China. In 1964, the 19th map in the New World Atlas[155] which was recommended by the Japanese Foreign Minister Masayoshi Ohira, has the annotation of "the Nansha (China)", which indicates that the Nansha Islands belong to China. As the Foreign Minister of the state that once invaded China, Okazako Katsuo and Masayoshi Ohira's statements clearly recognize that the Nansha Islands belong to China, which evidently has special legal significances. A foreign minister is the administrative representative of Japan and his behavior can be regarded as Japan's state activities which can result in corresponding international legal responsibilities. Besides, other published Japanese literatures also admit that China has territorial sovereignty over the Nansha Islands. For example, "the Chinese coastal lines start from Liaodong Peninsula to the Nansha Islands, which is 11000 km in total."[156] "Besides the mainland territories, China has Hannan Islands, Taiwan and the Penghu, as well as the Dongsha, the Xisha, the Zhongsha and the Nansha Islands

[154] The 15th Map in *The Standard World Map,* (Japan) National Education Co., Ltd, 1952.
[155] The 19th Map in The *New World Atlas*, (Japan) Tokyo Press, 1964.
[156] Japan Institute of Chinese Studies (eds.) (1996, p. 114).

in South China Sea."[157] China's territory "extends to the Nansha Islands near the equator."[158]

4.6.2 The Recognition from Disputing Parties and Its Legal Significance

From the 1950s to the 1960s, Vietnam recognized that China had territorial sovereignty over the Nansha Islands for many times. On 15 June 1956, the Deputy Foreign Minister of the Democratic Republic of Vietnam, Ung Van Khiem, and the Director of Department of Asian Affairs, Le Loc, met with Li Zhimin, the ad hoc representative of the People's Republic of China to Hanoi. Ung Van Khiem said that "Both the Xisha Islands and the Nansha Islands belong to China according to Vietnamese documents." Meanwhile, Le Loc made a supplementary statement that "the Xisha and the Nansha Islands have been belonging to China ever since the Song Dynasty."[159] This was the first statement concerning the islands in the South China Sea from the Democratic Republic of Vietnam. On 14 January 1950 and 18 January 1950, the People's Republic of China and the Democratic Republic of Vietnam respectively recognized each other's independence. Since then, the People's Republic of China has been supporting the development of the Democratic Republic of Vietnam. From the perspective of the joint relationship between the Democratic Republic of Vietnam and the People's Republic of China, and the Vietnam's standoff position against the United States, the Democratic Republic of Vietnam would acknowledge that China has the territorial sovereign over Nansha Islands without doubt.

Two weeks after 4 September 1958 when China issued the statement on its territorial sea, Premier Phan Van Dong of Vietnamese government wrote to the Chinese Premier Zhou Enlai, and expressed that the government of the Democratic Republic of Vietnam agreed with China's statement on territorial sea. In the letter, Phan Van Dong pointed out that "the Democratic Republic of Vietnam respects China's decision, and will instruct responsible government agencies to follow the rules that China's territorial sea is 12 nautical miles in matters with the People's Republic of China in the water."[160] Even the textbooks of the Vietnamese schools recognize China's sovereignty over the Nansha Islands as follows: "The arc-shaped island chains from the Nansha and the Xisha Islands to Hainan, Taiwan, the Penghu, and Zhoushan Islands lead to the great wall to protect Chinese mainland.[161] The textbooks of Vietnamese middle schools recognize that China has territorial sovereignty

[157](Japan) *the World Almanac*, 1972, Kyodo News Agency, p. 193.

[158](Japan) *Modern Encyclopedia Dictionary*, Vol. 13, 1973, p. 338.

[159]Chen (1989, p. 53).

[160]*People's Daily*, the third page on 22 September 1958.

[161](Vietnam) *Geography Textbook for the Ninth Grade of Regular School*, "China" Section, Vietnam Education Press, 1974.

over the Nansha Islands, which indicates that the Vietnamese government and the Vietnamese people do not have any doubt on the fact that China has sovereignty over the Nansha Islands.

Even though the governments of the Philippines, Malaysia and Brunei do not directly recognize that China has sovereignty over the Nansha Islands, plenty documents show that these states have indirectly recognized that China has territorial sovereignty over the Nansha Islands.

When France illegally occupied the nine islands in south Hainan, the Chinese government made protests, and took diplomatic measures to negotiate with France. However, the government of the Philippines held that "This issue is irrelevant to the interests of the Philippines, and thus is not the concern of the Philippine government because the islands are not situated in the territorial sea of the Philippines." William Francis Murphy, the Governor-General of the Philippines at that moment, did not make any statement on this issue. In addition, the staff of the Philippine Coastal Measurement Agency stated that the locations of these islands were 200 nautical miles beyond the lines of territorial sea stipulated in the Paris Treaty.[162] After its independence, the Philippines explicitly admits that these islands are not in its territory and the Philippines does not have rights to claim the sovereignty of the islands. In 1956, a special committee of the Philippine government affirmed after a discussion that "the islands are not within the range of the Philippines's territory."[163]

On 27 October 1955, the International Civil Aviation Organization convened an Asian-Pacific region aviation meeting in Manila. Almost all the states in the Pacific attended this meeting, including the Philippines. No. 24 Resolution was adopted at this meeting, which demanded the government of Chinese Taiwan to strengthen upper-air observations in the Nansha Islands in order to make international flights more conveniently., No states raised any objections when the resolution was adopted and afterwards. The states' acquiescence indicated that the Philippines and Malaysia respected and acquiesced that China has sovereignty over the Nansha Islands. Moreover, these states have not raised any objections when the Cairo Declaration and the Potsdam Proclamation were approved and afterwards.

There are a series of rules in international laws concerning recognition, acquiescence and estoppel to maintain the stability of international legal relations. "However sufficient a right is…. R(r)ecognition means a denial of the possibility for the state to deny such a right at any time in the future."[164] The recognition is important to acquire territories because the judgement of an international court is likely to favour the state whose rights have been recognized by other states who also claim for the rights when every state in disputes can prove it has been exercising certain degree of control over the territories in disputes.[165] In the disputes between two states, the court

---

[162] *Shen Paper, August 23,* 1933.

[163] *Guangming Daily,* June 1, 1956.

[164] Legal Status of Eastern Green Land (Denmark–Norway), Schwarzenberger (1945, Appendix 4, pp. 316–317).

[165] Greig (1976, p. 148).

will naturally take into consideration whether each party has *de facto* recognized the other state's rights or claims to look for a more persuasive proof.[166]

Acquiescence is the silence or no protest against a situation which normally requires explicit reactions to show an opposed position.[167] As to the legal significance of acquiescence, the high court of the United States pointed out in a judgement in 1923 by stating that it had been established and never doubted before this court that a state's acquiescence of the occupations and exercising sovereignty and jurisdiction of another state confirmed the latter state's legal rights and authorities over the lands.[168]

Therefore, recognition and acquiescence are of vital significance in territorial sovereignty disputes. Vietnam explicitly recognized China has territorial sovereignty over the Nansha Islands. Even if the Philippines, Malaysia and Brunei did not explicitly recognize that China has sovereignty over the Nansha Islands, these states did not explicitly raise any objections to the provisions in the Cairo Declaration or the Potsdam Proclamation, or to the warships sent by the Republic of China to take over the Nansha Islands, or to the dash boundary lines delaminated in 1947 and among others. No objection means silence, which can be regarded as acquiescence. In order words, these states have acquiescence that China has sovereignty over the Nansha Islands.

Recognition and acquiesce lead to another legal principle—estoppel. "Recognition cannot be withdrawn between the states who made the unilateral statement and the recognized state."[169] "It is believable that any legal system shall accept such a rule that once a person makes or approves a statement, but he changes his position in relation to the statement on other basis, the former different statement should be changed concerning the latest circumstances"[170] It is the same situation in international law. "A state shall adopt consistent legal positions to any specific factual circumstances or legal circumstances based on the requirement of good faith and fairness in order to prevent other states suffering from damages due to the inconsistent positions." Therefore, if a state has already expressed its positions or taken action concerning certain specific issue, and other states have been obligated or conferred rights or interests based on the reliance by expressions or actions, the former state is not allowed to adopt opposite activities or legal positions. Other states can raise objection against the opposite activities or legal positions, and the International Court of Justice and international arbitrary tribunals shall refute the opposite positions. A Rome aphorism is frequently cited by the International Court of Justice and international arbitrary tribunals, which states that paradox claims are not supported; anyone is not allowed to cause damages to others by changing positions; anyone is not allowed to acquire

[166]Evans (1922, p. 107).

[167]Jennings (1961, p. 36).

[168]Hackworth (1940, p. 436).

[169]Legal Status of Eastern Green Land (Denmark–Norway), Schwarzenberger (1945, Appendix 4, p. 317).

[170]Jennings (1961, p. 41).

interests by invading others; activities contradicting to a person's claim is invalid.[171] Studies of estoppel indicate that "the State who has recognized particular territorial rights of other states cannot deny the rights of the latter states."[172]

Judges pointed out in the award of Legal Status of Eastern Greenland held by the International Court of Justice that: Norway has recognized that Greenland is the colony of Denmark in many bilateral or multilateral treaties. In 1919, Nils Claus Ihlen, the Norwegian Minister of Foreign Affairs, wrote to a Danish envoy. In the letter he promised that he did not object to the sovereignty request to the whole Greenland by Denmark. The Minister of Foreign Affairs is the representative of a State. Therefore, his letter shall be regarded as a pledge of the Norwegian government. Thus, Norway has recognized that Denmark has territorial sovereignty of Greenland. And Norway cannot turn back on its acknowledgement.

In the case of Argentine-Chile border Arbitration, the arbitrary tribunal held that "estoppel" is not only a rule of evidence, but also a rule of positive law in international law. The court cited the opinion of Alfaro, the vice-president of International Court of Justice, in the case concerning the Temple of Preah Vihear. He stated that in international litigations, a state is bound to its activities and expressed attitudes if its claims contradict with its former attitudes.

To conclude, Vietnam, Philippines, Malaysia and other states have recognized that China has territorial sovereignty over the Nansha Islands. This recognition or acquiescence has corresponding legal force. However, these states' activities contradicted their recognitions, which have violated the rule of estoppel. Therefore, they should take relevant legal responsibility according to international law.

4.6.3 The Recognition by Other States

After the second World War, the peace treaties with Japan deals with the territorial issues related to Japan. The United States, the United Kingdom, China and the Soviet Union definitely have the responsibilities, derived from relevant provisions in the Cairo Declaration, the Yalta Agreement and the Potsdam Proclamation.

In these provisions, the territories that have been isolated from China shall be indisputably returned to China—the People's Republic of China currently. The rights over these territories shall be regarded as the rights of China.

With respect to the draft of the Treaty of Peace with Japan proposed by the United States and the United Kingdom, delegation of the Soviet Union believed that Taiwan, the Penghu, the Xisha Islands and other islands that had been encroached by Japan are inseparable parts of China's territory, and should be returned to China unconditionally. However, this draft severely undermined China's legal rights. The draft only stipulated that Japan renounced rights to the territories, but did not mention the sovereignty of these territories. The purpose was to remain the ambiguity of the

[171] Li (1988, pp. 596–597). Cited from Zhang (1996, pp. 3–13).

[172] Greig (1976, pp. 148–149).

legal status of the above regions because the United States intended to legitimize its occupation over the above regions in a long term. Anyhow, the territories must be returned to its owner—the People's Republic of China.

When severely criticizing the draft, the Soviet Union proposed an amendment to the draft as follows: Japan confirmed China's complete sovereignty over China's inviolable territories by abandoning Japan's rights and claims over Taiwan, the Penghu, the Xisha Islands, the nearby Dongsha Islands and the Nansha Islands, including the Xiniao Islands, which had been occupied by Japan.[173] The government of the Soviet Union noted the Chinese government by stating that they completely supported China's statement on territorial sea. Further, the Soviet Union's domestic public voice was in favor of China's sovereignty over the Nansha Islands.

In 1971, a higher commissioner of the United Kingdom to Singapore said that the Spratly Island is China's territory, and is part of Guangdong Province. The Nanwei Island has been resturned to China after the war. We cannot find any sign that signify the island to be occupied by other states. Therefore, the conclusion is that China owns the island.[174]

Even Indonesia, as China's neighbor in the South China Sea, admitted that the Nansha Islands belong to China. Melek, the Foreign Minister of Indonesia, made the statement to journalists that "if we take a look to current maps, it is clear that Paracel Islands (the Xisha Islands) and Spratly Islands (the Nansha Islands) belong to China. No one has ever raised any objections to this fact." Daily News of Bangkok, Thailand, published an editorial titled "The Opinion of Indonesia". It was stated in the editorial that "the Foreign Minister of Indonesia said the Indonesian government recognized the government of People's Republic of China as the only government of China based on facts. Therefore, the Nansha Islands belong to China. Looking at the widely-distributed maps, it is obviously an indisputable fact that the Xisha Islands and the Nansha Islands belong to China. The conversation made by the Foreign Minister of Indonesia may hit the vulnerability of South Vietnam because South Vietnam claimed that the Xisha Islands and the Nansha Islands belong to them. At least, South Vietnam has become one of the biggest states in Southeast Asia that objects to the claims of South Vietnam."[175]

In April 1971, Michael Mansfield, an American senate, pointed out that "China has claimed sovereignty over all these islands, including Taiwan, Diaoyu Island (Senkaku Islands) which is the disputing area between Japan and the People's Republic of China, Spratly Island (the Nansha Islands) and Paracel Islands (the Xisha Islands). According to historical precedents, there is solid evidence for China's claims."[176]

The government of North Korea also made statements in many occasions to support that China has the territorial sovereignty over the Nansha Islands. The government of North Korea condemned the conspiracy that Vietnam attempted to occupy the Nansha Islands. In addition, Romania, Czech, Bulgaria, Hungary, East Germany,

---

[173] *People's Daily*, page 1–4 on Septempber 9, 1951.

[174] (HK) *Far Eastern Economic Review*, December 31, 1973, p. 39.

[175] Cited from Han (eds.) (1988, p. 553).

[176] Cited from Han (eds.) (1988, p. 557).

Mongolia, and other states also made statements to support China's sovereignty over the Nansha Islands. They also supported China's statements on territorial sea and the statements by the Ministry of Foreign Affairs on the sovereignty of the South China Sea.

Articles were published based on the international public voice to support China's sovereignty over the Nansha Islands until 1990s. These articles believed that "China has very solid historical evidence to support its claims to the islands in the South China Sea."[177] "China's attitude is understandable because it is the consistent attitude towards China's territory. States in Southeast Asia do not forget the meaning of Zheng He's expedition."[178] "Territorial claims to Spratly Islands (the Nansha Islands) proposed by the Philippines, Malaysia, and Brunei are mainly based on the unilateral interpretations on ever-changing law of the sea, and lack historic evidence as China has."[179] Even Philippine newspapers held the opinion that China has solid evidence to supporter its claim to the Nansha Islands, and that "Philippines's claims to the Nansha Islands is lack of historic basis."[180]

Major states in the world support and admit that China has territorial sovereignty over the Nansha Islands, which is not only of political significance, but also of legal significance. As stated in the International Law written by Oppenheim that another factor concerning territorial acquirement should be taken into consideration in modern international law…How does the ways and roots of traditional system of acquiring ownership develop into a more completed system includes various factors, concerns and interactions of factual possession. One of the most important new factors is the attitude of international community expressed by the United Nations in acknowledgement procedures. Obviously, the attitude of international community is critical in the process of strengthening historical rights and for the United Nations to decide whether taking arm forces to deal with territorial issues.[181] Oppenheim has already taken the attitudes of international community as the major factor to settle international boundary disputes. This would be an important legal support for China to maintain its sovereignty over Nansha Islands. International community, including the disputing parties, and states that have had close relation with Nansha Islands such as France, Japan and United States, to a different extent recognize or tacitly approve that China enjoys sovereignty over Nansha Islands.

[177](Australia) *The Sydney Morning Herald*, June 30, 1995.

[178](Malaysia) *Sin Chew Daily,* December 24, 1992.

[179](England) *Survival*, 1995, Summer.

[180](the Philippines) *Business News*, December 3, 1987.

[181]Jennings and Watts (Revised) (1995, pp. 94–95).

References

J. Basdevant, Dictionnair De La Terminologie Du Droit International, 1960, p. 237.

Yu Binhua, *International Law* Vol. 1, China University of Political Science and Law Press: 1997, p. 236.

Yehuda Blum, *Historic Titles in International Law*. The Hague: Matinus Nijhoff, 1965, pp. 247–248.

Bureau of Surveying and Mapping of English Navy (eds.), *Guidance for the South China Seas*, 1923, Vol. 3.

Lin Chunsheng, *The Geography of the Islands Occupied by Frence in the South China Sea, printed in Monthly Fang Zhi*, Vol. 7, Period 4, April 1934.

Anthony D'amato, International Law, International Problems, R. Bernhardt, ed. *Encyclopedia of Public International Law*, vol. 9, 1986, p. 192.

Xu Daoling, *Issues on France Seizing Nine Islands of Hainan*, printed in Semimonthly *Yu Gong*, Compilation 123 of Volume 7. July, 1937, p. 270.

Emerich de Vatel, *Law of Nations*, Le droit des gens, Washington, 1906, p. 207.

Matin Dixon, *Textbook on International Law*, Blackston Press Limited, Great Britain, 1990, p. 83.

Lawrence B. Evance, *Leading Cases on International Law*, Second Edition, Chicago, Callaghan and Company, 1922, p. 283. p. 132.

Green Haywood Hackworth, *Digest of International Law*, Volume I, United States, Government Printing Office, Washington, 1940. p. 436.

D. W. Greig, *International Law*, Second Edition, Butter Worths, London, 1976.

Li Haopei, *Introduction of Treaty Laws*, Law Press China, 1988, pp. 596–597.

FAFVD Heydte, "Discovery, Symbolic Annexation and Virtual Effectiveness in International Law", *American Journal of International Law*, 1935, 29(3): pp. 453–454. (U.S.A).

Louis Henkin, *International Law, Cases and Materials*, West Publishing Co., 1980.

Norman Hill, *Claims to Territory in International Law and Relations*. 1945, p. 149.

Zhang Hongzeng, "the China's Sovereignty to the Xisha and Nansha Islands according to the International Law", printed in *Xisha and Nansha Islands has been parts of China from the ancient time*, Chinese People's Publishing House, 1982.

Hu Huangyong, "Intention of France and Japan to Occupy South China Sea Islands", printed in *Review of Foreign Affairs*, Volume 3, Period 5, 1934.

Wang Huhua, Ding Chengyue (eds.) *International Treaties and Conventions*(International Law Volume), East China University of Science and Technology Press, 1994, pp. 3–4.

Wang Huhua, Ding Chengyue (eds.) *International Treaties and Conventions*, East China University of Science and Technology Press, 1994, p. 464.

Japan Institute of Chinese Studies (eds.) *The People's Republic of China Yearbook* (1996), Tokyo Press, p. 114.

R. Y. Jennings, *The Acquisition of Territory in International Law*, Manchester University Press, U.S.A. Ocean Publications INC, 1961, p. 36.

R. Y. Jenings, *The Acquistion of Territory in International Law*, Manchester University Press, 1963, pp. 31–35.

Robert Jenning, *The Acquisition of Territory in International Law*, 1963, p. 28.

R.Y. Jennings, A. Watts (Revised). *Oppenheim's International Law* Vol 1, Sub-volume 2, Encyclopedia of China Publishing House, 1995, p. 92.

Liu Jiachen, Chen Zhizhong (eds.,). *International Law Cases*. China Law Press 1998.

Chen Jinghe, *Xisha Islands and Nansha Islands-Historical Review*. Chuangda Asia Study, 1989, Vol, 10, p. 53.

Li Jinming, "9 Intermittent Border Lines of the South China Sea and Related Issues. China's Borderland" Printed in *History and Geography Studies,* 2001, Vol. 2, p. 16.

He Jisheng. Historical Achievements for Development and Management among Xisha and Nansha Islands by Hainan Island Fishermen, in *Xisha and Nansha Islands has been parts of China from the ancient time*. People's Publishing House, 1981, p. 49.

Kriangsak Kittichaisaree, *The Law of The Sea and Maritime Boundary Delimitation in South-East Asia.* Oxford University Press, 1987, p. 141.
Gary Knight, Law of the Sea: Case, *Documents and Readings*, 1980, pp. 5–90.
Wolf-Dietrich Krause-AblaB, Intertemporales Volkerrecht-Der zeitliche Anwendungsbereich von Volkerrchtsnormen, Hamburg, 1970.
Fu Kuncheng, *Study on the Legal Status of the South (China) Sea.* Taiwan: 123 Information Press, 1995, pp. 62–85.
Law Dictionary of International Relations, Japanese Association of International Law (eds.,). Sanseido Publishing House, 1995, p. 379.
Zhao Lihai, "China has Iindisputable Sovereignty over the Nansha Islands from the Perspective of Intertemporal International Law", Journal of Peking University(Philosophy and Social Sciences), Vol. 3 1992, p. 32.
J. Moore, *International Law*, Vol. IV. Washington, 1906, p. 259.
O'Connell, *International Law* Vol.1, Second Edition, 1970.
B. Orent, P. Reinsch, "Sovereignty over Islands in Pacific". *American Journal of International Law*, 1994, 35(3): p. 443.
Choon-Ho Park, *East Asia and the Law of the Sea.* 1979, p. 183.
Choon-Ho Park, *East Asia and the Law of the Sea.* 1983, p. 220.
A. G. Roche, *The Minquiers, and Ecrehos Case*, 1959, p. 79.
Georg Schwarzenberger, *International Law*, Vol. 1, Stevens & Sons, Limited 119 & 120 Chanery Lane, Law Publishers, 1945.
G. Schwarzenberger, A Manual of International Law, 5th ed., 1967, p. 635.
Sankei Shimbun, A Japanese newspaper 1974, 1.20.
Wu Shicun, *Compilation of the South China Sea issue*, Hainan Publishing House, 2001 , p. 51.
J Simsarian, "The Acquisition of Legal Title to Terra Nullius", Politicalence Quarterly, 1938, 53(1): p. 128.
State Oceanic Administration People's Republic of China (eds.) *Compiles of Maritime Legislations of the People's Republic of China.* China Ocean Press, 1998, p. 1.
Mahesh Prasad Tandon and Rajesh Tandon, *Public International Law*, 14th Edition, Allahabad Law Agency, Law Publishers, 1974.
TangZhou, *Zheng De Qiong Tai Zhi*, Vol. 9, 1964, p. 14.
Chen Tianci, *Xisha and Dongsha Islands Development History*, 1982.
Wang Tieya, *Introduction of International Law*, Peking University Press:1998, p. 104.
Zhang Wenbin, "Comparison Study on Legal Basis of China and Related Countries in Terms of the Sovereignty of the Nansha Islands", printed in *Jurists Review*, Vol. 2, 1996, pp. 3–13.
RuoLin XiuShi et al. *New History of the Nansha Islands.* Printed in *Taiwan Times*: Vol 2, Period 3–4, May 20 in the 14th year of Zhaohe, 20 May 1939.
Huang Yuanlong, "Intertemporal law in International Law", Cass Journal of Foreign Law Vol. 2, 2000, p. 75.
Li Zhaojie, *The Principle of Intertemporal Law in International Law*, Chinese Yearbook of International Law, 1989, p. 97.
Wu Zhicun ed., *Compilation of the South China Sea issue*, Hainan Publishing House, 2001.
Han Zhenhua, (eds.) *Historical Data Compilation of the Islands in Southern China Sea.* Oritental Publishing Center, 1988.
Han Zhenhua, *Historical and Geographical Study on the South China Sea Islands*, Social Sciences Academic Press, 1996, p. 52.
Cheng Zhizhong, ed., *Cases of International Law*, Law Press. China, 1998, p. 121.

Chapter 5
Claims and Defenses to the Nansha Islands by Vietnam, the Philippines, Malaysia and Brunei

The sovereignty dispute of the Nansha Islands involves five states and six parties. Among them, Vietnam and China claim the entire sovereignty over the Nansha Islands. The Philippines, Malaysia and Brunei claimed sovereignty over some islands in the Nansha Islands to different extents. In recent years, conflicts have arisen between Mainland China and Taiwan on the sovereignty disputes of the Nansha Islands. It can be said without any exaggeration that the territorial dispute of the Nansha Islands is the most complicated dispute in contemporary world. The Nansha Islands contain abundant petroleum resources. Its location is of strategic importance, which makes the disputing parties reluctant to renounce their own claims easily. Furthermore, due to the intervention of some super powers, it is becoming more and more difficult to settle the dispute.

5.1 The Defenses and Claims to the Nansha Islands from Vietnam

Vietnam claimed "sovereignty" over the Nansha Islands and the Xisha Islands. The claims can be found in the following statements and documents published by the Vietnamese government.

In May 12, 1977, the Vietnamese government published the *Statement on the Territorial sea, the Contiguous Zone, the Exclusive Economic Zone and the Continental Shelf of Vietnam.*

This statement emphasized that Vietnam has 12-nautical mile territorial sea, contiguous zone with 24 nautical miles, and 200 nautical miles of exclusive economic zone. Article 5 of the statement prescribed that the islands and archipelagos have their own territorial seas, contiguous zones, exclusive economic zones and continental shelves, in accordance with the provisions of Articles 1, 2, 3, and 4, of this statement. And islands and archipelagos form integral parts of Vietnamese territory

C. Yang and Q. Zhang, *Legal Study on China's Sovereignty over the Nansha Islands*,
https://doi.org/10.1007/978-981-15-8715-3_5

and beyond the Vietnamese territorial sea mentioned in Article 1.[1] In this statement, the Vietnamese government only generally mentioned the boundaries of territorial waters, contiguous zones and exclusive economic zones, but did not clearly point out that the Nansha Islands and the Xisha Islands belong to Vietnam. Nevertheless, in the Statement of Vietnam on Hoang Sa and Truong Sa Archipelagos on August 7 1979, Article 1 stipulated that "Hoang Sa (the Xisha Islands) and Truong Sa (the Nansha Islands) Archipelagos are parts of Vietnamese territory."[2] This is the first time when Vietnam has incorporated the Nansha Islands and the Xisha Islands, which are indeed China's territories, in their map.

On December 12 1982, the Vietnamese government issued a *Declaration on Baseline of Territorial Waters.* Article 4 of this declaration stipulated that the baseline used to measure the width of the territorial waters of the Hoang Sa and Truong Sa Archipelagoes[3] should be determined in an ensuing text in conformity with Article 5 of the declaration of May 12, 1977 made by the Government of the Socialist Republic of Vietnam.[4] Not only Vietnam made the statement in which they claimed sovereignty over the Xisha and Nansha Islands, but also did the Vietnamese Ambassador to the U.N, who issued a *Memorandum concerning Truong Sa Archipelagoes* on 12 February 1987. In the memorandum, Vietnam stated that the Philippines, as a signatory and ratifying state of the 1982 United Nations Convention on the Law of the Sea, claimed its sovereignty over the Klayan Islands according to the C.N.7.1983 Treaties—1 submitted by Secretary-General on 23 February 1983, C.N.104.1984 Treaties—3 submitted on 22 May 1984. Besides, China has sovereignty over the Klayan Islands according to C.N.171.1985 Treaties—12 submitted by Secretary-General on 12 June 1985. The above-mentioned Klayan Islands (the Nansha Islands) are in fact the Truong Sa Archipelagoes administered by the Socialist Republic of Vietnam.[5]

In addition, on 9 September 1979 and 8 January 1982, the Vietnamese government published white papers to state that "Vietnam has sovereignty over the Hoang Sa and Truong Sa Archipelagos" and "The Hoang Sa and Truong Sa Archipelagos are Vietnamese Territory". In April 1988, the Vietnamese government published a book titled "*Hoang Sa Archipelagos, Truong Sa Archipelagos and International Law*". In the book, 19 Vietnamese official records, maps, and colonial documents in total since the 17th century were listed. Vietnam attempted to justify that Vietnam was the first country that conducted measures, explorations, occupations, declarations of "sovereignty" and exercising "sovereignty" over the Nansha Islands.

---

[1]Association of International Sea Issues (1984, pp. 117–119).

[2]Hongyu (1997, p. 242). Refer to Shicun (2001, pp. 211–212).

[3]According to the research of Chinese experts, the Hoang Sa and Truong Sa Archipelagoes claimed by Vietnamese in fact refers to the small islands in the noth of the Culao Rayand. It is not the Xisha Islands and Nansha Islands which belong to China. However, Vietnam blustered it out that t the Xisha Islands and Nansha Islands which belong to China are her territory.

[4]Association of International Sea Issues (1984, pp. 120).

[5]Refer to Shicun (2001, p. 227), Hongyu (1997, p. 252).

From above declarations and relevant documents by the Vietnamese government, they claimed a complete sovereignty over the Nansha Islands and even the Xisha Islands.

The legal basis of Vietnam's "sovereign claim" is the principles such as "pre-occupation", "historical facts", "effective occupation", "succession of state" and among others. Such legal basis includes the system of continental shelf and exclusive economic zone, *Cairo Declaration*, *Treaty of San Francisco*, and issues of the Truong Sa Archipelagos.

Now, I will analyze the above-mentioned principles on which Vietnam importunately insists.

First of all, Vietnam has mentioned that the Truong Sa Archipelago is the Nansha Islands for many times. Professor Dai Kelai has written an essay titled "Huangsha" and "Changsha" in which he mentioned that ancient Vietnamese books do not refer to the Xisha and Nnansha Islands of China—objections to the historical geology basis of Vietnam on the sovereignty over the Nansha Islands. He stated that the Hoang Sa and the Truong Sa in Vietnamese Ancient Books are not China's Xisha and Nansha Island. He denounced the Vietnamese historical arguments concerning the sovereignty over the Xisha and Nansha Islands. Prof. Dai did textual research on the exact geographic locations of Truong Sa Archipelago. And he pointed out in this essay that "the 'big and little' Truong Sa" or "Truong Sa Archipelagos" refer to the islands, allusions and sand belts nearby the coast of Thua Thien-Hue in Vietnamese according to ancient books including *Brief History of Vietnam*, *Book of History of Vietnam*, *Records of Wu Zhou* and *Miscellaneaof Fu Bian*.[6] After a study in *Zuan Ji Tian Nan Si Zhi Lu Tu Shu*, he pointed out the "Truong Sa" in the map is the coastal islands and shoals from the north Da Zhan Men to the south Sha Rong Men. Da Zhan Men and Sha Rong Men are islands and shoals from Cham Island, Youngjongdo to Guang Lie Islands areas today. It is why the Vietnamese Du Bo said that it takes one day and a half to go from Da Zhan Men to here; it takes half a day to go from Sha Qi Men to here by sea; it takes two whole days to go from Zhou Mei Men to here. From the perspective of navigation technology of ancient Vietnam, it is impossible to only take half a day, one and a half day, even two days to reach Nansha Islands, no matter which port in the Vietnam to start out. Therefore, "Truong Sa" mentioned by Du Bo could only be the islands in the coastal waters of Vietnam.[7] Mr. Wu Shicun referred to both Vietnamese and Chinese historical materials in the *Origination and Development of the Nansha Disputes*. These materials include volumn four, eight and nine of the *History of Song*, Map of Annan, Map of Ming Annan and Yue Nan Di Yu Tu Shuo in *Wu Bei Zhi*. It can be seen from these historical materials that "Tsuong Sa" is the coastal islands and shoals from Shun Hua to Fu Rong Harbor (today's Si Xian Harbor) along the Vietnamese seas.[8] Professor Han Zhenhua pointed out after

[6]Dai Kelai. "'Huangsha' and 'Changsha' in ancient Vietnamese books do not refer to the Xisha and Nnansha Islands of China—objections to the historical geology basis of Vietnam on the sovereignty of the Nansha Islands".

[7]See Footnote 6.

[8]Shicun (1999, p. 98).

textual research that the "Hoang Sa" and "Truong Sa" mentioned by Vietnam are not China's Xisha and Nansha Islands at all. They are indeed today's shallow waters and shoals among Guangdong Archipelagos and the Vietnamese coasts.[9] Professor Li Jinming also agreed that the "Hoang Sa" and "Truong Sa" are not China's Xisha and Nansha Islands.[10] Therefore, it is evident that Vietnam is confusing the public on purpose.

From the perspective of pre-emption claimed by Vietnam, it is obviously inconsistent with historical facts. According to international law, the objects of pre-emption can only be *terra nullius*. As early as in the Han Dynasty, the Chinese people started cruising and producing in the Nansha Islands, when they discovered and managed the Nansha Islands. It is 1800 years earlier than the time–1816, when the Vietnamese claimed they had pre-empted the Nansha Islands. Since Shi Mi, the general of Kublai Khan made expeditions to Java by passing the Xisha and Nansha Islands. It is 524 years earlier than the tributes paid by Annamese in 1292 when he occupied these islands. According to Zheng He's Expedition (from A.D 1411 to A.D 1421), the time of China's pre-emption is 400 years earlier than Vietnam's.[11] During the two Song Dynasties, the Chinese navy cruised around the Nansha Islands to declare China's sovereignty. In the year 424, the Chinese navy reached south Linyi.[12] Therefore, Vietnam's claimed pre-emption of the Nansha Islands is inconsistent with historic facts. Thus, Vietnam's claimed pre-emption lacks solid legal basis.

The next discussion is from the perspective of "historical facts". Vietnam believed that Annamese historically once fished around the Nansha Islands. This view is unreasonable because Annam per se was dependent states to China. It is natural that Annamese, nationals of dependent states to China, came to the Nansha Islands and fished around the water. There is no need to claim sovereignty based on the activities. If Vietnam claimed sovereignty over the Nansha Islands on this ground, it is 2000 years earlier when the Chinese people fished around Nansha Islands than the Vietnamese.

Another discussion is from the principle of "effective occupation". In April 1988, the Vietnamese Ministry of Foreign Affairs published an article titled "The Hoang Sa Islands, The Truong Sa Islands and International Law". In the article, it is stated that "during the process of dealing with the sovereignty over *terra nullius* of various states in the world, the principle of effectiveness has been established to determine a state's sovereignty. This principle is an international customary law." Based on this, Vietnam asserted that China does not have sovereignty over the Nansha Islands because China did not effectively occupy the Nansha Islands, but only discovered the Nansha Islands.

The principle of "effective occupation" can be found in Oppenheim International law revised by Robert Yewdall J Fennings and Arthur Watts. The author stated that

[9]Refer to Zhenhua (1996, pp. 154–180).

[10]Refer to Jinming (1999, pp. 68–86).

[11]Zhao Guocai, *Analysis on the Sovereign Disputes of the Nansha Islands in accordance with the Existing Sea Laws.*

[12]Li Daoyuan, *the Commentary on the Waterways Classic*, Volume 36, Yushui and Linyi.

"Possession and administration are the two essential facts that constitute an effective occupation. In former times the two conditions of possession and administration which now make the occupation effective were not considered necessary for the acquisition of territory through occupation." "And although later on a real taking possession of the territory was considered necessary for its occupation, it was not until the eighteenth century that the writers on the Law of Nations postulated an effective occupation as necessary, and it was not until the nineteenth century that the practice of the States accorded with this postulate."[13] According to international law, the principle of *Ex Post Facto* prohibition means that the determination of a legal activity shall be based on laws when the activity is conducted, instead of laws when disputes arouse. In other words, China's activities of pre-emption and jurisdiction shall be judged according to international law principles at that time, rather than modern law. Hence, it lacks legal basis for Vietnam to assert that China has not effectively occupied the Nansha Islands which results in reckless invasion of the Nansha Islands by Vietnam.

From the perspective of "state succession", Vietnam believes that after France ended its colonial rule over Indo-China Peninsula, Vietnam is the successor to the rights that French had owned. This is inconsistent with facts. Vietnam was a dependent state to China before France occupied this region, and France was expelled by Japanese invaders in the 1930s during the second World War. France sent warships to intrude the Nansha Islands, and the Chinese government immediately made protests against such invasions. When the French warships erected flags and marked on North Danger Reefs, the Taiping Island, the Thitu Island, the Nanwei Island and other islands, the Chinese fishermen protested against such activities by destroying the French flags and marks. All these facts indicate that what France did has constituted invasions to China's territorial sea. In the end of the 19th century and the beginning of the 20th century, peace-loving people in the world endeavored to maintain world peace. They urge states to abandon war as the tool to implement states' foreign policies. In 1928, the Kellog-Briand Pact was concluded in Paris. With the development of national independent movements, the colonial system is not as popular as usual. Acquisition of territory by conquest or merger was not legal means anymore. Therefore, it is a violation of international law for France to illegally occupy China's Nansha Islands. After the second World War, China has retrieved the Nansha Islands, and France had no foothold in the area any longer. It is ridiculous that Vietnam takes "state succession" as the ground to claim its sovereignty over the Nansha Islands.

Moreover, the treaties concluded between China and France never delimited the Nansha Islands into French Annam. There are three provisions that involved boundaries in the Treaty of Tientsin of 1885.[14] The first provision is about how to punish bandits and enhance cooperation of supervising layabouts in the boundary between China and Vietnam. The second one is about settlement in the boundary Beiqi areas between Chinese and French officials. The third one is about how to manage the personnel exchanges after boundary issue is settled. This treaty has not involved

[13] Jennings and Watts (Revised) (1998, pp. 75–76).

[14] Yuebo et al. (1935, pp. 89–90).

maritime boundaries. Then the Sino-France Treaty of 1887 particularly stipulates the maritime boundary is delimited by a red line. Islands to the east of the line belong to China, while islands and Jiutou Mountains to the west of the line as belong to Vietnam. According to Article 17 of the treaty on March 22 in the 12th year of Emperor Guangxu, if there is a Chinese who vilotes the law and flees to mountains as Jiutou, the person will be arrested and handed over by the local Franch officer.[15] This treaty was concluded on 26 June 1887, and exchanged on 7 August 1896. The content of the treaty does not involve the sovereignty over the Nansha Islands or the sovereignty over other islands in the South China Sea, which reflectes that France recognized that China's sovereignty over the Nansha Islands. Therefore, France did not propose any claims over Islands in the South China Sea. Since France does not claim titles and sovereignty over islands in the South China Sea in these treaties, Vietnam does not have rights to inherit the titles of the islands form France.

Furthermore, France illegally occupied and seized nine islands in the South Chinas Sea in the 1930s as a response to Japan's invasion to China, and its threat of French strategic interests in Vietnam and other areas. In other words, when Japan gradually implemented continental policy by invading China, and threatened the border regions between China and Indo-China, France took such steps as a precaution. It does not mean that nine islands in the South China Sea are the territory of Annam.

In order to maintain control over Indo-China Peninsula, France gradually occupied islands in the South China Sea effectively. These islands were regarded as the strategic chokes. On 4 December 1934, France declared to China that France had sovereignty over the Xisha Islands. After Japan quitted from the League of Nations in 1933, France sent troops to occupy the Nansha Islands step by step, and declared it to the world on 21 July 1933.

Vietnam believes that the Cairo Declaration and Treaty of Peace with Japan do not return the Nansha Islands to China. In fact, the Cairo Declaration concluded by Chiang Khai Shek, Theodore Roosevelt, and Winston Churchilin 1943, clearly stipulated Japan's restoration of China's territories (including the Nansha Islands). The declaration stipulates that three states are fighting in this war to restrain and punish the aggression of Japan. They covet no gains for themselves and have no intentions of territorial expansion. It is their purpose that Japan shall be stripped of all the islands in the Pacific which it has seized or occupied since the beginning of first World War in 1914. All the territories Japan has stolen from China, such as the Manchuria, the Taiwan, and the Penghu, shall be restored to the Republic of China.[16] Since the islands were under the jurisdiction of Kaohsiung city of Taiwan during the period of Japan's occupation, the restoration should naturally contain islands in the South China Sea, including the Nansha Islands according to Cairo Declaration. Professor Urano Tatseo, the famous Japanese scholar in international politics, also supports this point of view.[17]

---

[15]Yuebo et al. (1935, p. 90).

[16]*Collected International Treaties* (1934–1944), World Affairs Press, 1961, p. 407.

[17]Urano Tatseo is a doctor of philosophy in politics. He is a professor in Law School of Nihon University and a visiting professor in Chung-Ang University, Korea National Defence University

Concerning the issue of the Treaty of Peace with Japani in 1951, since China did not participate in this conference, the draft of the Treaty of Peace adopted in the conference only stipulates as follows: Japan shall renounce all the rights, titles and claims to Taiwan and the Penghu. Japan shall renounce all rights, titles and claims to the Nanwei Islands and the Xisha Islands.[18] The treaty has not clearly mentioned the returning of sovereignty over the above regions to China. However, according to the Cairo Declaration and the Potsdam Proclamation, provisions concerning the Nanwei Islands and the Xisha Islands can only be interpreted and understood as returning the islands to China. Particularly, France, as the state concerned, did not clearly demand the stipulation of sovereignty over the Nansha Islands in the conference. This fact demonstrated that France did not support Vietnam's claims.

In addition, it is not worthwhile to refute that Vietnam attempted to claim sovereignty over the Nansha Islands based on rules of continental shelves and exclusive economic zones provided in the United Nations Convention on the Law of the Sea. Because Vietnam cannot gain rights based on contemporary laws, and Vietnam's rights cannot undermine China's historic rights. In order to settle the demarcation of maritime boundary, China and Vietnam have to negotiate and seek settlement based on principle of equity.

5.2 Claims and Defenses to the Philippines's Titles of Partial Islands in the Nansha Islands

The Philippines has claimed sovereignty over the Nansha Islands according to promulgated laws, decrees, and president proclamations. Among these, the Philippines mostly relies on No. 5446 Act on Modification of No.3046 Act of determination of Philippines's Territorial Sea Baseline (Chap. 1), issued on 18 September 1968, No. 1596 President Decree of the Philippines and No. 1599 President Decree of the Philippines on the establishment of exclusive economic zones, issued on 11 June 1978, and the Philippines's declaration on the 1982 United Nations Convention on the Law of the Sea, issued on 10 December 1982.

No. 5446 Act of Republic[19] has explicitly stipulated the baseline of territorial sea of the Philippines.

In order to highlight claims to sovereignty over the Nansha Islands, Ferdinand Marcos, President of the Philippines, proclaimed to exercise administrative jurisdiction over islands in the South China Sea in 1978. The Philippines segmented the

---

and Peking University. He is a prolific scholar who has published dozens of monographs about international relations and international politics. In August 2000, when he passed Chengdu on his way to Tibetan for travelling, he had a meeting with the author of this book. In the talking, he definitely said that when Japan restored the territories including Taiwan stolen from China, the restoration should naturally contain islands in the South China Sea because the islands were under the jurisdiction of Kaohsiung city of Taiwan.

[18] *Collected International Treaties* (1950–1952), World Affairs Press, 1959, p. 335.

[19] Association of International Sea Issues (1984, pp. 61–72).

Nansha Islands and called them "the Kalayaan Islands" with the following scope: stretching westwards along the area, 7°40′N from the crossing point between the area, 7°40′N and the area, Greenwich 116°00′E (at the limit specified in the Philippines Treaty), until the crossing point at the area, 112°10′E; then move northwards to the area, 9° N along the area, 112°10′E; afterwards, move northeastwards to the crossing point between the area, 12°N and the area, 114°30′E and move southwards to reach to the crossing point between the area, 12°N and the area, 118°E; finally, stretch southwards to the area, 10°N along the area, 118°E and move back to the start point, namely, the crossing point between the area, 7°40′N and the area, 116°00′E.[20] According to ranges delimited by the Philippines, large numbers of China's islands and waters have been delimited into the Philippines's boundaries. This delimitation severely violates China's territorial integrity and sovereignty.

The Philippines announced that: the above areas, including its seabed, subsoil, continental margins and the air were within the Philippine's sovereignty. This area became an independent autonomous region of Palawan, which was renamed as Kalayaan.[21]

In No. 1599 President Order, the Philippines proposed to establish exclusive economic zones of 200 nautical miles.[22] The exclusive economic zones of 200 nautical miles proposed by the Philippines include the Scarborough Shoal and most areas of the Nansha Islands, which constitutes a violation of China' s sovereignty.

Article 4 of the Philippines's declaration on the 1982 United Nations Convention on the Law of the Sea, issued on 10 December 1982, stated that "this signature shall not harm the Philippines's territorial rights, such as its rights over the kalayaan Islands and its seas.[23]

Main reasons for the Philippines's "sovereignty" claims to so-called "Kalayaan Islands" are as follows: 1. The islands are of vital importance to the Philippines's security and economy. 2. According to the law of the sea, the Philippines enjoys 200 nautical miles exclusive economic zones. These islands are the Philippines's parts of continental margin. According to the principle of natural prolongation of continental shelf, the Philippines has sovereignty over the islands. These islands are situated in the vicinity of the Philippines. 3. These islands are legally *terra nullius*. 4. The Philippines has effectively occupied and controlled this area. 5. The original owner had renounced sovereignty over the islands. 6. The so-called "historical facts."

The first reason the Philippines relies on obviously lacks legal basis. It cannot be deemed that the Philippines can take these islands which shall belong to China as her territory simply because they are of safe and economic importance to the Philippines. If we followed the logic, China could take the Taiwan Strait as an inland sea strait because it is of vital importance to China's security and economy, This is clearly inconsistent with international law. Therefore, the first reason is invalid.

---

[20] Association of International Sea Issues (1984, pp. 74–75).

[21] Association of International Sea Issues (1984, p. 76).

[22] Hongyu (1997, p. 72).

[23] Hongyu (1997, p. 72).

The Philippines claims that it enjoys 200 nautical miles exclusive economic zones according to the United Nations Convention on the Law of the Sea. However, according to Paragraph 1 of Article 74 concerning Delimitation of exclusive economic zones between states with opposite or adjacent coasts, the delimitation of exclusive economic zones between states with opposite or adjacent coasts shall be effected by agreements on the basis of international law in order to achieve an equitable solution, as mentioned in Article 38 of the Statue of the International Court of Justice. Paragraph 2 stipulates that "if no agreement can be reached within a reasonable period of time, the State concerned shall resort to the procedures provided for in the Part XV."[24] Therefore, when delimiting exclusive economic zones, the Philippines shall follow the United Nations Convention on the Law of the Sea to negotiate with China, rather than delimit the lines unilaterally. Furthermore, the establishment of exclusive economic zones does not affect China's sovereignty over the islands within the area.

The Philippines claims that east Nansha Island is located at the continental margin of the Philippines. Hence, according to the principle of "natural prolongation" in maritime law, the islands should belong to the Philippines. In fact, according to surveys conducted by maritime geologists, the slop body of continental shelf between Philippine islands and Nansha Islands is ruptured, which has formed North Luzon trough, West Luzon Trough, and Mariana Trench.[25] The depth of North Luzon Trough is 3000–3500 m. The West Luzon Trough is 2200–2600 m, and width of the trough bottom is around 55 km. The Mariana Trench is situated at west of the West Luzon Trough, whose average depth is 4800 m, deepest point is at 5577 m, and width of the bottom is around 10 km.[26] The troughs and trench were resulted from sub-ducting movement of pacific plates to Eurasian plate. Therefore, the Nansha Islands is not situated at the continental margin of the Philippines. Hence, the principle of "natural prolongation" cannot be applied to the maritime delimitation between China and the Philippines.

The principle of "vicinity" has been involved in the Philippines's second argument. The Philippines claims its sovereignty over east Nansha Islands because these islands are situated in the vicinity of the Philippines. Nevertheless, acquiring territory by "vicinity" has been denied in the international law theories and practices. In the case of the Islands of Palmas, Arbitrator M. Huber, pointed out that "vicinity" lacks legal basis. The United States cannot acquire the islands just because these islands are in the vicinity of the Philippines.[27] "It should never be a rule that a state's territorial sovereignty can be assumed only by the vicinity of a state's territory."[28] In the case

[24] *The United Nations Convention on the Law of the Sea* (both Chinese and English). China Ocean Press, 1996, p. 61.

[25] Ju Jiwu, "Nature's Masterpiece the Impact of Coral-Formation of the South China Sea and Islands", printed in (Keqin 1996, p. 61).

[26] Ju Jiwu, "Nature's Masterpiece the Impact of Coral-Formation of the South China Sea and Islands", printed in (Keqin 1996, pp. 61–62).

[27] Zhizhong (1998, p. 123).

[28] Jidichaisali (1987, p. 141).

of the Minquiers and Ecrehos arbitration, the International Court of Justice did not support that islands belong to France on the ground of principle of vicinity. The islands are only 8 nautical miles away from France, and 49 nautical miles away from the United Kingdom. So the islands are closer to France than United Kingdom. The International Court of Justice drew the rule based on legal relations rather than geological locations. In the Clipperton case, the arbitrator ruled that France which is across the Atlantic to the island has sovereignty over the island.[29] St. Pierre Island and Miquelon are only 3 nautical miles away from Newfoundland but they belong to France. Many Greek islands in Aegean Sea are only 3 nautical miles away from Turkey's coasts. In the North Sea Continental Shelf case, the international court of justice denied the "vicinity" claimed by German.[30] Therefore, sovereignty over the islands should be determined by legal relations instead of geological locations. No state has rights to claim sovereignty over the islands just because they are near its coast. Thus, it lacks legal basis that the Philippine's sovereignty claims over certain Nansha Islands based on principle of vicinity.

The Philippines's third argument is that the Nansha Islands is "*terra nullius*". The Treaty of Peace with Japan has not clearly mentioned about sovereignty over the Nansha Islands after Japan's renouncement. In accordance with "*terra nullius*" and pre-emption, the Philippines allowed Tomas Cloma, a lunatic, to occupy the Nansha Islands. He established the so-called "Kingdom of Humanity". In this regard, such arguments of the Philippines are illegal. The Nansha Islands has been China's territories since many years ago. The Chinese people occupied, developed and managed this area thousands of years earlier than Filipino did. Even if in the Treaty of Peace with Japan, sovereignty over the Nansha Islands has not been stated, so the islands cannot be regarded as "*terra nullius*". Furthermore, according to Oppenheim's interpretation, a land cannot be regarded as *terra nullius* if its sovereignty remains unclear or controversial. For example, if two states have disputes over a certain border region, a third state cannot acquire the sovereignty over this area by occupation.[31] Therefore, the Philippines's argument is untenable no matter based on facts or international customary rules.

In addition, the content and conclusion of the Treaty of Peace with Japan are flawed. China, which had been fighting against Japan for eight years, made greatest contributions to the victory of the Anti-Japanese War. However, China was unable to participate in and send delegations to the Peace Conference with Japan in San Francisco in 1951. This conference was of vital significance, but China did not have its own representatives in this conference and France coveted sovereignty over the Nansha Islands, so the results of the conference went against China's interests. Furthermore, the cold war just begun at that time, western states represented by the United States deliberately opposed the socialism camp represented by the Soviet Union. Thus, the results of the conference were reached against China's interests. On

---

[29] The Clippertton Island Arbitration Case, 1932, *UN Reports of International Arbitration Awards*, Vol. 11, p. 1055, pp. 1110–1111.

[30] *International Court of Justice Reports*, 1969, paras, 41–42, pp. 30–31.

[31] Jennings and Watts (Revised) (1998, p. 143, Annotation 320).

5 September 1951, in the second session of the peace conference, the representative of the Soviet Union clearly demanded the immediate restoration of China's territory that had been invaded by Japan back to China unconditionally. However, because the Soviet Union's demands had not been satisfied, and the People's Republic of China's sovereignty over the Nansha Islands was refused to be recognized, the Soviet Union refused to sign the Treaty.[32]

Therefore, because of the fact that China was unable to participate in the Peace Conference, influence of cold war and other reasons, the Treaty of Peace with Japan did not stipulate sovereignty over the Nansha Islands. However, this treaty cannot nullify the Yalta Agreement, the Cairo Declaration and other international treaties which have stated that the Nansha Islands belong to China, as well as other historic facts and legal basis. Therefore, it is extremely ridiculous for the Philippines to claim that the Nansha Islands are *terra nullius*.

All the "historic treaties" relating to the Philippines have not incorporated the Nansha Islands into the Philippines's territory.

On 12 December 1898, after the war between the United States and Spain, the two states concluded the Peace Treaty in Paris. Article 3 of the Treaty stipulates that "Spain ceded islands called Philippine Islands and islands within the following boundary line to America: draw a straight line from the west to the east along with or near the area 20°N to go through the navigable Bashi Channel; then reach the area 127°E from the area 118°E; afterwards, go to the area 4°45' N along the area127°E and reach the crossing point at the area 119° 35'E along the area 4°45' N; reach the area 7°40'N from the area 119° 35'E; reach the crossing point at the area 116°E along the area 7°40' N; draw a straight line to the crossing point of 10°N and 118°E and then come back to the starting point along 118°E."[33] However, geological coordinates of the Nansha Islands is 3°36′N–11°57′N, 109°06′ E–117°50′E.[34] Therefore, the boundary delimited in the Paris Peace Treaty between United State and Spain does not contain the Nansha Islands.

The Peace Treaty in Paris between the United States and Spain has been reconfirmed in the Treaty of Peace between the United States and Spain signed on 7 November 1900. One article in the Treaty stipulates, "Spain transfers to America all islands which belong to the Philippines Islands ceded to Spain and beyond the scope stated in Article 3 of this Treaty when concluding the Peace Treaty of Paris, especially, Cagayan, Saltanah Sulu and Sibutu as well as the rights and claims of the annexed territory and agrees that all these islands are fully included in islands transferred and are also within the above-mentioned scope."[35]

---

[32]*The Conference Records of Proceeds,* U.S. State Dept. Publication 4392 (Dec. 1952), p. 292.

[33]Hongyu (1997, pp. 29–30).

[34]Baoyin (1996, p. 1). In addition, in Ju Jiwu, "The treasure islands of Chian—the Scattered Islands in South Chia Sea", the coordinates described is 3°58′N–11°55′N, 109°44′E–117°50′E. See Chen Keqin (Keqin 1996, p. 140).

[35]Sea Technology Information, 1979, Period 4, translated based on *CCOP No.9 Conference Report Association of International Sea Issues,* cited from Association of International Sea Issues (1984, p. 81).

On 1 January 1930, in order to clarify the boundaries of the Philippines Islands and North Borneo protected by the United Kingdom, the United States and the United Kingdom concluded Convention between the United States of America and the Great Britain delimiting the boundary between the Philippine archipelago and the State of North Borneo. According to this convention, part of the boundaries established in the treaty between the United States and Spain in 1898 will be replaced by the boundaries of the line separating the islands belonging to the Philippine Archipelago on the one hand and the islands belonging to the State of North Borneo which is under British protection on the other hand.[36] Location of the boundary is as follows:

The boundary of the Philippines in the Convention between the United States of America and Great Britain delimiting the boundary between the Philippine archipelago and the State of North Borneo

Northern latitude	Eastern latitude		
	East	North	East
4°45′	120°00′	6°00′	118°20′
4°23′	120°00′	6°17′	117°58′
4°23′	119°00′	6°52′	117°58′
4°42′	119°00′	7°24′45″	117°25′30″
5°16′	119°35′	7°40′	117°00′
6°00′	118°50′		

It can be seen that the Nansha Islands have not been included in the treaty. According to international laws, non-private treaties shall be inherited by States. Therefore, the Philippines cannot change the existing boundaries determined by treaties. According to the Vienna Convention on Succession in respect of Treaties 1978, Article 11 stipulates that a succession of States does not as such affect a boundary established by a treaty or obligations and rights established by a treaty and relating to the regimé of a boundary. Article 65 of the Vienna Convention on the Law of the Treaties 1969 provides the exclusion of a state to invoke the change as a ground for suspending the operation of the treaty if the treaty establishes a boundary. Besides, according to the Vienna Convention on the Law of Treaties between States and International Organizations or between International Organizations, Article 62 also stipulates that a fundamental change of circumstances, which has occurred with regard to those existing at the time of the conclusion of a treaty, and which was not foreseen by the parties, may not be invoked as a ground for terminating or withdrawing from the treaty unless the existence of the circumstances constituted an essential basis for the consent of the parties to be bound by the treaty.[37]

---

[36]Sea Technology Information, 1979, Period 4, translated based on CCOP No.9 *Conference Report Association of International Sea Issues*, cited from Association of International Sea Issues (1984, p. 80).

[37]Jennings and Watts (Revised) (1998, p. 61).

On 17 June 1961, No. 3046 Act of the Republic issued by the Philippines did not delimit the Nansha Islands in the Philippines's maps. On 18 September 1968, the House and Senate of the Philippines adopted No. 5446 Act which corrected the typographical error in No. 3046 Act. The baseline of territorial sea of the Philippines in the act did not mention that the Philippines enjoyed sovereignty over the Nansha Islands.[38]

Philippines's fourth argument is "effective occupation" and "effective control." The Philippines holds that China did not effectively occupy and actually control the Nansha Islands in the past. From this point of view, the Philippines, in fact, has admitted China's sovereignty over the Nansha Islands (at least nominal sovereignty over the Nansha Islands). The Philippines just takes that China has not effectively occupied and actually controlled the Nansha Islands as an excuse in order to claim parts of the Nansha Islands. There are abundant historical documents to prove that China discovered the Nansha Islands in the Han Dynasty. The Chinese government has exercised effective administrative jurisdiction over the Nansha Islands since the Song Dynasty. After the second World War, China has retrieved sovereignty over the Nansha Islands and sent troops to garrison the islands. The rules of international laws for occupations on islands with hostile environment are not strict. Additionally, for the condition of the natural environment of the Philippines, such arguments cannot hold water. The Philippines is constituted of 7083 islands. Among these islands, there are 2600 islands with habitants, and only 1095 habited islands have been named. The majority of the Philippines's islands are inhabited and unnamed. Therefore, the Philippines cannot regard the Nansha Islands as *terra nullius* only because the islands are inhabited.[39] China has declared its sovereignty over the Nansha Islands, included the Nansha Islands into national administrative systems, sent troops to cruise and garrison, and delimited the islands into Chinese map. All the activities have demonstrated that China has exercised effective jurisdiction and effective control over the Nansha Islands.

Currently, the Philippines has illegally occupied the Lawak Island, the Patag Island, the Thitu Island, the Loaita Island, the Northeast Cay, the West York Island, the Reed Tablemount, the Tizard Banks, the Commodore Reef, the Lankiam Cay, the Cailun Reef and among others. The Philippines has built military airfields on and emigrated to some islands. The Philippines has attempted to achieve so-called "effective occupation" and "effective control" by means of military force and resources development.

With regard to whether the former sovereignty owner renounces the islands, the fact is that all previous Chinese government has never renounced sovereignty over the Nansha Islands. Therefore, the Philippines's arguments cannot be established.

---

[38] Shicun (1999, p. 120).

[39] Zhao Guocai, *Analysis on the Sovereign Disputes of the Nansha Islands in accordance with the Existing Sea Laws.*

5.3 Claims and Defenses to Malaysia and Brunei's Titles of Partial Nansha Islands

Malaysia and Brunei's claims to titles of the Nansha Islands and their legal basis are not complicated. In the first place, Malaysia did not claim sovereignty over the Nansha Islands. In 1968, Malaysia took waters of 80,000 km^2, including South Luconia Shoals, North Luconia Shoals, James Shoals, as resource zones, and lent them to Sarawak Shell Company to exploit petroleum.[40] From the maps published by Malaysia and the continental shelf boundary delimited by Malaysia and Indonesia, Malaysia has demarcated 10 islands into its map.[41] Currently, Malaysia has illegally occupied the Swallow Reef, the Ardasier Reef, the Mariveles Reef, the Ardasier Breakers, the Louisa Reef and among others. In 1993, Malaysia named the controlled waters as "the Sabah Sea".

Malaysia's "legal basis" of the claims to the region is provisions concerning the continental shelf and exclusive economic zones in the United Nations Convention on the Law of the Sea.

Brunei has claimed sovereignty over the Ardasier Breakers, and announced to establish exclusive economic zones of 200 nautical miles.

The legal basis of Brunei's claim, the same as Malaysia's, is based on the system of continental shelf and exclusive economic zones. Article 56 of the United Nations Convention on the Law of the Sea stipulates that: in the exclusive economic zone, the coastal States has: (a) sovereign rights for the purpose of exploring and exploiting, conserving and managing the natural resources, whether living or non-living, of the waters superjacent to the seabed and of the seabed and its subsoil, and with regard to other activities for the economic exploitation of the zone, such as the production of energy from the water, currents and winds; (b) jurisdiction as provided for in the relevant provisions of this Convention with regard to: (i) the establishment and use of artificial islands, installations and structures; (ii) marine scientific research; (iii) the protection and preservation of the marine environment; (c) other rights and duties provided for in this convention.[42] Therefore, this convention does not involve sovereignty over the islands within the zone. Subparagraph C does not stipulate sovereignty over the islands either.

Article 77 of the United Nations Convention on the Law of the Sea stipulates: the coastal States exercises over the continental shelf sovereignty rights for the purpose of exploring it and exploiting its natural resources.[43] Relevant provisions of the Convention do not involve sovereignty over the islands on the continental shelf.

In conclusion, according to a Roman legal proverb, an exercise of right shall not damage others' rights. When delimiting the baseline of territorial sea, establishing

---

[40] Shicun (1999, p. 122).

[41] Day (1982, p. 126).

[42] *The United Nations Convention on the Law of the Sea* (both Chinese and English). China Ocean Press, 1996, p. 27.

[43] *The United Nations Convention on the Law of the Sea* (both Chinese and English). China Ocean Press, 1996, p. 40.

exclusive economic zones and continental shelves, states shall not undermine the interests of other states. Coastal states with conflict of interests shall negotiate with each other to reach a settlement. More importantly, states cannot take islands that are located within exclusive economic zones or continental shelves as their own territories. It is an important rule in customary international law that land governs the sea instead of sea governs the land. A state must possess land, by which it can enjoy relevant sovereignty over the sea. "Under no circumstances shall sovereign rights (different form sovereignty) deriving from continental shelves and exclusive economic zones depend on occupation, no matter whether it is "effective" or "symbolic", unless they might be dependent territories."[44] Oppenheim has made a very clear explanation that sovereign rights of continental shelves and exclusive economic zones are different from sovereignty. A state cannot acquire sovereignty over the region, including the islands, because of sovereign rights that are derived from continental shelves and exclusive economic zones. "It is wrong that exclusive economic zones provided in the Convention on the Law of the Sea can establish territorial sovereignty. States may enjoy some rights in the zones, but have no sovereignty over the islands within the zones."[45] Furthermore, the continental shelves of the Nansha Islands are constituted of accumulation shelf and continental slopes. The continental shelf is an undivided integration.

References

Alan. J. Day, *Border and Territorial Disputes*. London 1982.

Association of International Sea Issues, *Selected Collection of Sea Regulations and Treaties of Countries Adjacent to China Sea*. China Ocean Press, 1984.

Chen Hongyu, *Collection for Seas Law and Treaties of Southeast Asian Countries*. Sanmin Book Store, 1997.

Chen Keqin, (ed.) *The Islands in The South China Sea*, Hainan International News Press 1996.

Chen Zhizhong, *Cases of International Law*. Law Press. China, 1998.

Han Zhenhua, *Historical and Geographical Study on the South China Sea Islands*, Social Sciences Academic Press, 1996, pp. 154–180.

Huang Yuebo et al., *Collection of Chinese and Foreign Treatie*, The Commercial Press, 1935.

Jidichaisali, *The Sea Law and Sea Border of the South China Sea*, 1987.

Li Jinming, *A Study on South China Sea Boundaries*. Fujian People's Publishing House, 1999.

Liu Baoyin, *The Nansha Islands, the Dongsha Islands and the Penghu Islands*, China Ocean Press: 1996.

R.Y. Jennings, A. Watts (Revised). *Oppenheim's International Law*, Vol 1, Sub-volume 2, Encyclopedia of China Publishing House, 1998.

Wu Shicun, *The Origin and Development of the Dispute of the Nansha Islands*. China Ocean Press, 1999.

Wu Shicun, *Compilation of the South China Sea issue*, Hainan Publishing House, 2001.

---

[44] Jennings and Watts (Revised) (1998, p. 75).

[45] *Far Eastern Economic Review*, January 21, 1999, p. 61.

Chapter 6
Conclusion: China Has Indisputable Sovereignty and Sovereign Rights Over the Nansha Islands and Its Nearby Waters

From above analysis, it can be concluded that China's sovereignty over the Nansha Islands has sufficient legal basis.

First, China should comprehensively consider various relevant elements with respect to the maintenance and protection of sovereignty over the Nansha Islands. Professor Brownlie holds that what the court concerns is evidence of exercising a state's sovereignty at the key date. Traditional analysis cannot be applied to describe the judgement procedures. The dispute of territorial sovereignty is always very complicated which involves applications of legal principles of important facts. Oppenheim also holds that the key date or the time itself should be taken into consideration with various factors in particular cases. These factors include continuous and effective occupation or administration, acquiescence or objections, relative strong or weak opposing claims, impact of intertemporal laws, principle of stability of territory and boundaries, the principle of "occupation", geographical and historical factors, the attitude of international community, requirement of self-defense, possible illegal resource of original possession.[1] Above elements are of theoretical and practical significance for protecting China's sovereignty over the Nansha Islands. When discussing the issue of sovereignty over the Nansha Islands, we cannot merely depend on modern international laws and maritime laws, but have to consider that China has discovered, named, pre-empted, effectively occupied, managed, explored, declared its sovereignty over the Nansha Islands, and exercised administrative and judicial jurisdiction over the Nansha Island for more than 2000 years. Besides, the Chinese troops patrolled and combated piracy around the Nansha Islands. Other facts including the recognitions and acquiescence by various states, intertemporal international laws, the key date, historic titles, existence of dash boundary lines, protests of the Chinese government, China's national powers, legal force of the maps and among others shall also be considered.

[1] Jennings and Watts (Revised) (1998, p. 95).

C. Yang and Q. Zhang, *Legal Study on China's Sovereignty over the Nansha Islands*,
https://doi.org/10.1007/978-981-15-8715-3_6

Second, China has acquired territorial sovereignty over the Nansha Islands based on "discovery", "pre-emption", "effective occupation" and other principles of international laws. When Vietnam, the Philippines, Malaysia and other states claim sovereignty over the Nansha Islands, the islands have already been under administrative and judicial jurisdiction of China. Obviously, it cannot hold water that Vietnam and the Philippines claim sovereignty over the Nansha Islands on the ground of "discovery", because the object of "discovery" and "pre-emption" is confined to *terra nullius*, and the states cannot take the Nansha Islands which is China's territory as the object of occupation.

Third, China discovered the Nansha Islands as early as in the Qin and Han Dynasty. In the Song Dynasty, China exercised administrative jurisdiction of the Nansha Islands. Therefore, when dealing with sovereignty dispute of the Nansha Islands, international laws before the 15th–16th century should be the rules to settle the dispute, rather than contemporary international law. In other words, the law for the purpose of settlement of disputes should be the law when the rights have been generated, rather than the law when claims have been proposed or when disputes have arisen. The rule of "intertemporal law" has become the universally accepted criterion of international law.

Forth, China can merely depend on "discovery" of the Nansha Islands so as to gain the "preliminary right" and the "incomplete right" that can prevent other States fro occupying the Nansha Islands. In the Qin and Han Dynasty, the Nansha Islands were discovered, developed, and explored by the Chinese people. Therefore, the Nansha Islands have become the "Forbidden Land" to Vietnam, the Philippines, Malaysia, Brunei and other states.

Fifth, in the early time, private acts are of vital importance for the acquisition of territory, which has been widely accepted by many scholars of international law. O'Connell,Daniel said, "No preempting can be realized without the private behaviors." Moore, the judge of the Permanent Court of International Justice, said, "The empowered private discovery is allowable, to which there are no objections in the International Law and the Common Law". Judge Carneiro also believed that if two countries claim for sovereignty to the territory located in the border regions, the private behaviors are very vital. Private acts conducted by the Chinese people in the Nansha Islands are the earliest, the most frequent, of the large scale, and remain the most trail of living and production. Exploration and management of Nansha Islands by the Chinese people can constitute pre-emption, which can effectively prevent the sovereignty claim proposed by other States.

Sixth, the modern international law requires that "symbolic activities, such as rising flags, firing cannons, erecting tablets of sovereignty, inserting cross, publishing announcement on the newspaper" can constitute pre-emption, or if a state has exercised administrative or judicial jurisdiction over some area, which can also be regarded as pre-emption. When Vietnam, the Philippines, Malaysia and Brunei claimed the sovereignty over Nansha Islands, China had conducted not only symbolic activities, but also sovereign activities such as administrative and judicial jurisdiction, patrolling and garrison. All in all, China has satisfied the requirements of "pre-emption" and "effective occupation" in international law.

Seventh, it is not solid that the Philippines, Malaysia and Brunei claimed sovereignty over Nansha Islands based on the principle of "vicinity". Because, there is no such rule in international law, and such rule is not accepted by the International Court of Justice, the Permanent Court of Arbitration, and other well-known scholars of international law. The proposition of "vicinity" not only lacks recognition, but also is denied for many time in the cases of international law.

Eighth, in accordance with the UN Convention on the Law of the Sea, the Philippines, Vietnam, Malaysia and Brunei claim sovereignty of Nansha Islands, which is inconsistent with the principle of the convention. First of all, this convention is not to solve the dispute of sovereignty. System of continental shelf and exclusive economic zone do not involve the sovereignty of islands. Secondly, when exercising their own right, the states cannot abuse them, and undermine the interests and rights of others, which is the generally accepted rule of law.

Ninth, Vietnam, the Philippines, Malaysia, Brunei and other states have given recognition and acquiescence that China has the sovereignty over the Nansha Islands. Such recognition and acquiescence are conducted by the government, and has generated relevant legal force of international law, which cannot be changed. Estoppel in international law can effectively prevent these states from claiming sovereignty over the Nansha Islands. A modern civilized state cannot adopt contradictory attitudes, positions or courses of action, otherwise, the state shall be condemned by the international community, and take relevant legal responsibility.

Tenth, in regard to the fact that China has the sovereignty over Nansha Islands, international treaties, bilateral agreements, various states, and even Japan who has invaded Nansha Islands admitted and recognized this fact. There are abundant maps and documents that clearly record that the Nansha Islands belong to China. Even western states called this area as "South China Sea", instead of "Vietnam Sea", or "East Vietnam Sea", or "Philippine Sea", or "West Philippine Sea", or "Malaysia Sea", or "West Malaysia Sea", or "Brunei Sea", because the Chinese people, have developed, explored, managed, and navigated around the Nansha Islands since it was in the ancient time. These facts cannot be distorted. Some states in Southeast Asia attempt to rename South China Sea as "Southeast Asia Sea", which can not be accepted by China.

Today, more than 40 islands of the Nansha Islands have been illegally occupied, large areas of waters have been carved up, and petroleum resources are continuously exploited by states illegally. The Nansha Islands are crying and bleeding. Nevertheless, since "illegal gains shall not generate any rights", these states cannot take the Nansha Islands as their own territory by military means.

Reference

R.Y. Jennings, A. Watts (Revised). *Oppenheim's International Law*, Vol 1, Sub-volume 2, Encyclopedia of China Publishing House, 1998.

Appendix A

See Fig. A.1

C. Yang and Q. Zhang, *Legal Study on China's Sovereignty over the Nansha Islands*,
https://doi.org/10.1007/978-981-15-8715-3

中国地图

审图号：GS(2019)1658号 自然资源部 监制

Fig. A.1 Map of China (vertical version)

Appendix B

Declaration of The Government of the People's Republic of China on China's Territorial Sea

Beijing, September 4, 1958

The Govemment of the People's Republic of China declares:

1. The breadth of the territorial sea of the People's Republic of China shall be twelve nautical miles. This provision applies to all territories of the People's Republic of China including the Chinese mainland and its coastal islands, as well as Taiwan and its surrounding islands, the Penghu Islands, the Dongsha Islands, the Xisha Islands, the Zhongsha Islands, the Nansha Islands and all other islands belonging to China which are separated from the mainland and its coastal islands by the high seas.
2. China's territorial sea along the mainland and its coastal islands takes as its baseline the line composed of the straight lines connecting base-points on the mainland coast and on the outermost coastal islands; the water area extending twelve nautical miles outward from this baseline is China's territorial sea. The water areas inside the baseline, including Bohai Bay and the Qiongzhou Straits, are Chinese inland waters. The islands inside the base line, including Dongyin Island. Gaodeng Island, the Mazu Islands, the Baiquan Islands, Wuqiu Island, the Greater And Lesser Jinmen Islands, Dadan Island, Erdan Island and Dongding Island, are islands of the Chinese inland waters.
3. No foreign aircraft and no foreign vessels for military use may enter China's territorial sea and the air space above it without the permission of the Goverment of the People's Republic of China.
   While navigation Chinese territorial sea, every foreign vessel must observe the relevant laws and regulations laid down by the Government of rhe People's Republic of China.
4. The principles provided in paragraphs 2) and 3) likewise apply to Taiwan and its surrounding islands, the Penghu Islands, the Dongsha Islands, the Xisha Islands.

C. Yang and Q. Zhang, *Legal Study on China's Sovereignty over the Nansha Islands*,
https://doi.org/10.1007/978-981-15-8715-3

the Zhongsha Islands, the Nansha islands, and all other islands belonging to China.

The Taiwan and Penghu areas are still occupied by the United States armed force. This is an unlawful encroachment on the territorial integrity and sovereignty of the People's Republic of China. Taiwan, Penghu and such other areas are yet to be recovered, and the Government of the People's Republic of china has the right to recover these areas by all suitable means at a suitable time. This is China's internal affair, in which no foreign interference is tolerated.

Appendix C

Law of the PRC on the Territoral Sea and the Contiguous Zone (adopted at the 24th meeting of the standing committee of the seventh national people's congress on february 25, 1992, promulgated by order no. 55 of the president of the people's republic of china on february 25, 1992, and effective as of the date of promulgation).

Article 1 this law is enacted for the people's republic of china to exercise its sovereignty over its territorial sea and the control over its contiguous zone, and to safeguard its national security and its maritime rights and interests.

Article 2 the territorial sea of the people's republic of china is the sea belt adjacent to the land territory and the internal waters of the people's republic of china. The land territory of the people's republic of china includes the mainland of the people's republic of china and its coastal islands; taiwan and all islands appertaining thereto including the diaoyu islands; the penghu islands; the dongsha islands; the xisha islands; the zhongsha islands and the nansha islands; as well as all the other islands belonging to the people's republic of china. The waters on the land ward side of the baselines of the territorial sea of the people's republic of china constitute the internal waters of the people's republic of china.

Article 3 the breadth of the territorial sea of the people's republic of china is twelve nautical miles, measured from the baselines of the territorial sea. The method of straight baselines composed of all the straight lines joining the adjacent base points shall be employed in drawing the baselines of the territorial sea of the people's republic of china. The outer limit of the territorial sea of the people's republic of china is the line every point of which is at a distance equal to twelve nautical miles from the nearest point of the baseline of the territorial sea.

Article 4 the contiguous zone of the people's republic of china is the sea belt adjacent to and beyond the territorial sea. the breadth of the contiguous zone is twelve nautical miles. The outer limit of the contiguous zone of the people's republic of china is the line every point of which is at a distance equal to twenty-four nautical miles from the nearest point of the baseline of the territorial sea.

Article 5 the sovereignty of the people's republic of china over its territorial sea extends to the air space over the territorial sea as well as to the bed and subsoil of the territorial sea.

C. Yang and Q. Zhang, *Legal Study on China's Sovereignty over the Nansha Islands*,
https://doi.org/10.1007/978-981-15-8715-3

Article 6 foreign ships for non-military purposes shall enjoy the right of innocent passage through the territorial sea of the people's republic of china in accordance with the law. Foreign ships for military purposes shall be subject to approval by the government of the people's republic of china for entering the territorial sea of the people's republic of china.

Article 7 foreign submarines and other underwater vehicles, when passing through the territorial sea of the people's republic of china, shall navigate on the surface and show their flag.

Article 8 foreign ships passing through the territorial sea of the people's republic of china must comply with the laws and regulations of the people's republic of china and shall not be prejudicial to the peace, security and good order of the people's republic of china. Foreign nuclear-powered ships and ships carrying nuclear, noxious or other dangerous substances, when passing through the territorial sea of the people's republic of china, must carry relevant documents and take special precautionary measures. The government of the people's republic of china has the right to take all necessary measures to prevent and stop non-innocent passage through its territorial sea. Cases of foreign ships violating the laws or regulations of the people's republic of china shall be handled by the relevant organs of the people's republic of china in accordance with the law.

Article 9 the government of the people's republic of china may, for maintaining the safety of navigation or for other special needs, request foreign ships passing through the territorial sea of the people's republic of china to use the designated sea lanes or to navigate according to the prescribed traffic separation schemes. The specific regulations to this effect shall be promulgated by the government of the people's republic of china or its competent authorities concerned.

Article 10 in the case of violation of the laws or regulations of the people's republic of china by a foreign ship for military purposes or a foreign government ship for noncommercial purposes when passing through the territorial sea of the people's republic of china, the competent authorities of the people's republic of china shall have the right to order it to leave the territorial sea immediately and the flag state shall bear international responsibility for any loss or damage thus caused.

Article 11 all international organizations, foreign organizations or individuals shall obtain approval from the government of the people's republic of china for carrying out scientific research, marine operations or other activities in the territorial sea of the people's republic of china, and shall comply with the laws and regulations of the people's republic of china. All illegal entries into the territorial sea of the people's republic of china for carrying out scientific research, marine operations or other activities in contravention of the provisions of the preceding paragraph of this article, shall be dealt with by the relevant organs of the people's republic of china in accordance with the law.

Article 12 no aircraft of a foreign state may enter the air space over the territorial sea of the people's republic of china unless there is a relevant protocol or agreement between the government of that state and the government of the people's republic of china, or approval or acceptance by the government of the people's republic of china or the competent authorities authorized by it.

Article 13 the people's republic of china has the right to exercise control in the contiguous zone to prevent and impose penalties for activities infringing the laws or regulations concerning security, the customs, finance, sanitation or entry and exit control within its land territory, internal waters or territorial sea.

Article 14 the competent authorities concerned of the people's republic of china may, when they have good reasons to believe that a foreign ship has violated the laws or regulations of the people's republic of china, exercise the right of hot pursuit against the foreign ship. Such pursuit shall be commenced when the foreign ship or one of its boats or other craft engaged in activities by using the ship pursued as a mother ship is within the internal waters, the territorial sea or the contiguous zone of the people's republic of china. If the foreign ship is within the contiguous zone of the people's republic of china, the pursuit may be undertaken only when there has been a violation of the rights as provided for in the relevant laws or regulations listed in article 13 of this law the pursuit, if not interrupted, may be continued outside the territorial sea or the contiguous zone until the ship pursued enters the territorial sea of its own country or of a third state. The right of hot pursuit provided for in this article shall be exercised by ships or aircraft of the people's republic of china for military purposes, or by ships or aircraft on government service authorized by the government of the people's republic of china.

Article 15 the baselines of the territorial sea of the people's republic of china shall be promulgated by the government of the people's republic of china.

Article 16 the government of the people's republic of china formulates the relevant regulations in accordance with this law. This law shall come into force on the date for promulgation.

Appendix D

≪Declaration of the Government of the People's Republic of China on the Baselines of the Territorial Sea of the People's Republic of China≫

(May 15, 1996 State Council)

In accordance with the Law of the People's Republic of China on the Territorial Sea and the Contiguous Zone adopted and promulgated on February 25, 1992, the Government of the People's Republic of China hereby announces some of the baselines of its territorial sea adjacent to the mainland and those of the territorial sea adjacent to its Xisha Islands as follows:

1. the straight lines joining the following adjacent base points shall be a part of the baseline of the territorial sea adjacent to the mainland:

(1) shandong gaojiao (1) 37° 24.0 min n

122° 42.3 min e

(2) shandong gaojiao (2) 37° 23.7 min n

122° 42.4 min e

(3) the moye island (1) 36° 57.8 min n

122° 34.2 min e

(4) the moye island (2) 36° 55.1 min n

122° 32.7 min e

(5) the moye island (3) 36° 53.7 min n

122° 31.1 min e

(6) the sushan island 36° 44.8 min n

C. Yang and Q. Zhang, *Legal Study on China's Sovereignty over the Nansha Islands*,
https://doi.org/10.1007/978-981-15-8715-3

122° 15.8 min e

(7) the chaolian island 35° 53.6 min n

120° 53.1 min e

(8) the dashan island 35° 00.2 min n

119° 54.2 min e

(9) macaihang 33° 21.8 min n

121° 20.8 min e

(10) waikejiao 33° 00.9 min n

121° 38.4 min e

(11) the sheshan island 31° 25.3 min n

122° 14.6 min e

(12) haijiao 30° 44.1 min n

123° 09.4 min e

(13) dongnanjiao 30° 43.5 min n

123° 09.7 min e

(14) the brother-two island 30° 10.1 min n

122° 56.7 min e

(15) the yushan islands 28° 53.3 min n

122° 16.5 min e

(16) the taizhou islands (1) 28° 23.9 min n

121° 55.0 min e

(17) the taizhou islands (2) 28° 23.5 min n

121° 54.7 min e

(18) daotiaoshan 27° 27.9 min n

121° 07.8 min e

(19) the dongyin island 26° 22.6 min n

120° 30.4 min e

(20) the dongsha island 26° 09.4 min n

120° 24.3 min e

(21) the niushan island 25° 25.8 min n

119° 56.3 min e

(22) the wuqiu island 24° 58.6 min n

119° 28.7 min e

(23) the dongding island 24° 09.7 min n

118° 14.2 min e

(24) daganshan 23° 31.9 min n

117° 41.3 min e

(25) the nanpeng islands (1) 23° 12.9 min n

117° 14.9 min e

(26) the nanpeng islands (2) 23° 12.3 min n

117° 13.9 min e

(27) shibeishanjiao 22° 56.1 min n

116° 29.7 min e

(28) zhenshiyan 22° 18.9 min n

115° 07.5 min e

(29) the jiapeng islands 21° 48.5 min n

113° 58.0 min e

(30) the weijia island 21° 34.1 min n

112° 47.9 min e

(31) dafanshi 21° 27.7 min n

112° 21.5 min e

(32) the qizhou islands 19° 58.5 min n

111° 16.4 min e

(33) shuangfan 19° 53.0 min n

111° 12.8 min e

(34) the dazhou island (1) 18° 39.7 min n

110° 29.6 min e

(35) the dazhou island (2) 18° 39.4 min n

110° 29.1 min e

(36) shuangfanshi 18° 26.1 min n

110° 08.4 min e

(37) lingshuijiao 18° 23.0 min n

110° 03.3 min e

(38) dongzhou (1) 18° 11.0 min n

109° 42.1 min e

(39) dongzhou (2) 18° 11.0 min n

109° 41.8 min e

(40) jinmujiao 18° 09.5 min n

109° 34.4 min e

(41) shenshijiao 18° 14.6 min n

109° 07.6 min e

(42) the xigu island 18° 19.3 min n

108° 57.1 min e

(43) yinggezui (1) 18° 30.2 min n

108° 41.3 min e

(44) yinggezui (2) 18° 30.4 min n

108° 41.1 min e

(45) yinggezui (3) 18° 31.0 min n

108° 40.6 min e

(46) yinggezui (4) 18° 31.1 min n

108° 40.5 min e

(47) ganenjiao 18° 50.5 min n

108° 37.3 min e

(48) sigengshajiao 19° 11.6 min n

108° 36.0 min e

(49) junbijiao 19° 21.1 min n

108° 38.6 min e

2. the staight lines joining the following adjacent base points shall be the baseline of the territorial sea adjacent to the xisha islands:

(1) the dongdao island (1) 16° 40.5 min n

112° 44.2 min e

(2) the dongdao island (2) 16° 40.1 min n

112° 44.5 min e

(3) the dongdao island (3) 16° 39.8 min n

112° 44.7 min e

(4) langhuajiao (1) 16° 04.4 min n

112° 35.8 min e

(5) langhuajiao (2) 16° 01.9 min n

112° 32.7 min e

(6) langhuajiao (3) 16° 01.5 min n

112° 31.8 min e

(7) langhuajiao (4) 16° 01.0 min n

112° 29.8 min e

(8) the zhongjian island (1) 15° 46.5 min n

111° 12.6 min e

(9) the zhongjian island (2) 15° 46.4 min n

111° 12.1 min e

(10) the zhongjian island (3) 15° 46.4 min n

111° 11.8 min e

(11) the zhongjian island (4) 15° 46.5 min n

111° 11.6 min e

(12) the zhongjian island (5) 15° 46.7 min n

111° 11.4 min e

(13) the zhongjian island (6) 15° 46.9 min n

111° 11.3 min e

(14) the zhongjian island (7) 15° 42.7 min n

111° 11.4 min e

(15) beijiao (1) 17° 04.9 min n

111° 26.9 min e

(16) beijiao (2) 17° 05.4 min n

111° 26.9 min e

(17) beijiao (3) 17° 05.7 min n

111° 27.2 min e

(18) beijiao (4) 17° 06.0 min n

111° 27.8 min e

(19) beijiao (5) 17° 06.5 min n

111° 29.2 min e

(20) beijiao (6) 17° 07.0 min n

111° 31.0 min e

(21) beijiao (7) 17° 07.1 min n

111° 31.6 min e

(22) beijiao (8) 17° 06.9 min n

111° 32.0 min e

(23) the zhaoshu island (1) 16° 59.9 min n

112° 14.7 min e

(24) the zhaoshu island (2) 16° 59.7 min n

112° 15.6 min e

(25) the zhaoshu island (3) 16° 59.4 min n

112° 16.6 min e

(26) the beidao island 16° 58.4 min n

112° 18.3 min e

(27) the zhongdao island 16° 57.6 min n

112° 19.6 min e

(28) the nandao island 16° 56.9 min n

112° 20.5 min e

(29) the dongdao island (1) 16° 40.5 min n

112° 44.2 min e

The other part of the baseline of the territorial sea of the people's republic of china shall be announced separately by the government of the people's republic of china.

Appendix E

Law on the Exclusive Economic Zone and the Continental Shelf of the People's Republic of China (Adopted at the 3rd Meeting of the Standing Committee of the Ninth National People's Congress on June 26, 1998).

Article 1. This Law is enacted to ensure that the People's Republic of China exercise its sovereign rights and jurisdiction over its exclusive economic zone and its continental shelf and to safeguard its national marine rights and interests.

Article 2. The exclusive economic zone of the People's Republic of China covers the area beyond and adjacent to the territorial sea of the People's Republic of China, extending to 200 nautical miles from the baselines from which the breadth of the territorial sea is measured.

The continental shelf of the People's Republic of China comprises the sea-bed and subsoil of the submarine areas that extend beyond its territorial sea throughout the natural prolongation of its land territory to the outer edge of the continental margin, or to a distance of 200 nautical miles from the baselines from which the breadth of the territorial sea is measured where the outer edge of the continental margin does not extend up to that distance.

The People's Republic of China shall determine the delimitation of its exclusive economic zone and continental shelf in respect of the overlapping claims by agreement with the states with opposite or adjacent coasts, in accordance with the equitable principle and on the basis of international law.

Article 3. The People's Republic of China exercises its sovereign rights over the exclusive economic zone for the purpose of exploring, exploiting, conserving and managing the natural resources of the waters superjacent to the sea-bed and of the sea-bed and its subsoil, and in its other activities for economic exploitation and exploration of the zone, such as production of energy from water, currents and winds.

The People's Republic of China exercises jurisdiction over the establishment and use of artificial islands, installations and structures, marine scientific research, and the protection and preservation of the marine environment in the exclusive economic zone.

The natural resources in the exclusive economic zone referred to in this Law consist of living and non-living resources.

C. Yang and Q. Zhang, *Legal Study on China's Sovereignty over the Nansha Islands*,
https://doi.org/10.1007/978-981-15-8715-3

Article 4. The People's Republic of China exercises its sovereign rights over the continental shelf for the purpose of exploring it and exploiting its natural resources.

The People's Republic of China exercises jurisdiction over the establishment and use of artificial islands, installations and structures, marine scientific research, and the protection and preservation of the marine environment on the continental shelf.

The People's Republic of China has the exclusive right to authorize and regulate drilling on the continental shelf for all purposes.

The natural resources of the continental shelf referred to in this Law consist of the mineral and other non-living resources of the sea-bed and subsoil, and the living organisms that belong to sedentary species—organisms which, at the harvestable stage, either are immobile on or under the sea-bed or are unable to move except in constant physical contact with the sea-bed or the subsoil.

Article 5. All international organizations, foreign organizations or individuals that wish to enter the exclusive economic zone of the People's Republic of China for fishing shall be subject to approval of the competent authorities of the People's Republic of China and shall comply with its laws and regulations as well as the accords and agreements it has signed with the states concerned.

The competent authorities of the People's Republic of China shall have the right to take all necessary conservation and management measures to ensure that the living resources in the exclusive economic zone are protected from the danger of over-exploitation.

Article 6. The competent authorities of the People's Republic of China shall have the right to conserve and manage straddling species, highly migratory species, marine mammals, anadromous stocks that originate in the rivers of the People's Republic of China, and catadromous species that spend the greater part of their life cycle in the waters of the People's Republic of China.

The People's Republic of China enjoys the primary interests in the anadromous stocks that originate in its rivers.

Article 7. All international organizations, foreign organizations or individuals that wish to explore the exclusive economic zone of the People's Republic of China or exploit the natural resources on its continental shelf or for any purpose to drill on the continental shelf shall be subject to approval of the competent authorities of the People's Republic of China and shall comply with the laws and regulations of the People's Republic of China.

Article 8. The People's Republic of China has the exclusive right to construct and to authorize and regulate the construction, operation and use of the artificial islands, installations and structures in its exclusive economic zone and on its continental shelf.

The People's Republic of China exercises exclusive jurisdiction over the artificial islands, installations and structures in its exclusive economic zone and on its continental shelf, including jurisdiction with regard to customs, fiscal, health and safety laws and regulations, and laws and regulations governing entry into and exit from the territory of the People's Republic of China.

The competent authorities of the People's Republic of China shall have the right to establish safety belts around the artificial islands, installations and structures in the exclusive economic zone and on the continental shelf and may take appropriate measures in these belts to ensure safety both of navigation and of the artificial islands, installations and structures.

Article 9. All international organizations, foreign organizations or individuals that wish to conduct marine scientific research in the exclusive economic zone or on the continental shelf of the People's Republic of China shall be subject to approval of the competent authorities of the People's Republic of China and shall comply with the laws and regulations of the People's Republic of China.

Article 10. The competent authorities of the People's Republic of China shall have the right to take all necessary measures to prevent, reduce and control pollution of the marine environment for the protection and preservation of the marine environment in the exclusive economic zone and on the continental shelf.

Article 11. All states shall, on the premise that they comply with international law and the laws and regulations of the People's Republic of China, enjoy the freedom of navigation in and flight over its exclusive economic zone, the freedom to lay submarine cables and pipelines and the convenience of other lawful uses of the sea related to the freedoms mentioned above in the exclusive economic zone and on the continental shelf of the People's Republic of China. The routes for the submarine cables and pipelines shall be subject to consent of the competent authorities of the People's Republic of China.

Article 12. The People's Republic of China may, in the exercise of its sovereign rights to explore its exclusive economic zone and to exploit, conserve and manage the living resources there, take such necessary measures as visit, inspection, arrest, detention and judicial proceedings in order to ensure that the laws and regulations of the People's Republic of China are complied with.

The People's Republic of China has the right to take necessary measures against violations of its laws and regulations in its exclusive economic zone and on its continental shelf and to investigate for legal responsibility according to law, and may exercise the right of hot pursuit.

Article 13. The People's Republic of China exercises, in accordance with international law and other relevant laws and regulations of the People's Republic of China, the rights in its exclusive economic zone and on its continental shelf that are not provided for in this Law.

Article 14. The provisions in this Law shall not affect the rights that the People's Republic of China has been enjoying ever since the days of the past.

Article 15. The Government of the People's Republic of China may formulate relevant regulations on the basis of this Law.

Article 16. This Law shall go into effect as of the date of promulgation.

Appendix F

Excerpts from United Nations Convention on the Law of the Sea

Part II

Territorial Sea and Contiguous Zone

Section 1. General Provisions

Article 2

Legal status of the territorial sea, of the air space over the territorial sea and of its bed and subsoil

1. The sovereignty of a coastal State extends, beyond its land territory and internal waters and, in the case of an archipelagic State, its archipelagic waters, to an adjacent belt of sea, described as the territorial sea.
2. This sovereignty extends to the air space over the territorial sea as well as to its bed and subsoil.
3. The sovereignty over the territorial sea is exercised subject to this Convention and to other rules of international law.

Section 2. Limits of the Territorial Sea

Article 3

Breadth of the territorial sea Every State has the right to establish the breadth of its territorial sea up to a limit not exceeding 12 nautical miles, measured from baselines determined in accordance with this Convention.

Article 4

Outer limit of the territorial sea
The outer limit of the territorial sea is the line every point of which is at a distance from the nearest point of the baseline equal to the breadth of the territorial sea.

C. Yang and Q. Zhang, *Legal Study on China's Sovereignty over the Nansha Islands*,
https://doi.org/10.1007/978-981-15-8715-3

Article 5

Normal baseline

Except where otherwise provided in this Convention, the normal baseline for measuring the breadth of the territorial sea is the low-water line along the coast as marked on large-scale charts officially recognized by the coastal State.

Article 6

Reefs

In the case of islands situated on atolls or of islands having fringing reefs, the baseline for measuring the breadth of the territorial sea is the seaward low-water line of the reef, as shown by the appropriate symbol on charts officially recognized by the coastal State.

Article 7

Straight baselines

1. In localities where the coastline is deeply indented and cut into, or if there is a fringe of islands along the coast in its immediate vicinity, the method of straight baselines joining appropriate points may be employed in drawing the baseline from which the breadth of the territorial sea is measured.
2. Where because of the presence of a delta and other natural conditions the coastline is highly unstable, the appropriate points may be selected along the furthest seaward extent of the low-water line and, notwithstanding subsequent regression of the low-water line, the straight baselines shall remain effective until changed by the coastal State in accordance with this Convention.
3. The drawing of straight baselines must not depart to any appreciable extent from the general direction of the coast, and the sea areas lying within the lines must be sufficiently closely linked to the land domain to be subject to the regime of internal waters.
4. Straight baselines shall not be drawn to and from low-tide elevations, unless lighthouses or similar installations which are permanently above sea level have been built on them or except in instances where the drawing of baselines to and from such elevations has received general international recognition.
5. Where the method of straight baselines is applicable under paragraph 1, account may be taken, in determining particular baselines, of economic interests peculiar to the region concerned, the reality and the importance of which are clearly evidenced by long usage.
6. The system of straight baselines may not be applied by a State in such a manner as to cut off the territorial sea of another State from the high seas or an exclusive economic zone.

Article 8

Internal waters

1. Except as provided in Part IV, waters on the landward side of the baseline of the territorial sea form part of the internal waters of the State.
2. Where the establishment of a straight baseline in accordance with the method set forth in article 7 has the effect of enclosing as internal waters areas which had not previously been considered as such, a right of innocent passage as provided in this Convention shall exist in those waters.

Article 9

Mouths of rivers

If a river flows directly into the sea, the baseline shall be a straight line across the mouth of the river between points on the low-water line of its banks.

Article 10

Bays

1. This article relates only to bays the coasts of which belong to a single State.
2. For the purposes of this Convention, a bay is a well-marked indentation whose penetration is in such proportion to the width of its mouth as to contain land-locked waters and constitute more than a mere curvature of the coast. An indentation shall not, however, be regarded as a bay unless its area is as large as, or larger than, that of the semi-circle whose diameter is a line drawn across the mouth of that indentation.
3. For the purpose of measurement, the area of an indentation is that lying between the low-water mark around the shore of the indentation and a line joining the low-water mark of its natural entrance points. Where, because of the presence of islands, an indentation has more than one mouth, the semi-circle shall be drawn on a line as long as the sum total of the lengths of the lines across the different mouths. Islands within an indentation shall be included as if they were part of the water area of the indentation.
4. If the distance between the low-water marks of the natural entrance points of a bay does not exceed 24 nautical miles, a closing line may be drawn between these two low-water marks, and the waters enclosed thereby shall be considered as internal waters.
5. Where the distance between the low-water marks of the natural entrance points of a bay exceeds 24 nautical miles, a straight baseline of 24 nautical miles shall be drawn within the bay in such a manner as to enclose the maximum area of water that is possible with a line of that length.
6. The foregoing provisions do not apply to so-called "historic" bays, or in any case where the system of straight baselines provided for in article 7 is applied.

Article 11

Ports

For the purpose of delimiting the territorial sea, the outermost permanent harbour works which form an integral part of the harbour system are regarded as forming part of the coast. Off-shore installations and artificial islands shall not be considered as permanent harbour works.

Article 12

Roadsteads which are normally used for the loading, unloading and anchoring of ships, and which would otherwise be situated wholly or partly outside the outer limit of the territorial sea, are included in the territorial sea.

Article 13

Low-tide elevations

1. A low-tide elevation is a naturally formed area of land which is surrounded by and above water at low tide but submerged at high tide. Where a low-tide elevation is situated wholly or partly at a distance not exceeding the breadth of the territorial sea from the mainland or an island, the low-water line on that elevation may be used as the baseline for measuring the breadth of the territorial sea.
2. Where a low-tide elevation is wholly situated at a distance exceeding the breadth of the territorial sea from the mainland or an island, it has no territorial sea of its own.

Article 14

Combination of methods for determining baselines

The coastal State may determine baselines in turn by any of the methods provided for in the foregoing articles to suit different conditions.

Article 15

Delimitation of the territorial sea between States with opposite or adjacent coasts
Where the coasts of two States are opposite or adjacent to each other, neither of the two States is entitled, failing agreement between them to the contrary, to extend its territorial sea beyond the median line every point of which is equidistant from the nearest points on the baselines from which the breadth of the territorial seas of each of the two States is measured. The above provision does not apply, however, where it is necessary by reason of historic title or other special circumstances to delimit the territorial seas of the two States in a way which is at variance therewith.

Article 16

Charts and lists of geographical coordinates

1. The baselines for measuring the breadth of the territorial sea determined in accordance with articles 7, 9 and 10, or the limits derived therefrom, and the lines of delimitation drawn in accordance with articles 12 and 15 shall be shown on charts

of a scale or scales adequate for ascertaining their position. Alternatively, a list of geographical coordinates of points, specifying the geodetic datum, may be substituted.

2. The coastal State shall give due publicity to such charts or lists of geographical coordinates and shall deposit a copy of each such chart or list with the Secretary-General of the United Nations.

Section 3. Innocent Passage in the Territorial Sea

Subsection A. Rules Applicable to All Ships

Article 17

Right of innocent passage

Subject to this Convention, ships of all States, whether coastal or land-locked, enjoy the right of innocent passage through the territorial sea.

Article 18

Meaning of passage

1. Passage means navigation through the territorial sea for the purpose of: (a) traversing that sea without entering internal waters or calling at a roadstead or port facility outside internal waters; or (b) proceeding to or from internal waters or a call at such roadstead or port facility.
2. Passage shall be continuous and expeditious. However, passage includes stopping and anchoring, but only in so far as the same are incidental to ordinary navigation or are rendered necessary by force majeure or distress or for the purpose of rendering assistance to persons, ships or aircraft in danger or distress.

Article 19

Meaning of innocent passage

1. Passage is innocent so long as it is not prejudicial to the peace, good order or security of the coastal State. Such passage shall take place in conformity with this Convention and with other rules of international law.
2. Passage of a foreign ship shall be considered to be prejudicial to the peace, good order or security of the coastal State if in the territorial sea it engages in any of the following activities:

   a. any threat or use of force against the sovereignty, territorial integrity or political independence of the coastal State, or in any other manner in violation of the principles of international law embodied in the Charter of the United Nations;
   b. any exercise or practice with weapons of any kind;
   c. any act aimed at collecting information to the prejudice of the defence or security of the coastal State;

d. any act of propaganda aimed at affecting the defence or security of the coastal State;
e. the launching, landing or taking on board of anyaircraft;
f. the launching, landing or taking on board of any military device;
g. the loading or unloading of any commodity, currency or person contrary to the customs, fiscal, immigration or sanitary laws and regulations of the coastal State;
h. any act of wilful and serious pollution contrary to this Convention;
i. any fishing activities;
j. the carrying out of research or survey activities;
k. any act aimed at interfering with any systems of communication or any other facilities or installations of the coastal State;
l. any other activity not having a direct bearing on passage.

Article 20

Submarines and other underwater vehicles

In the territorial sea, submarines and other underwater vehicles are required to navigate on the surface and to show their flag.

Article 21

Laws and regulations of the coastal State relating to innocent passage

1. The coastal State may adopt laws and regulations, in conformity with the provisions of this Convention and other rules of international law, relating to innocent passage through the territorial sea, in respect of all or any of the following:
   a. the safety of navigation and the regulation of maritime traffic;
   b. the protection of navigational aids and facilities and other facilities or installations;
   c. the protection of cables and pipelines;
   d. the conservation of the living resources of the sea;
   e. the prevention of infringement of the fisheries laws and regulations of the coastal State;
   f. the preservation of the environment of the coastal State and the prevention, reduction and control of pollution thereof;
   g. marine scientific research and hydrographic surveys;
   h. the prevention of infringement of the customs, fiscal, immigration or sanitary laws and regulations of the coastal State.
2. Such laws and regulations shall not apply to the design, construction, manning or equipment of foreign ships unless they are giving effect to generally accepted international rules or standards.
3. The coastal State shall give due publicity to all such laws and regulations.
4. Foreign ships exercising the right of innocent passage through the territorial sea shall comply with all such laws and regulations and all generally accepted international regulations relating to the prevention of collisions at sea.

Article 22

Sea lanes and traffic separation schemes in the territorial sea

1. The coastal State may, where necessary having regard to the safety of navigation, require foreign ships exercising the right of innocent passage through its territorial sea to use such sea lanes and traffic separation schemes as it may designate or prescribe for the regulation of the passage of ships.
2. In particular, tankers, nuclear-powered ships and ships carrying nuclear or other inherently dangerous or noxious substances or materials may be required to confine their passage to such sea lanes.
3. In the designation of sea lanes and the prescription of traffic separation schemes under this article, the coastal State shall take into account:

    a. the recommendations of the competent international organization;
    b. any channels customarily used for international navigation;
    c. the special characteristics of particular ships and channels; and
    d. the density of traffic.

4. The coastal State shall clearly indicate such sea lanes and traffic separation schemes on charts to which due publicity shall be given.

Article 23

Foreign nuclear-powered ships and ships carrying nuclear or other inherently dangerous or noxious substances.

Foreign nuclear-powered ships and ships carrying nuclear or other inherently dangerous or noxious substances shall, when exercising the right of innocent passage through the territorial sea, carry documents and observe special precautionary measures established for such ships by international agreements.

Article 24

Duties of the coastal State

1. The coastal State shall not hamper the innocent passage of foreign ships through the territorial sea except in accordance with this Convention.
   In particular, in the application of this Convention or of any laws or regulations adopted in conformity with this Convention, the coastal State shall not:
   (a) impose requirements on foreign ships which have the practical effect of denying or impairing the right of innocent passage; or (b) discriminate in form or in fact against the ships of any State or against ships carrying cargoes to, from or on behalf of any State.
2. The coastal State shall give appropriate publicity to any danger to navigation, of which it has knowledge, within its territorial sea.

Article 25

Rights of protection of the coastal State

1. The coastal State may take the necessary steps in its territorial sea to prevent passage which is not innocent.
2. In the case of ships proceeding to internal waters or a call at a port facility outside internal waters, the coastal State also has the right to take the necessary steps to prevent any breach of the conditions to which admission of those ships to internal waters or such a call is subject.
3. The coastal State may, without discrimination in form or in fact among foreign ships, suspend temporarily in specified areas of its territorial sea the innocent passage of foreign ships if such suspension is essential for the protection of its security, including weapons exercises. Such suspension shall take effect only after having been duly published.

Article 26

Charges which may be levied upon foreign ships

1. No charge may be levied upon foreign ships by reason only of their passage through the territorial sea.
2. Charges may be levied upon a foreign ship passing through the territorial sea as payment only for specific services rendered to the ship. These charges shall be levied without discrimination.

Subsection B. Rules Applicable to

Merchant Ships and Government Ships Operated for Commercial Purposes

Article 27

Criminal jurisdiction on board a foreign ship

1. The criminal jurisdiction of the coastal State should not be exercised on board a foreign ship passing through the territorial sea to arrest any person or to conduct any investigation in connection with any crime committed on board the ship during its passage, save only in the following cases:

    a. if the consequences of the crime extend to the coastal State;
    b. if the crime is of a kind to disturb the peace of the country or the good order of the territorial sea;
    c. if the assistance of the local authorities has been requested by the master of the ship or by a diplomatic agent or consular officer of the flag State; or
    d. if such measures are necessary for the suppression of illicit traffic in narcotic drugs or psychotropic substances.

2. The above provisions do not affect the right of the coastal State to take any steps authorized by its laws for the purpose of an arrest or investigation on board a foreign ship passing through the territorial sea after leaving internal waters.
3. In the cases provided for in paragraphs 1 and 2, the coastal State shall, if the master so requests, notify a diplomatic agent or consular officer of the flag State before taking any steps, and shall facilitate contact between such agent or officer and the ship's crew. In cases of emergency this notification may be communicated while the measures are being taken.
4. In considering whether or in what manner an arrest should be made, the local authorities shall have due regard to the interests of navigation.
5. Except as provided in Part XII or with respect to violations of laws and regulations adopted in accordance with Part V, the coastal State may not take any steps on board a foreign ship passing through the territorial sea to arrest any person or to conduct any investigation in connection with any crime committed before the ship entered the territorial sea, if the ship, proceeding from a foreign port, is only passing through the territorial sea without entering internal waters.

Article 28

Civil jurisdiction in relation to foreign ships

1. The coastal State should not stop or divert a foreign ship passing through the territorial sea for the purpose of exercising civil jurisdiction in relation to a person on board the ship.
2. The coastal State may not levy execution against or arrest the ship for the purpose of any civil proceedings, save only in respect of obligations or liabilities assumed or incurred by the ship itself in the course or for the purpose of its voyage through the waters of the coastal State.
3. Paragraph 2 is without prejudice to the right of the coastal State, in accordance with its laws, to levy execution against or to arrest, for the purpose of any civil proceedings, a foreign ship lying in the territorial sea, or passing through the territorial sea after leaving internal waters.

Subsection C. Rules Applicable to Warships and Other Government Ships Operated for Non-commercial Purposes

Article 29

Definition of warships

For the purposes of this Convention, "warship" means a ship belonging to the armed forces of a State bearing the external marks distinguishing such ships of its nationality, under the command of an officer duly commissioned by the government of the State and whose name appears in the appropriate service list or its equivalent, and manned by a crew which is under regular armed forces discipline.

Article 30

Non-compliance by warships with the laws and regulations of the coastal State. If any warship does not comply with the laws and regulations of the coastal State concerning passage through the territorial sea and disregards any request for compliance therewith which is made to it, the coastal State may require it to leave the territorial sea immediately.

Article 31

Responsibility of the flag State for damage caused by a warship or other government ship operated for non-commercial purposes The flag State shall bear international responsibility for any loss or damage to the coastal State resulting from the non-compliance by a warship or other government ship operated for non-commercial purposes with the laws and regulations of the coastal State concerning passage through the territorial sea or with the provisions of this Convention or other rules of international law.

Article 32

Immunities of warships and other government ships operated for non-commercial purposes. With such exceptions as are contained in subsection A and in articles 30 and 31, nothing in this Convention affects the immunities of warships and other government ships operated for non-commercial purposes.

Part V

Exclusive Economic Zone

Article 55

Specific legal regime of the exclusive economic zone

The exclusive economic zone is an area beyond and adjacent to the territorial sea, subject to the specific legal regime established in this Part, under which the rights and jurisdiction of the coastal State and the rights and freedoms of other States are governed by the relevant provisions of this Convention.

Article 56

Rights, jurisdiction and duties of the coastal State in the exclusive economic zone

1. In the exclusive economic zone, the coastal State has:

    a. sovereign rights for the purpose of exploring and exploiting, conserving and managing the natural resources, whether living or non-living, of the waters superjacent to the seabed and of the seabed and its subsoil, and with regard to other activities for the economic exploitation and exploration of the zone, such as the production of energy from the water, currents and winds;

b. jurisdiction as provided for in the relevant provisions of this Convention with regard to:
    i. the establishment and use of artificial islands, installations and structures;
    ii. marine scientific research;
    iii. the protection and preservation of the marine environment;
    iv. other rights and duties provided for in this Convention.

2. In exercising its rights and performing its duties under this Convention in the exclusive economic zone, the coastal State shall have due regard to the rights and duties of other States and shall act in a manner compatible with the provisions of this Convention.
3. The rights set out in this article with respect to the seabed and subsoil shall be exercised in accordance with Part VI.

Article 57

Breadth of the exclusive economic zone

The exclusive economic zone shall not extend beyond 200 nautical miles from the baselines from which the breadth of the territorial sea is measured.

Article 58

Rights and duties of other States in the exclusive economic zone

1. In the exclusive economic zone, all States, whether coastal or land-locked, enjoy, subject to the relevant provisions of this Convention, the freedoms referred to in article 87 of navigation and overflight and of the laying of submarine cables and pipelines, and other internationally lawful uses of the sea related to these freedoms, such as those associated with the operation of ships, aircraft and submarine cables and pipelines, and compatible with the other provisions of this Convention.
2. Articles 88 to 115 and other pertinent rules of international law apply to the exclusive economic zone in so far as they are not incompatible with this Part.
3. In exercising their rights and performing their duties under this Convention in the exclusive economic zone, States shall have due regard to the rights and duties of the coastal State and shall comply with the laws and regulations adopted by the coastal State in accordance with the provisions of this Convention and other rules of international law in so far as they are not incompatible with this Part.

Article 59

Basis for the resolution of conflicts regarding the attribution of rights and jurisdiction in the exclusive economic zone

In cases where this Convention does not attribute rights or jurisdiction to the coastal State or to other States within the exclusive economic zone, and a conflict rises between the interests of the coastal State and any other State or States, the conflict should be resolved on the basis of equity and in the light of all the relevant circumstances, taking into account the respective importance of the interests involved to the parties as well as to the international community as a whole.

Article 60

Artificial islands, installations and structures in the exclusive economic zone

1. In the exclusive economic zone, the coastal State shall have the exclusive right to construct and to authorize and regulate the construction, operation and use of:
   a. artificial islands;
   b. installations and structures for the purposes provided for in article 56 and other economic purposes;
   c. installations and structures which may interfere with the exercise of the rights of the coastal State in the zone.
2. The coastal State shall have exclusive jurisdiction over such artificial islands, installations and structures, including jurisdiction with regard to customs, fiscal, health, safety and immigration laws and regulations.
3. Due notice must be given of the construction of such artificial islands, installations or structures, and permanent means for giving warning of their presence must be maintained. Any installations or structures which are abandoned or disused shall be removed to ensure safety of navigation, taking into account any generally accepted international standards established in this regard by the competent international organization. Such removal shall also have due regard to fishing, the protection of the marine environment and the rights and duties of other States. Appropriate publicity shall be given to the depth, position and dimensions of any installations or structures not entirely removed.
4. The coastal State may, where necessary, establish reasonable safety zones around such artificial islands, installations and structures in which it may take appropriate measures to ensure the safety both of navigation and of the artificial islands, installations and structures.
5. The breadth of the safety zones shall be determined by the coastal State, taking into account applicable international standards. Such zones shall be designed to ensure that they are reasonably related to the nature and function of the artificial islands, installations or structures, and shall not exceed a distance of 500 metres around them, measured from each point of their outer edge, except as authorized by generally accepted international standards or as recommended by the competent international organization. Due notice shall be given of the extent of safety zones.
6. All ships must respect these safety zones and shall comply with generally accepted international standards regarding navigation in the vicinity of artificial islands, installations, structures and safety zones.
7. Artificial islands, installations and structures and the safety zones around them may not be established where interference may be caused to the use of recognized sea lanes essential to international navigation.

8. Artificial islands, installations and structures do not possess the status of islands. They have no territorial sea of their own, and their presence does not affect the delimitation of the territorial sea, the exclusive economic zone or the continental shelf.

Article 61

Conservation of the living resources

1. The coastal State shall determine the allowable catch of the living resources in its exclusive economic zone.
2. The coastal State, taking into account the best scientific evidence available to it, shall ensure through proper conservation and management measures that the maintenance of the living resources in the exclusive economic zone is not endangered by over-exploitation. As appropriate, the coastal State and competent international organizations, whether subregional, regional or global, shall cooperate to this end.
3. Such measures shall also be designed to maintain or restore populations of harvested species at levels which can produce the maximum sustainable yield, as qualified by relevant environmental and economic factors, including the economic needs of coastal fishing communities and the special requirements of developing States, and taking into account fishing patterns, the interdependence of stocks and any generally recommended international minimum standards, whether subregional, regional or global.
4. In taking such measures the coastal State shall take into consideration the effects on species associated with or dependent upon harvested species with a view to maintaining or restoring populations of such associated or dependent species above levels at which their reproduction may become seriously threatened.
5. Available scientific information, catch and fishing effort statistics, and other data relevant to the conservation of fish stocks shall be contributed and exchanged on a regular basis through competent international organizations, whether subregional, regional or global, where appropriate and with participation by all States concerned, including States whose nationals are allowed to fish in the exclusive economic zone.

Article 62

Utilization of the living resources

1. The coastal State shall promote the objective of optimum utilization of the living resources in the exclusive economic zone without prejudice to article 61.
2. The coastal State shall determine its capacity to harvest the living resources of the exclusive economic zone. Where the coastal State does not have the capacity to harvest the entire allowable catch, it shall, through agreements or other arrangements and pursuant to the terms, conditions, laws and regulations referred to in paragraph 4, give other States access to the surplus of the allowable catch, having

particular regard to the provisions of articles 69 and 70, especially in relation to the developing States mentioned therein.

3. In giving access to other States to its exclusive economic zone under this article, the coastal State shall take into account all relevant factors, including, inter alia, the significance of the living resources of the area to the economy of the coastal State concerned and its other national interests, the provisions of articles 69 and 70, the requirements of developing States in the subregion or region in harvesting part of the surplus and the need to minimize economic dislocation in States whose nationals have habitually fished in the zone or which have made substantial efforts in research and identification of stocks.
4. Nationals of other States fishing in the exclusive economic zone shall comply with the conservation measures and with the other terms and conditions established in the laws and regulations of the coastal State. These laws and regulations shall be consistent with this Convention and may relate, inter alia, to the following:
   a. licensing of fishermen, fishing vessels and equipment, including payment of fees and other forms of remuneration, which, in the case of developing coastal States, may consist of adequate compensation in the field of financing, equipment and technology relating to the fishing industry;
   b. determining the species which may be caught, and fixing quotas of catch, whether in relation to particular stocks or groups of stocks or catch per vessel over a period of time or to the catch by nationals of any State during a specified period;
   c. regulating seasons and areas of fishing, the types, sizes and amount of gear, and the types, sizes and number of fishing vessels that may be used;
   d. fixing the age and size of fish and other species that may be caught;
   e. specifying information required of fishing vessels, including catch and effort statistics and vessel position reports;
   f. requiring, under the authorization and control of the coastal State, the conduct of specified fisheries research programmes and regulating the conduct of such research, including the sampling of catches, disposition of samples and reporting of associated scientific data;
   g. the placing of observers or trainees on board such vessels by the coastal State;
   h. the landing of all or any part of the catch by such vessels in the ports of the coastal State;
   i. terms and conditions relating to joint ventures or other cooperative arrangements;
   j. requirements for the training of personnel and the transfer of fisheries technology, including enhancement of the coastal State's capability of undertaking fisheries research;
   k. enforcement procedures.
5. Coastal States shall give due notice of conservation and management laws and regulations.

Article 63

Stocks occurring within the exclusive economic zones of two or more coastal States or both within the exclusive economic zone and in an area beyond and adjacent to it

1. Where the same stock or stocks of associated species occur within the exclusive economic zones of two or more coastal States, these States shall seek, either directly or through appropriate subregional or regional organizations, to agree upon the measures necessary to coordinate and ensure the conservation and development of such stocks without prejudice to the other provisions of this Part.
2. Where the same stock or stocks of associated species occur both within the exclusive economic zone and in an area beyond and adjacent to the zone, the coastal State and the States fishing for such stocks in the adjacent area shall seek, either directly or through appropriate subregional or regional organizations, to agree upon the measures necessary for the conservation of these stocks in the adjacent area.

Article 64

Highly migratory species

1. The coastal State and other States whose nationals fish in the region for the highly migratory species listed in Annex I shall cooperate directly or through appropriate international organizations with a view to ensuring conservation and promoting the objective of optimum utilization of such species throughout the region, both within and beyond the exclusive economic zone. In regions for which no appropriate international organization exists, the coastal State and other States whose nationals harvest these species in the region shall cooperate to establish such an organization and participate in its work.
2. The provisions of paragraph 1 apply in addition to the other provisions of this Part.

Article 65

Marine mammals Nothing in this Part restricts the right of a coastal State or the competence of an international organization, as appropriate, to prohibit, limit or regulate the exploitation of marine mammals more strictly than provided for in this Part. States shall cooperate with a view to the conservation of marine mammals and in the case of cetaceans shall in particular work through the appropriate international organizations for their conservation, management and study.

Article 66

Anadromous stocks

1. States in whose rivers anadromous stocks originate shall have the primary interest in and responsibility for such stocks.
2. The State of origin of anadromous stocks shall ensure their conservation by the establishment of appropriate regulatory measures for fishing in all waters landward of the outer limits of its exclusive economic zone and for fishing provided for

in paragraph 3(b). The State of origin may, after consultations with the other States referred to in paragraphs 3 and 4 fishing these stocks, establish total allowable catches for stocks originating in its rivers.

3. (a) Fisheries for anadromous stocks shall be conducted only in waters landward of the outer limits of exclusive economic zones, except in cases where this provision would result in economic dislocation for a State other than the State of origin. With respect to such fishing beyond the outer limits of the exclusive economic zone, States concerned shall maintain consultations with a view to achieving agreement on terms and conditions of such fishing giving due regard to the conservation requirements and the needs of the State of origin in respect of these stocks.
   (b) The State of origin shall cooperate in minimizing economic dislocation in such other States fishing these stocks, taking into account the normal catch and the mode of operations of such States, and all the areas in which such fishing has occurred.
   (c) States referred to in subparagraph (b), participating by agreement with the State of origin in measures to renew anadromous stocks, particularly by expenditures for that purpose, shall be given special consideration by the State of origin in the harvesting of stocks originating in its rivers.
   (d) Enforcement of regulations regarding anadromous stocks beyond the exclusive economic zone shall be by agreement between the State of origin and the other States concerned.
4. In cases where anadromous stocks migrate into or through the waters landward of the outer limits of the exclusive economic zone of a State other than the State of origin, such State shall cooperate with the State of origin with regard to the conservation and management of such stocks.
5. The State of origin of anadromous stocks and other States fishing these stocks shall make arrangements for the implementation of the provisions of this article, where appropriate, through regional organizations.

Article 67

Catadromous species

1. A coastal State in whose waters catadromous species spend the greater part of their life cycle shall have responsibility for the management of these species and shall ensure the ingress and egress of migrating fish.
2. Harvesting of catadromous species shall be conducted only in waters landward of the outer limits of exclusive economic zones. When conducted in exclusive economic zones, harvesting shall be subject to this article and the other provisions of this Convention concerning fishing in these zones.
3. In cases where catadromous fish migrate through the exclusive economic zone of another State, whether as juvenile or maturing fish, the management, including harvesting, of such fish shall be regulated by agreement between the State mentioned in paragraph 1 and the other State concerned. Such agreement shall

ensure the rational management of the species and take into account the responsibilities of the State mentioned in paragraph 1 for the maintenance of these species. Article 68 Sedentary species. This Part does not apply to sedentary species as defined in article 77, paragraph 4.

Article 69

Right of land-locked States

1. Land-locked States shall have the right to participate, on an equitable basis, in the exploitation of an appropriate part of the surplus of the living resources of the exclusive economic zones of coastal States of the same subregion or region, taking into account the relevant economic and geographical circumstances of all the States concerned and in conformity with the provisions of this article and of articles 61 and 62.
2. The terms and modalities of such participation shall be established by the States concerned through bilateral, subregional or regional agreements taking into account, inter alia:

   a. the need to avoid effects detrimental to fishing communities or fishing industries of the coastal State;
   b. the extent to which the land-locked State, in accordance with the provisions of this article, is participating or is entitled to participate under existing bilateral, subregional or regional agreements in the exploitation of living resources of the exclusive economic zones of other coastal States;
   c. the extent to which other land-locked States and geographically disadvantaged States are participating in the exploitation of the living resources of the exclusive economic zone of the coastal State and the consequent need to avoid a particular burden for any single coastal State or a part of it;
   d. the nutritional needs of the populations of the respective States.

3. When the harvesting capacity of a coastal State approaches a point which would enable it to harvest the entire allowable catch of the living resources in its exclusive economic zone, the coastal State and other States concerned shall cooperate in the establishment of equitable arrangements on a bilateral, subregional or regional basis to allow for participation of developing land-locked States of the same subregion or region in the exploitation of the living resources of the exclusive economic zones of coastal States of the subregion or region, as may be appropriate in the circumstances and on terms satisfactory to all parties. In the implementation of this provision the factors mentioned in paragraph 2 shall also be taken into account.
4. Developed land-locked States shall, under the provisions of this article, be entitled to participate in the exploitation of living resources only in the exclusive economic zones of developed coastal States of the same subregion or region having regard to the extent to which the coastal State, in giving access to other States to the living resources of its exclusive economic zone, has taken into account the need to

minimize detrimental effects on fishing communities and economic dislocation in States whose nationals have habitually fished in the zone.

5. The above provisions are without prejudice to arrangements agreed upon in subregions or regions where the coastal States may grant to land-locked States of the same subregion or region equal or preferential rights for the exploitation of the living resources in the exclusive economic zones.

Article 70

Right of geographically disadvantaged States

1. Geographically disadvantaged States shall have the right to participate, on an equitable basis, in the exploitation of an appropriate part of the surplus of the living resources of the exclusive economic zones of coastal States of the same subregion or region, taking into account the relevant economic and geographical circumstances of all the States concerned and in conformity with the provisions of this article and of articles 61 and 62.
2. For the purposes of this Part, "geographically disadvantaged States" means coastal States, including States bordering enclosed or semi-enclosed seas, whose geographical situation makes them dependent upon the exploitation of the living resources of the exclusive economic zones of other States in the subregion or region for adequate supplies of fish for the nutritional purposes of their populations or parts thereof, and coastal States which can claim no exclusive economic zones of their own.
3. The terms and modalities of such participation shall be established by the States concerned through bilateral, subregional or regional agreements taking into account, inter alia:
    a. the need to avoid effects detrimental to fishing communities or fishing industries of the coastal State;
    b. the extent to which the geographically disadvantaged State, in accordance with the provisions of this article, is participating or is entitled to participate under existing bilateral, subregional or regional agreements in the exploitation of living resources of the exclusive economic zones of other coastal States;
    c. the extent to which other geographically disadvantaged States and land-locked States are participating in the exploitation of the living resources of the exclusive economic zone of the coastal State and the consequent need to avoid a particular burden for any single coastal State or a part of it;
    d. the nutritional needs of the populations of the respective States.
4. When the harvesting capacity of a coastal State approaches a point which would enable it to harvest the entire allowable catch of the living resources in its exclusive economic zone, the coastal State and other States concerned shall cooperate in the establishment of equitable arrangements on a bilateral, subregional or regional basis to allow for participation of developing geographically disadvantaged States of the same subregion or region in the exploitation of the living

resources of the exclusive economic zones of coastal States of the subregion or region, as may be appropriate in the circumstances and on terms satisfactory to all parties.

In the implementation of this provision the factors mentioned in paragraph 3 shall also be taken into account.

5. Developed geographically disadvantaged States shall, under the provisions of this article, be entitled to participate in the exploitation of living resources only in the exclusive economic zones of developed coastal States of the same subregion or region having regard to the extent to which the coastal State, in giving access to other States to the living resources of its exclusive economic zone, has taken into account the need to minimize detrimental effects on fishing communities and economic dislocation in States whose nationals have habitually fished in the zone.
6. The above provisions are without prejudice to arrangements agreed upon in subregions or regions where the coastal States may grant to geographically disadvantaged States of the same subregion or region equal or preferential rights for the exploitation of the living resources in the exclusive economic zones.

Article 71

Non-applicability of articles 69 and 70 The provisions of articles 69 and 70 do not apply in the case of a coastal. State whose economy is overwhelmingly dependent on the exploitation of the living resources of its exclusive economic zone.

Article 72

Restrictions on transfer of rights

1. Rights provided under articles 69 and 70 to exploit living resources shall not be directly or indirectly transferred to third States or their nationals by lease or licence, by establishing joint ventures or in any other manner which has the effect of such transfer unless otherwise agreed by the States concerned.
2. The foregoing provision does not preclude the States concerned from obtaining technical or financial assistance from third States or international organizations in order to facilitate the exercise of the rights pursuant to articles 69 and 70, provided that it does not have the effect referred to in paragraph 1.

Article 73

Enforcement of laws and regulations of the coastal State

1. The coastal State may, in the exercise of its sovereign rights to explore, exploit, conserve and manage the living resources in the exclusive economic zone, take such measures, including boarding, inspection, arrest and judicial proceedings, as may be necessary to ensure compliance with the laws and regulations adopted by it in conformity with this Convention.

2. Arrested vessels and their crews shall be promptly released upon the posting of reasonable bond or other security.
3. Coastal State penalties for violations of fisheries laws and regulations in the exclusive economic zone may not include imprisonment, in the absence of agreements to the contrary by the States concerned, or any other form of corporal punishment.
4. In cases of arrest or detention of foreign vessels the coastal State shall promptly notify the flag State, through appropriate channels, of the action taken and of any penalties subsequently imposed.

Article 74

Delimitation of the exclusive economic zone between States with opposite or adjacent coasts

1. The delimitation of the exclusive economic zone between States with opposite or adjacent coasts shall be effected by agreement on the basis of international law, as referred to in Article 38 of the Statute of the International Court of Justice, in order to achieve an equitable solution.
2. If no agreement can be reached within a reasonable period of time, the States concerned shall resort to the procedures provided for in Part XV.
3. Pending agreement as provided for in paragraph 1, the States concerned, in a spirit of understanding and cooperation, shall make every effort to enter into provisional arrangements of a practical nature and, during this transitional period, not to jeopardize or hamper the reaching of the final agreement. Such arrangements shall be without prejudice to the final delimitation.
4. Where there is an agreement in force between the States concerned, questions relating to the delimitation of the exclusive economic zone shall be determined in accordance with the provisions of that agreement.

Article 75

Charts and lists of geographical coordinates

1. Subject to this Part, the outer limit lines of the exclusive economic zone and the lines of delimitation drawn in accordance with article 74 shall be shown on charts of a scale or scales adequate for ascertaining their position. Where appropriate, lists of geographical coordinates of points, specifying the geodetic datum, may be substituted for such outer limit lines or lines of delimitation.
2. The coastal State shall give due publicity to such charts or lists of geographical coordinates and shall deposit a copy of each such chart or list with the Secretary-General of the United Nations.

Part VI

Continental Shelf

Article 76

Definition of the continental shelf

1. The continental shelf of a coastal State comprises the seabed and subsoil of the submarine areas that extend beyond its territorial sea throughout the natural prolongation of its land territory to the outer edge of the continental margin, or to a distance of 200 nautical miles from the baselines from which the breadth of the territorial sea is measured where the outer edge of the continental margin does not extend up to that distance.
2. The continental shelf of a coastal State shall not extend beyond the limits provided for in paragraphs 4 to 6.
3. The continental margin comprises the submerged prolongation of the land mass of the coastal State, and consists of the seabed and subsoil of the shelf, the slope and the rise. It does not include the deep ocean floor with its oceanic ridges or the subsoil thereof.
4. (a) For the purposes of this Convention, the coastal State shall establish the outer edge of the continental margin wherever the margin extends beyond 200 nautical miles from the baselines from which the breadth of the territorial sea is measured, by either:

   i. a line delineated in accordance with paragraph 7 by reference to the outermost fixed points at each of which the thickness of sedimentary rocks is at least 1% of the shortest distance from such point to the foot of the continental slope; or
   ii. a line delineated in accordance with paragraph 7 by reference to fixed points not more than 60 nautical miles from the foot of the continental slope.

   (b) In the absence of evidence to the contrary, the foot of the continental slope shall be determined as the point of maximum change in the gradient at its base.
5. The fixed points comprising the line of the outer limits of the continental shelf on the seabed, drawn in accordance with paragraph 4 (a)(i) and (ii), either shall not exceed 350 nautical miles from the baselines from which the breadth of the territorial sea is measured or shall not exceed 100 nautical miles from the 2,500 m isobath, which is a line connecting the depth of 2,500 m.
6. Notwithstanding the provisions of paragraph 5, on submarine ridges, the outer limit of the continental shelf shall not exceed 350 nautical miles from the baselines from which the breadth of the territorial sea is measured. This paragraph does not apply to submarine elevations that are natural components of the continental margin, such as its plateaux, rises, caps, banks and spurs.
7. The coastal State shall delineate the outer limits of its continental shelf, where that shelf extends beyond 200 nautical miles from the baselines from which the breadth of the territorial sea is measured, by straight lines not exceeding 60 nautical miles in length, connecting fixed points, defined by coordinates of latitude and longitude.
8. Information on the limits of the continental shelf beyond 200 nautical miles from the baselines from which the breadth of the territorial sea is measured shall be submitted by the coastal State to the Commission on the Limits of the

Continental Shelf set up under Annex II on the basis of equitable geographical representation. The Commission shall make recommendations to coastal States on matters related to the establishment of the outer limits of their continental shelf. The limits of the shelf established by a coastal State on the basis of these recommendations shall be final and binding.

9. The coastal State shall deposit with the Secretary-General of the United Nations charts and relevant information, including geodetic data, permanently describing the outer limits of its continental shelf. The Secretary-General shall give due publicity thereto.
10. The provisions of this article are without prejudice to the question of delimitation of the continental shelf between States with opposite or adjacent coasts.

Article 77

Rights of the coastal State over the continental shelf

1. The coastal State exercises over the continental shelf sovereign rights for the purpose of exploring it and exploiting its natural resources.
2. The rights referred to in paragraph 1 are exclusive in the sense that if the coastal State does not explore the continental shelf or exploit its natural resources, no one may undertake these activities without the express consent of the coastal State.
3. The rights of the coastal State over the continental shelf do not depend on occupation, effective or notional, or on any express proclamation.
4. The natural resources referred to in this Part consist of the mineral and other non-living resources of the seabed and subsoil together with living organisms belonging to sedentary species, that is to say, organisms which, at the harvestable stage, either are immobile on or under the seabed or are unable to move except in constant physical contact with the seabed or the subsoil.

Article 78

Legal status of the superjacent waters and air space and the rights and freedoms of other States.

1. The rights of the coastal State over the continental shelf do not affect the legal status of the superjacent waters or of the air space above those waters.
2. The exercise of the rights of the coastal State over the continental shelf must not infringe or result in any unjustifiable interference with navigation and other rights and freedoms of other States as provided for in this Convention.

Article 79

Submarine cables and pipelines on the continental shelf

1. All States are entitled to lay submarine cables and pipelines on the continental shelf, in accordance with the provisions of this article.

2. Subject to its right to take reasonable measures for the exploration of the continental shelf, the exploitation of its natural resources and the prevention, reduction and control of pollution from pipelines, the coastal State may not impede the laying or maintenance of such cables or pipelines.
3. The delineation of the course for the laying of such pipelines on the continental shelf is subject to the consent of the coastal State.
4. Nothing in this Part affects the right of the coastal State to establish conditions for cables or pipelines entering its territory or territorial sea, or its jurisdiction over cables and pipelines constructed or used in connection with the exploration of its continental shelf or exploitation of its resources or the operations of artificial islands, installations and structures under its jurisdiction.
5. When laying submarine cables or pipelines, States shall have due regard to cables or pipelines already in position. In particular, possibilities of repairing existing cables or pipelines shall not be prejudiced.

Article 80

Artificial islands, installations and structures on the continental shelf Article 60 applies mutatis mutandis to artificial islands, installations and structures on the continental shelf.

Article 81

Drilling on the continental shelf The coastal State shall have the exclusive right to authorize and regulate drilling on the continental shelf for all purposes.

Article 82

Payments and contributions with respect to the exploitation of the continental shelf beyond 200 nautical miles

1. The coastal State shall make payments or contributions in kind in respect of the exploitation of the non-living resources of the continental shelf beyond 200 nautical miles from the baselines from which the breadth of the territorial sea is measured.
2. The payments and contributions shall be made annually with respect to all production at a site after the first five years of production at that site. For the sixth year, the rate of payment or contribution shall be 1% of the value or volume of production at the site. The rate shall increase by 1% for each subsequent year until the twelfth year and shall remain at 7% thereafter. Production does not include resources used in connection with exploitation.
3. A developing State which is a net importer of a mineral resource produced from its continental shelf is exempt from making such payments or contributions in respect of that mineral resource.
4. The payments or contributions shall be made through the Authority, which shall distribute them to States Parties to this Convention, on the basis of equitable sharing criteria, taking into account the interests and needs of developing States, particularly the least developed and the land-locked among them.

Article 83

Delimitation of the continental shelf between States with opposite or adjacent coasts

1. The delimitation of the continental shelf between States with opposite or adjacent coasts shall be effected by agreement on the basis of international law, as referred to in Article 38 of the Statute of the International Court of Justice, in order to achieve an equitable solution.
2. If no agreement can be reached within a reasonable period of time, the States concerned shall resort to the procedures provided for in Part XV.
3. Pending agreement as provided for in paragraph 1, the States concerned, in a spirit of understanding and cooperation, shall make every effort to enter into provisional arrangements of a practical nature and, during this transitional period, not to jeopardize or hamper the reaching of the final agreement. Such arrangements shall be without prejudice to the final delimitation.
4. Where there is an agreement in force between the States concerned, questions relating to the delimitation of the continental shelf shall be determined in accordance with the provisions of that agreement.

Article 84

Charts and lists of geographical coordinates

1. Subject to this Part, the outer limit lines of the continental shelf and the lines of delimitation drawn in accordance with article 83 shall be shown on charts of a scale or scales adequate for ascertaining their position. Where appropriate, lists of geographical coordinates of points, specifying the geodetic datum, may be substituted for such outer limit lines or lines of delimitation.
2. The coastal State shall give due publicity to such charts or lists of geographical coordinates and shall deposit a copy of each such chart or list with the Secretary-General of the United Nations and, in the case of those showing the outer limit lines of the continental shelf, with the Secretary-General of the Authority.

Article 85

Tunnelling This Part does not prejudice the right of the coastal State to exploit the subsoil by means of tunnelling, irrespective of the depth of water above the subsoil.

The manufacturer's authorised representative in the EU is Springer Nature Customer Service Centre GmbH, Europaplatz 3, 69115 Heidelberg, Germany. If you have any concerns regarding our products, please contact ProductSafety@springernature.com

Printed and bound by CPI Group (UK) Ltd, Croydon, CR0 4YY
30/09/2026
02225289-0001